Interpretation in Jungian Analysis

Analytic interpretation is fundamental to the process of psychoanalysis, Jungian analysis, and psychoanalytic psychotherapy. Interpretation is the medium by which the psychoanalytic art form is transmitted. What one chooses to say in analysis, why one chooses it, how one says it, when one says it; these are the building blocks of the interpretive process and the focus of *Interpretation in Jungian Analysis: Art and Technique*.

This volume is the first of its kind in the literature of Analytical Psychology. Until now, the process of interpretation has been addressed only briefly in general Jungian texts. *Interpretation in Jungian Analysis* provides an in-depth exploration of the process, including the history of analytic technique, the role of language in analytic therapy, the poetics and metaphor of interpretation, and the relationship between interpretation and the analytic attitude. In addition, the steps involved with the creation of clear, meaningful, and transformative interpretations are plainly outlined. Throughout the book, clinical examples and reader exercises are provided to deepen the learning experience. The influence of the Jungian perspective on the interpretative process is outlined, as are the use of analytic reverie and confrontation during the analytic process.

In addition to the historical, technical, and theoretical aspects of interpretation, this book also focuses on the artistic and creative elements that are often overlooked in the interpretive process. Ultimately, cultivating fluidity within the interpretive process is essential to engaging the depth and complexity of the psyche. *Interpretation in Jungian Analysis* will be of great interest to psychoanalysts and psychotherapists of all theoretical orientations and will be essential reading for students of Analytical Psychology.

Mark Winborn is a Jungian psychoanalyst in private practice in Memphis, USA. He is a training analyst of the Inter-Regional Society of Jungian Analysts and the C. G. Jung Institute, Zurich, and an author of several books on Jungian psychoanalysis. He lectures nationally and internationally on analytic technique and comparative psychoanalysis.

Interpretation in Jungian Analysis

Art and Technique

Mark Winborn

 Routledge
Taylor & Francis Group

LONDON AND NEW YORK

First published 2019
by Routledge
2 Park Square, Milton Park, Abingdon, Oxon OX14 4RN

and by Routledge
711 Third Avenue, New York, NY 10017

Routledge is an imprint of the Taylor & Francis Group, an informa business

© 2019 Mark Winborn

British Library Cataloguing in Publication Data
A catalogue record for this book is available from the British Library

Library of Congress Cataloging in Publication Data
Names: Winborn, Mark, author.
Title: Interpretation in Jungian analysis : art and technique / Mark
    Winborn.
Description: Abingdon, Oxon ; New York, NY : Routledge, 2019. |
    Includes bibliographical references and index.
Identifiers: LCCN 2018009395 (print) | LCCN 2018011176 (ebook) |
    ISBN 9781315164489 (Master e-book) | ISBN 9781138058088
    (hardback : alk. paper) | ISBN 9781138058118 (pbk. : alk. paper)
Subjects: LCSH: Jungian psychology. | Psychoanalysis.
Classification: LCC BF173.J85 (ebook) | LCC BF173.J85 W528 2019
    (print) | DDC 150.19/54—dc23
LC record available at https://lccn.loc.gov/2018009395

ISBN: 978-1-138-05808-8 (hbk)
ISBN 978-1-138-05811-8 (pbk)
ISBN: 978-1-315-16448-9 (ebk)

Typeset in Times New Roman
by Swales & Willis Ltd, Exeter, Devon, UK

Dedicated to the patients, supervisees, and students who have graciously permitted me to participate in their life journeys. In doing so, they have all contributed to this volume.

Contents

Figures

Acknowledgments

This book has been gestating for nearly twenty years. I am grateful to the patients, supervisees, students, and colleagues who have assisted in shaping my ideas about the process of interpretation. Special gratitude goes to the students of the Memphis-Atlanta Jungian Seminar and the C. G. Jung Institute in Zurich where much of my teaching has taken place. My appreciation also extends to my wife Lisa for her support and the sacrifices made during the writing process.

I wish to express my appreciation for the great jazz artists of the 1950s and 1960s whose recordings inspired me and kept me company during the long hours spent researching, writing, and editing. Those musicians include: Miles Davis, John Coltrane, Wayne Shorter, Dave Brubeck, John Desmond, Joe Pass, Grant Green, Wes Montgomery, Art Pepper, Chet Baker, Art Blakey, Lester Young, McCoy Tyner, Stan Getz, Charles Mingus, Thelonious Monk, Eric Dolphy, Jim Hall, Kenny Burrell, and Bill Evans. While the list could go on, these are some of the most cherished.

My thanks to Susannah Frearson, Editor for Analytical Psychology at Routledge, for the warm reception she provided this project. Finally, deep gratitude to my two friends and colleagues, Dianne Braden and Deborah Bryon, who provided feedback throughout the writing process.

Permissions and credits

Introduction

During my analytic training, I often wrestled with the question, "What distinguishes Jungian analysis from other forms of therapy?" In many respects, when not engaged in dream work, it seemed that I was unable to clearly differentiate the Jungian model of therapy from other models of therapy. As I wrestled with this issue during my training, I noticed a few of my teachers and supervisors seemed to approach analytic intervention in a distinctly different manner than the other analysts to whom I was exposed. Most notable among these was Mel Marshak, who had received her analytic training in London through the Society of Analytical Psychology. Early in my training, as she would read from the process notes of her cases, I would be astonished at the clarity, emotional engagement, and specificity of her interventions. At the time, I did not yet realize that she was providing examples of interpretation. My idealizing fantasy was that her ability to intervene in this manner reflected a unique gift that only she possessed. Eventually, I found my way into the psychoanalytic literature and discovered that there was an underlying method to what Marshak was doing. More importantly, I came to recognize that analytic interpretation was a process that could be learned and taught. By incorporating a focus on the technique of analysis, in particular interpretation, I began to see how analytic work truly differs from other therapeutic modalities; not just when interpreting dreams but throughout the analytic interaction. Of equal significance, my study of interpretive processes awakened me to the creative, artistic elements of the analytic process.

The subject of interpretation is fundamental to the process of analysis or analytic psychotherapy. In analysis, many factors contribute to the cultivation of transformative experience, for example, a deep sense of engagement, the analyst's capacity to listen in depth, and the capacity to tolerate long periods of ambiguity. However, the analytic interpretation remains the most salient medium by which the analytic art form is communicated. If the analytic vessel is thought of as the canvas, then interpretations are the paints the depth psychologist uses, along with the patient,[1] to create the analytic painting. What the analyst chooses to say in analysis, why the analyst chooses that particular thing to say, how the analyst says it, and when the analyst says it – these are the fundamental building blocks of the interpretive process.[2]

At times, when first hearing about interpretation and technique,[3] there can be a perception that interpretation and technique are somehow dry and mechanical. However, the interpretive process is where the creative aspect of analysis truly comes alive; when the analyst becomes the poet – carefully weighing words, sensing into the feeling of those words, imagining how the words will fit with the emotional context of what has come before and what will come after. Ultimately, an interpretation is an attempt to capture in language and tone the essence of something only partially seen, still dancing behind a veil. As Loewald (1980) puts it, "Language in its most specific function in analysis, as interpretation, is thus a creative act similar to that in poetry where language is found for phenomena, contexts, connections, and experiences not previously known and speakable" (p. 242). According to Hillman (1983, p. 108), a fundamental shift occurs when we begin seeing therapy as an artistic process, that is, to allow an "art fantasy" to exist outside of the existing fantasy of therapy. This is a shift that allows therapy to be de-literalized and that guards against the overvaluation of either therapy or art.

However, interpretation is like other creative processes; developing fluidity and spontaneity requires effort and practice. The artist, whether poet, dancer, musician, painter, sculptor, or composer, spends thousands of hours practicing the techniques of their craft. Before they can improvise fluidly, jazz musicians spend years learning scales, chord structure, modes, standard progressions, and the technique of their particular instrument. Aspiring novelists practice the effective use of literary techniques such as character development, back story, plot twists, foreshadowing, and narrative hooks. Poets develop proficiency with techniques such as rhythm, form, rhyme, metaphor, allusion, and alliteration. Interpretation is an essential skill for the analytic therapist, but it can be used effectively only if fluency and comfort with interpretation have been cultivated. Engaging in analysis without learning the art and craft of interpretation is somewhat like a painter desiring to paint only with one brush and one color. Yes, a painting can be created with those materials, but the possibilities are greatly constricted.

Technique addresses the process of the analytic work rather than the content that emerges during the work. When combined with an analytic attitude, it is a set of tools that facilitates the engagement of the unconscious while minimizing factors that interfere with the emergence of unconscious material. Technique provides an underlying structure to the analytic process – the unseen but necessary support for the art of analysis. An understanding of technique provides a bird's-eye view of the analytic process. As Lear (2009) emphasizes, understanding the structure of analysis informs the analyst's awareness of the overall arc of analysis during the moment-to-moment shifts in the analytic session:

> If one is to have a clear sense of why one is doing what one is doing in an analytic moment, one needs to have a sense of what psychoanalysis is for; conversely, one cannot have a textured sense of what psychoanalysis is all about unless one also understands how that overall conception of its value filters down and informs the analytic moment.
>
> (p. 1299)

Yet, within this common set of underlying patterns, designed to maximize the emergence and engagement of unconscious processes, each analysis also unfolds in its own unique way, still ultimately shaped by the personalities of the patient and the analyst. As Jung (1953b), citing an alchemical dictum, reminds us, "*Ars totum requirit hominem*" – that is, the art requires the whole person (para. 6).

For most psychoanalytic institutes,[4] the study of technique is foundational to their training programs, and they have developed a model of analytic technique in which the concept of interpretation is central (Levy, 1990; Rubovits-Seitz, 1998, 2001a,b). Freud laid out the fundamental principles of technique in psychoanalysis in a series ten papers published between 1910 and 1919 (Freud, 1959). While these guidelines have been re-examined and modified (Fenichel, 1941; Greenson, 1967; Etchegoyen, 2005), Freud's primary guidelines on technique remain intact in most schools of contemporary psychoanalysis, even though many of Freud's theories regarding the nature of unconscious processes and development of the personality have been modified or discarded (Rubovits-Seitz, 2002). Levy (1990) highlights the centrality of technique and interpretation to the analytic process, "Certain principles of technique and especially systematic interpretative inventions remain at the core of all clinical psychotherapeutic and psychoanalytic work" (p. viii).

Jungians, however, have a more ambivalent attitude about guidelines regarding technique in general and interpretation in particular (Zinkin, 1969; Charlton, 1986). As Dieckmann (1991) points out, Jungians generally have an aversion to addressing technical guidelines for undertaking an analysis, with the exception of dream interpretation and active imagination. Numerous volumes have been written detailing guidelines for Jungian dream interpretation and active imagination, yet there are fewer than a handful of books that address the interpretation of the analytic interaction from a Jungian perspective.[5] However, as anyone practicing analytic therapy quickly becomes aware, there are often significant stretches of time in analytic sessions that are not focused on dream work or active imagination. In fact, some patients do not engage in dream work or active imagination throughout the course of their analytic process. As Bovensiepen (2002) puts it:

> Even today, several of my Jungian colleagues and I frequently experience a certain gap between Jung's topical theoretical conceptions of the unconscious and transformability of the psyche and his lack of theory for analytic technique. . . Or perhaps, to express it more poetically, Jungians like ourselves too often have our heads in the clouds, and we can learn from psychoanalytical treatment technique to bring us back down to earth.
>
> (p. 242)

Historically, the primary exception to the Jungian ambivalence toward the technical aspects of analysis has been Michael Fordham and the Society of Analytical Psychology (SAP) in London (Astor, 1995; Samuels, 1986). Fordham and other analysts of the SAP began incorporating elements of psychoanalytic technique and theory in areas where they felt there was inadequate development of the Jungian model. This group became known as the London School, in distinction from the Zurich School – that is, those analysts who were trained by Jung and his close colleagues in Zurich. As time has gone on, this emphasis on blending psychoanalytic approaches with the classical Jungian approach is no longer exclusive to London, and analysts practicing from this perspective are often referred to as "developmental Jungians" (Samuels, 1986).

Apart from the developmental perspective, for reasons to be discussed more fully later on, Jungian analytic training tends to underemphasize technique. As a result, an important tool for working analytically is not well developed. In my experience as a teacher and supervisor, most Jungian analytic candidates feel rather uncertain about how to proceed in the analytic situation when not involved with dream interpretation or active imagination. They often have difficulty recognizing and engaging the patient's emerging unconscious material when the symbolism is not readily identified as such within the analytic context.

The analytic activity of interpretation is an area where the rich reservoir of archetypal images and narratives cultivated during Jungian training can be brought to life. The immersion in mythology, religion, fairy tales, and alchemy during Jungian training serves to develop a strong facility in working metaphorically with analytic patients. The underlying metaphorical patterns observed in these archetypal motifs are also present in the implicit or unconscious patterning of the patient's verbalizations, fantasies, and behaviors. However, without developing the necessary facility with interpretation, it is difficult for students in Jungian training to effectively incorporate these rich archetypal-metaphorical resources in their analytic interactions. In my experience, blending the deep understanding of archetype, symbol, and metaphor from the Jungian tradition with competency in psychoanalytic interpretative technique creates a powerful therapeutic amalgam.

Many in the Jungian community are more comfortable operating primarily from intuition and inquiry; tending to overemphasize the passive, receptive, holding aspects of clinical interaction while neglecting to develop a balance in their analytic activity by engaging the active, penetrating, engaging end of the intervention continuum. Working from the metaphor of the mother–infant dyad, a clear, coherent, empathic interpretation is like the mother's firm, milk-engorged nipple that provides the infant something to attach to and be nourished by, whereas the passive-receptive stance can sometimes be experienced by the patient as being like the flaccid nipple that is difficult to grasp and receive nourishment from.

The following chapters will examine in more depth the historical, philosophical, and theoretical origins of interpretation, definitions of interpretation, research on interpretation, and the role of interpretation in various schools of analytic thought. Specific focus will be given to the place of interpretation in Jungian analysis and the unique contribution the Jungian perspective can bring to the interpretive process, particularly the use of interpretation in the transformation of complexes. Attention will also be given to the role of metaphor in interpretation, the differentiation between interpretive and non-interpretive interventions in analytic therapy, and the identification of different types of interpretation. Much of the focus involves a functional delineation of the process of interpretation in the analytic setting – including the structure, timing, wording, and style of interpretation. The poetic and musical bases of interpretation, as well as the analyst's use of reverie in the interpretive process, are also examined. Finally, the arc of interpretation, as an ongoing process that shifts and evolves throughout the analytic process, is addressed. Suggestions for learning to interpret fluidly are furnished, and clinical examples of interpretation are provided throughout. In most instances, the examples selected for this volume were chosen because they reflect the vicissitudes of everyday work in the analytic consulting room. Extensive patient histories are not provided; in fact, only minimal context is provided for each example, and in each instance all identifying information is intentionally altered in order to protect the identities of the patients involved. In a few instances, clinical montages using elements from similar cases have been created to illustrate scenarios commonly encountered in the analytic setting.

Without sacrificing the philosophical heart of Jung's approach to the psyche, Analytical Psychology has much to gain by incorporating the technique of interpretation. In fact, knowledge of interpretation expands one's sense of the symbolic by developing a greater awareness of, appreciation for, and understanding of the symbolic aspects of the analytic interaction. My hope is that the readers of this book will become excited about the therapeutic and creative possibilities associated with analytic interpretation. Hopefully, this volume will dispel old stereotypes that portray interpretation as distant, dry, mechanical, and overly intellectualized, and will help to close the lingering divide between the Jungian and psychoanalytic communities. Said another way, my intention is to re-narrate the normative perception of interpretation. Ultimately, my goal is to provide less experienced analytic therapists and analysts-in-training with an in-depth exposure to the art and technique of analytic interpretation, as well as providing more experienced practitioners with opportunities to re-evaluate their relationship with analytic technique and deepen their capacity to utilize interpretation as a tool for facilitating transformation.

Notes

1 Throughout this book, I utilize the terms "patient" and "analysand" interchangeably to refer to any individual engaged in an analytic process, regardless of the frequency or duration of that process. I intentionally avoid the use of the term "client," which, for me, evokes connotations of commercial or business transactions focused primarily on the exchange of money for services rather than a mutually created process that emerges out of relationship.
2 In this book, I will often refer to the role of the analytic clinician as "analyst," but I use the terms analyst, therapist, psychotherapist, psychoanalyst, depth psychologist, or analytic clinician interchangeably throughout. These roles share, as common denominators, the engagement with the unconscious, the coalescence of experience, and the creation of meaning.

3 Technique refers to the mechanics by which the analytic interaction takes place – for example, how the analyst: begins and ends an analysis, creates a secure analytic setting, works within the transference–countertransference matrix, engages the patient's defenses and resistance, and interprets the analytic interaction.

4 By "psychoanalytic institute," I am referring to institutes whose lineage is traced back to Freud rather than Jung – for example, object relations, intersubjective, Lacanian, self psychology, relational, or interpersonal. Very few contemporary psychoanalysts identify with or refer to themselves as "Freudian" or as "Freudian psychoanalysts." Hence I will use the term "psychoanalytic" when referring to psychoanalysts and institutes that practice a contemporary version of psychoanalysis that descends from Freud rather than Jung.

5 The interpretation of dreams and the facilitation of active imagination are also components of Jungian technique; however, since these aspects of technique are covered at length elsewhere, this volume will focus on interpreting the explicit and implicit aspects of the analytic interaction.

Chapter 1

An overview of technique and interpretation

Technique in Analytical Psychology

Before delving into interpretation, it is necessary to locate interpretation within the broader context of analytic therapy and training in analytic therapy. In most psychoanalytic institutes the training focuses on two areas, theory and technique, whereas in Jungian institutes the training focus includes theory, technique, and the study of archetypal content. However, the emphasis given to these areas differs significantly between psychoanalytic institutes and Jungian institutes. Psychoanalytic institutes give significantly greater weight to the technique of analysis, while Jungian institutes place significant emphasis on archetypal content such as fairytales, myths, religion, and alchemy. The technique of dream analysis[1] is emphasized in Jungian institutes, but the techniques associated with the ebb and flow of the interaction between analyst and analysand receive comparatively little attention.

As I mentioned in the Introduction, technique refers to the methods or processes by which the analytic interaction takes place. That is, how the analyst listens, begins and ends an analysis, establishes the analytic frame,[2] develops a therapeutic alliance,[3] works within the transference–countertransference matrix, engages the patient's defenses and resistance, interprets patient's dreams, and interprets the analytic interaction. These fundamental areas of technique were initially outlined by Freud (Ellman, 1991) but have been elucidated and expanded upon within the psychoanalytic world by Fenichel (1941), Stone (1961), Greenson (1967), Auld and Hyman (1991), and Etchegoyen (2005), among many others. The psychoanalytic literature also includes numerous texts focused on specific areas of analytic technique. Technique provides the underlying structure of the analytic process – the unseen but necessary support for the art of analysis. The integration of technique facilitates an understanding of why analytic therapy requires the unique shape it does and assists in cultivating a bird's-eye overview of the analytic process. However, each analysis unfolds in its own unique way despite relying on a common underlying structure of technique that serves to maximize the engagement of unconscious processes. Connolly (2008) highlights the intimate relationship between technique, theory, and the creative art of analysis:

> Technique... derives from Aristotle's notion of *techne* or *ars*, the name given to that skillful activity (*poesis*) that accomplishes its purpose in the production of a particular work that is never already given but which can or cannot appear and in which the certainty of success is always in doubt. In *techne*, method and theory emerge from the thoughtful examination of the way in which the production of the work is carried out.
>
> (p. 482)

In this regard, the structuring and creative aspects of analysis intermingle in the same manner as in jazz improvisation. The minimal but necessary form provided by the underlying chord structure, tempo, and rhythm serves to shape the musical exchange between soloists in the jazz setting (Barrett, 2000; Knoblauch, 2000). Barrett describes the improvisational process as follows:

> To say that jazz music is improvised means that jazz music is spontaneous and unrehearsed.... When improvising, one journeys into the unknown and is expected to create coherent musical ideas that are novel and unpredictable... the improviser makes connections between the old and new material and adds to the unfolding scheme.
>
> (pp. 232, 233, 238)

The structure is sufficiently minimal that significant variation of expression is encouraged, yet it provides a sufficient organizing influence to prevent disintegration into musical chaos. Enactments, acting out, and "wild analysis" (Freud, 1910) could be considered the equivalent of chaos in the analytic setting.

In contrast to the psychoanalytic literature, there is a relative scarcity of Jungian literature on analytic technique, with only a handful of books focused on the technique of Jungian analysis.[4] Most of the emphasis on technique in Analytical Psychology is on dream interpretation rather than the techniques associated with establishing and maintaining the analytic interaction when dream analysis is not occurring. Dozens, perhaps hundreds, of Jungian volumes have been written that focus on dream interpretation, but there is little Jungian literature on technique and the processes that occur during analytic sessions. The technique associated with analytic interaction receives the least attention during the training of Jungian analytic candidates. Informal surveys, conducted during seminars I have taught, revealed that most Jungian candidates had not had a seminar specifically focused on interpretation. During my own training, I did not have any courses specifically focused on analytic interpretation, but I was fortunate to have a few mentors who emphasized and modeled the importance of interpretation and technique. In contrast, psychoanalytic institutes typically have multiple courses on technique; often during each year of their curriculum.

The general avoidance of technique within the Jungian world can largely be traced back to Jung's attitude towards technique which carried over to many in the generations that followed him. Adler (1967) summarizes the traditional Jungian position as follows:

One of the main differences between Analytical Psychology and other schools lies in the undogmatic approach of Analytical Psychology to each individual case. The basic presupposition from which Analytical Psychology starts is that each patient has his own particular and "personal" psychology necessitating an approach which varies with each individual case. . . . Such a conception must obviously involve a considerable limitation on general technique, since the whole point of a technique is to provide certain universally applicable rules.

(p. 23)

Typologically, Jung was an intuitive (like many who have been drawn to his ideas) who had an aversion to methodological approaches. Dehing (1992, p. 42) indicates that Jung detested any sort of systemization. Jung also established his position as a reaction against elements of Freud's theory and technique (Zinkin, 1969). Additionally, Jung felt that the pursuit of Analytical Psychology was so unique to the individual personality of the practitioner that he did not believe one should provide specific guidelines as to the practice of Analytical Psychology. While Jung's adoption of an anti-methodological position may have been useful in differentiating Analytical Psychology from Freudian psychoanalysis, I propose that he also discarded an important element of the transformative process.

According to Fordham (1998), the lack of focus on technique had a detrimental effect on the development of well-rounded analysts, "The methods used by Jung, and more so by his followers, were not applicable often in the rough and tumble of everyday psychotherapy when the careful analysis of sexuality and childhood was often needed but neglected" (pp. 56–57). Fordham is alluding to the reality that many patients presenting for therapy or analysis are not initially well suited for a classical Jungian or archetypally focused analysis. Such a situation arises with patients who arrive for therapy not yet functioning at a symbolic level and still needing to address areas of immature psychological development, deficits in identity and self-structure, or experiencing difficulty with affective–behavioral regulation.

Kirsch (2000) captures the essence these two primary attitudes towards technique in Analytical Psychology:

Jung eschewed the word "technique," but there was a general way in which he worked. He used dream analysis, active imagination, and amplification in face-to-face, relatively infrequent sessions, and fostered an active dialectic between himself and his patient. Today there is wide variation in the use of these basic analytic methods. The more developmentally oriented Jungians use a couch, require more frequent sessions, interpret the transference, and focus less on dreams, amplification and active imagination.

(p. 247)

Zinkin (1969) argues that, "both models are essential and complementary" (p. 131). I maintain that the divide between these two positions can be diminished and that a greater emphasis on technique can be assimilated by Analytical Psychology without losing the analytic values so central to Jung's opus. With that perspective in mind, we can now turn our attention to a synopsis of interpretation.

What is an interpretation?

The origins of psychoanalytic interpretation can be traced back to a twelfth-century Latin term, *interpretati*, which means to explain, expound, or understand (Blue & Harrang, 2016). Interpretation is also connected to the field of hermeneutics, "the study of the methodological principles of interpretation" (Merriam-Webster, n.d.), often in reference to the textual analysis of literature, scripture, and alchemy as well as art and history. In analytic therapy, at the most fundamental level, "Interpretation seeks to make conscious the unconscious" (Etchegoyen, 2005, p. 386).

Contrary to some perceptions, a psychoanalytic interpretation is not everything that is spoken to the patient in a session. It is a specific type of verbal interaction set apart from other types of therapeutic utterances – such as asking questions, reframing patient statements, affective mirroring, empathic statements, or reassurance. As Oremland (1991) points out, while all of these interventions may contribute to the progress of an analysis, only interpretation is specifically intended to facilitate the engagement and understanding of the patient's unconscious:

> It is important, however, to recognize that interpretation is interactive and that all aspects of psychotherapeutic interaction are just that, various kinds of inter- actions. Yet, interpretation as an intervention is qualitatively different from other interactions in that its aim is solely to add explicit knowledge, whereas interactive interventions remain largely experiential. Most important, when transferential, interpretation makes the interaction itself the object of analysis.
>
> (p. 10)

In general, interventions that focus on reassurance, advice-giving, problem- solving, encouragement, consolidation of self-esteem, prevention of regression, maintenance of existing defense mechanisms, and maintenance of reality orienta- tion are considered to be supportive interventions (Klerman et al., 1984; Werman, 1984). While these interventions support the patient's conscious perception of the relationship as helpful, accepting, understanding, and supportive, they are not intended or expected to increase the patient's insight, engage unconscious patterns, or facilitate the transformation of psychological structures. All types of psychotherapy or counseling include supportive inventions to some degree, and some forms of therapy focus almost exclusively on supportive interventions. In contrast, analytic therapies seek to minimize the utilization of supportive or sug- gestive interventions while emphasizing interventions, such as interpretation, that engage unconscious processes, increase insight and consciousness, and carry the potential for psychic transformation (Auld & Hyman, 1991). Auld and Hyman indicate, "Psychoanalytic therapy is interpretive rather than suggestive.... Principally, the therapist helps through making interpretations" (p. 19), and that,

"The warm relationship is the necessary context for the interpretive actions of the therapist, because interpretations necessarily involve some narcissistic affront to the patient" (p. 35). Vivona (2013) offers a fuller explication of the interaction between the analytic relationship and the interpretive process:

> The relationship between analyst and patient fosters change when the analyst can articulate, clearly and with empathy, the nature of the relational experiences in which the two participate. It is not insight in the abstract that helps, not the dissemination of ideas separate from the emotional relational context that brings those ideas to mind. It is not warm or benevolent actions or attitudes, not the way the analyst is or seems, separate from what he thinks and says. It is the use of speech to articulate, with an attitude of empathy and openness, what is being experienced in relation to the other and the meaning that can be made of that experience. The interpretation is the analyst's authentic, empathic response to the patient.
>
> (p. 1131)

Jung (1954b), like Auld and Hyman, cautions against the use of suggestion in analytic therapy:

> Methods of treatment based on suggestion are deceptive makeshifts; they are incompatible with the principles of analytical therapy and should be avoided if at all possible. Naturally, suggestion can only be avoided if the doctor is conscious of its possibility. There is at the best of times always enough – and more than enough – unconscious suggestion.
>
> (para. 315)

In any analytic therapy, a balance is necessary between the supportive and interpretive aspects based on the needs, psychological makeup, and presenting problem of the patient. The greater the severity of the patient's psychological state and the lower the patient's resources, the greater the supportive element may need to be. There is rarely an optimal analytic hour in which only interpretive interventions are utilized; there is always an approximation and balancing of these therapeutic characteristics. In addition, within every session, there is a need for flexibility of technique that allows for moment-to-moment shifts to meet the needs of the situation. The goal is awareness of the continuum between supportive and analytic interventions with an ongoing intention of moving closer to the interpretive end of the continuum (see Figure 1.1).

The following exchange is an example of an intervention that could have remained primarily supportive but shifted to an interpretive intervention as the exchange progressed. The exchange takes place at the conclusion of a session. The patient, John, was a student in his late thirties. He manifested sociopathic tendencies and a previous history of drug and alcohol abuse. John had lived a marginal existence for much of his life but seemed to have arrived at a frame of

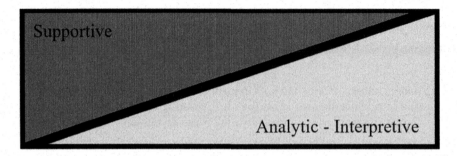

Figure 1.1 The supportive–interpretive continuum

mind where he could begin focusing on lasting transformation. In the session, we had been focused on John's anxiety regarding interactions with his mother. He had recently received a letter and check from his mother and was experiencing anxiety and ambivalence about feeling he should write her back. I made an observation about the level of anxiety she constellated in him and made reference to something he had said, during our previous session, about having to drink two beers before returning a call to his mother. The patient responded, "Oh you remembered." John was moved that I remembered what he had said in the previous session. From a supportive perspective, I could have concluded the session, or I could have said "Of course, I remembered," but neither of those interventional options would have helped John know anything about himself or how he utilizes me. Instead, I choose to continue with an observation of his surprise:

A: You seem surprised that I remembered.
P: I didn't mean any offense. I just meant that none of my therapists before have ever remembered what I've said from week to week.
A: I didn't think you were making a derogatory comment about me.
P: Good, because I wasn't. This therapy is really important to me.

At that point, I made an interpretation focused on his self-experience, that is, of not feeling memorable and his transferential expectation of me. An interpretation was offered to John in two parts with space for him to respond between the two elements of the interpretation.

A: I think you were telling me that you don't feel memorable, so it surprises you that I could hold you in my mind.
P: *(he grins somewhat sheepishly but mixed with some expression of pleasure)* Well, I know that you see a lot of patients and it must be hard to keep all of this stuff straight.
A: You seem to be wondering whether you're important enough to me for me to remember you as an individual among the other people who come into my office.

P: *(becoming tearful)* I know I'm important to you and it's really important that I
       stay with this and finish therapy this time. I've gotten started and quit so many
       times. I can't do that again.

The patient's internal narrative manifested in his belief that he was not memorable and in his anticipation that I would confirm this by not remembering him as a unique individual among my other patients. This exchange highlights the difference between supportive and interpretive interventions. While a supportive intervention would have been well received by the patient, it would not have deepened his understanding of himself or the role I play in his interior landscape.

Therapeutic intervention, which has previously been conceptualized as being either supportive or interpretative, has more recently been conceptualized by the Boston Change Process Study Group (BCPSG, 2010) as addressing implicit relational aspects of the analytic relationship and explicit interpretive aspects of the analytic interaction. The BCPSG have attempted to identify the mutative influences in analytic therapy without making theoretical attributions about those influences (Stern et al., 1998). Utilizing research from infant observation, developmental studies, systems theory, attachment theory, neurosciences, and clinical experience, the BCPSG describe the existence of two, equally important, "mutative phenomena": interpretation and "moments of meeting" (Stern et al., 1998, p. 904). They define "moments of meeting" as authentic person-to-person engagements that alter the patient's sense of self, and indicate "moments of meeting" are first experienced implicitly, that is, outside of conscious awareness.

In the BCPSG model, change or transformation in analytic therapy is brought about through both the relational (implicit) and interpretive (explicit) aspects of the analytic interaction (BCPSG, 2010). According to BCPSG, the interaction between "moments of meeting" and interpretation is not an either/or proposition. The BCPSG developed their position as a corrective to what they perceived as an historical emphasis on interpretation alone, particularly in relation to the stereotype of the analyst as an uninvolved, distant, objective observer of the patient's mind. Therefore, it is not that the work of the analyst and patient occurs in the implicit or explicit domain (i.e., interpretive activity); the two realms are in an ever-evolving mutually supportive relationship with each other. Often, the emergence of "moments of meeting" will be facilitated by interpretation, and interpretive interventions are enhanced by states of intersubjective intimacy created by "moments of meeting." Doctors (2009), working from a contemporary understanding of interpretation, proposes that interpretation is itself a relational process:

Any understanding achieved is a joint creation, emerging from the interaction, rather than an objective truth about one person discovered by another. Interpretations not only emerge from the interaction, but also recursively influence the relationship, for better or worse. In this ongoing reverberatory process, it is often useful to weave into interpretive activity one's sense of where the patient is and where the analyst is at any given intersubjective moment.

(p. 462)

From a Jungian perspective, there is a third mutative factor, the symbolic, that operates concurrently alongside these other two factors. Using Goodheart's (1980) terminology from "Theory of analytic interaction," a "secured symbolizing field" is constellated when all three of these mutative factors have the possibility of impacting the field (p. 8). The possibility of a "secured symbolizing field" increases when the analyst is able to simultaneously participate in the analytic activities of interpretation, symbolic inquiry, and relational "moments of meeting." When the analyst permits these three mutative elements to work synergistically, a more profound transformative experience becomes possible; whereas if the analyst relies on any one of these three factors in isolation, the mutative possibilities diminish.

Defining interpretation

Before looking at the component elements of interpretations, we will examine a few definitions of interpretation, from both psychoanalytic and Jungian perspectives, as well as examining the role interpretation plays in analysis. Psychoanalysis was slow to develop a definition of interpretation or a well-developed hypothesis regarding the mechanism by which interpretation impacts the psychic situation of the patient. It was not until the 1930s that more complete articulations of the interpretive process began to emerge, such as those by Glover (1930) and Strachey (1934). Freud (1914, p. 147) initially saw interpretation as a means for overcoming the patient's resistance to analysis. A short time later, Freud (1917) expanded his concept of interpretation to include a widening of the ego at the expense of the unconscious:

> By means of the work of interpretation, which transforms what is unconscious into what is conscious, the ego is enlarged at the cost of this unconscious; by means of instruction, it is made conciliatory towards the libido and inclined to grant it some satisfaction, and its repugnance to the claims of the libido is diminished by the possibility of disposing of a portion of it by sublimation. The more closely events in the treatment coincide with this ideal description, the greater will be the success of the psycho-analytic therapy.
>
> (p. 455)

In this passage, it is clear that Freud has not yet differentiated between the action of interpretation and the action of suggestion, seen here in his choice of the word "instruction," which is a hold-over from his earlier interest in the therapeutic effects of hypnosis.

Strachey (1934), in his classic article "The nature of the therapeutic action of psychoanalysis," proposes that therapeutic transformation takes place through interpretations, which gradually create lasting changes in the superego structure of the patient. In Strachey's model, the analyst stands in for the patient as "auxiliary superego," allowing a gradual introjection of a new element of the superego that is less punitive or hostile (p. 139). Conceptually, this is somewhat akin to Jung's observation that the analyst must often carry the patient's projection of the Self until a time when the patient is sufficiently able to maintain relationship with the Self independent of the analyst. While Strachey's explanation of the process of transformation through interpretation was a conceptual advance, most contemporary psychoanalysts would not limit the influence of interpretation to modification of the superego. The scope of interpretive interventions has widened considerably in contemporary analysis, with interpretations now focused on a much broader range of unconscious experience.

The persistent caricature of the traditional Freudian analyst – as distant and detached, mostly sitting silently, and interpreting infrequently from a position of observing authority – has at times created a bias against the use of analytic interpretation. The caricature does have an element of historical accuracy, particularly in the United States, from the 1940s through the 1970s. During this period, the New York Psychoanalytic Society and the American Psychoanalytic Association fostered a dogmatic attitude toward psychoanalysis and tried to enforce a rigid theoretical and technical approach to the practice of psychoanalysis (Rangell, 2006). Racker (1968), in a critique of such dogmatism, provides a description of the interpretative stance of analysts practicing from a position of objective authority, "For these analysts the interpretation must be given *when the analyst knows what the patient does not know, needs to know, and is capable of knowing*" (p. 41, italics in original). During the 1970s, the hegemony of ego psychology was diminished by the influence of the interpersonal school of psychoanalysis,[5] object relations theory, and the self psychology of Heinz Kohut, as new theoretical models and methods of analysis were introduced. The evolution of psychoanalytic theory and practice has continued with the emergence of the intersubjective and relational approaches to psychoanalysis. Few analysts practicing today would identify with the stereotype of the detached observing analyst who interprets what is transpiring in the patient's mind with absolute authority. In fact, this sort of *experience-distant* interpretation is not consistent with the description of effective interpretation offered by Strachey in 1934:

> Every mutative interpretation must be emotionally "immediate"; the patient must experience it as something actual. This requirement, that the interpretation must be "immediate", may be expressed in another way by saying that interpretations must always be directed to the "point of urgency".
>
> (p. 150)

In the simplest terms, an interpretation is an invitation for the patient to see their world in a new way. Ideally, it contains some element that comes as a surprise for the analyst first and then for the patient. That is, it reveals something previously unseen or not experienced consciously. Robert Frost (1972) offers a similar perspective about writing poetry, "No surprise for the writer, no surprise for the reader" (p. 440). An effective interpretation is somewhat like the well-known drawing of a woman that is seen by some as a picture of a young woman and by others as a picture of an old woman. There is typically an element of surprise for the viewer when the other possibility is made clear. Their surprise is accompanied by a shift in perception in which the viewer is able to see both the young woman and the old woman. Similar shifts in self-perception are facilitated by well-crafted interpretations. Interpretation also provides meaning to what is being experienced; the experience having previously lacked meaning or for which meaning was distorted.

Shifting now to a more formal definition of interpretation, according to Moore and Fine (1990) interpretation is:

> The central therapeutic activity of the analyst during treatment, a process whereby the analyst expresses in words what he or she comes to understand about the patient's mental life. This understanding is based upon the patient's descriptions of memories, fantasies, wishes, fears, and other elements of psychic conflict that were formerly unconscious or known to the patient only in incomplete, inaccurate, or otherwise distorted form. Interpretation is also based upon observation of the way the patient distorts the relationship with the analyst to meet unconscious needs and to relive old experiences. . . . An interpretation is a statement of new knowledge about the patient. Both patient and analyst may contribute to it, although it is usually initiated by the analyst. . . . An interpretation usually involves additions and modifications by both analyst and patient as new material emerges. The process of interpretation allows the patient to understand his or her past and present inner life in a new, less distorted, and more complete way, leading to the possibility of changes in feelings, attitudes, and behavior. *Working through* links the process of interpretation to therapeutic change.
>
> (pp. 103–104, italics in original)

More succinctly, Levy (1990) indicates that, "Interpretation. . . is the verbal expression of what is understood about the patient and his problems" (p. 4). As we can see, the two definitions just cited focus primarily on psychic conflicts, distortions, and problems. While these areas of focus are essential, important, and frequently present in most patients, these definitions leave out the forward-looking, transcendent aspect of the psyche articulated by Jung, for example, "The unconscious is continually active, combining its material in ways which serve the future" (Jung, 1953a, para. 197). This difference highlights the point that the technique of interpretation remains fundamentally the same across theoretical orientations, but the content and focus of the interpretations shift based upon the analyst's theoretical orientation (e.g., Pine, 1990, p. 8). The teleological thrust in Analytical Psychology is most strongly represented in Jung's (1916) concept of the transcendent function, the internal mechanism by which opposites of psychological experience are transformed via a higher synthesis into a new third, and in his concept of individuation.[6] Therefore, Jungian analysts also include the teleological aspect of the psyche among the various possibilities for interpretation. For example, a Jungian version of the Levy definition, cited above, might read,

"Interpretation is the verbal expression of what is understood about the unconscious situation of the patient," capturing a broader view of the psyche that looks both forwards and backwards, embracing the teleological aspects of psyche in addition to the disruptive elements.

Michael Fordham is the analyst primarily responsible for fostering the incorporation of psychoanalytic technique into Jungian analysis. Fordham (1978) indicates that an interpretation, "connects together statements of the patient that have a common source unknown to the patient. So when the analyst tells the patient about the source he makes an inference that goes beyond the actual material at hand" (p. 113). Fordham's definition highlights the element of surprise essential for effective interpretation and the necessary movement beyond the immediate concrete meaning of the patient's verbalizations. Therefore, analytic interpretation treats all patient interactions as symbolic; that is, they carry "a meaning that is darkly divined" (Jung, 1960b, para. 644). Elsewhere, Fordham (1991a) provides further elaboration on the specific construction of an interpretation:

> An interpretation is composed of that part of the patient's unconscious digested and thought about by the analyst. The result is then communicated to the patient in such a way as to give meaning to the patient's material. To do this it must have a clear structure and contain a verb.
>
> (p. 209)

This definition highlights the creation of meaning, the importance of the analyst's reflective capacities, and the need for clarity in the interpretive process. Having established a general overview of interpretation, we can now turn to Jung's views on interpretation along with various post-Jungian perspectives.

C. G. Jung's perspective on technique and interpretation

An examination of Jung's views on interpretation is complicated and fraught with ambiguity. As Dehing (1992) puts it, "Unfortunately, C. G. Jung is rarely explicit with regard to his analytical practice; he always refused to lay down technical rules and little is known of his actual psychotherapeutic interventions" (p. 31). In most instances, Jung utilized his published case studies to support theoretical constructs he was developing or to elaborate on the archetypal themes present in the material of his patients. Only infrequently does he provide glimmers of how he worked with his patients. In fact, according to Astor (1998), "Jung often sounded hostile to close discussion of technique that he feared might turn the individual relationship between therapist and patient into the application of a method" (p. 698).

In examining Jung's relationship with technique, it is important to hold in mind that one of Jung's principal agendas, particularly throughout much of his early post-Freudian writing, was to articulate the contrast between Freud's approach to analysis and the position he was advocating (Jung, 1958b), for example:

My difference with Freud begins with the interpretation of unconscious material. It stands to reason that you cannot integrate anything into consciousness without some measure of comprehension, i.e., insight. In order to make the unconscious material assimilable or understandable, Freud implies his famous sexual theory, which conceives the material brought to light through analysis mainly as sexual tendencies (or immoral wishes) that are incompatible with the conscious attitude. Freud's standpoint here is based on the rationalistic materialism of the scientific views current in the late nineteenth century.

(para. 541)

In this passage, it is clear that Jung's disagreement was not with the act of interpretation *per se*, but was instead with interpretations constructed from a limited range of theoretical possibilities resulting in foregone conclusions. However, psychoanalytic interpretation from a contemporary perspective does not resemble Jung's description.[7] Yet, Jung's portrayal of interpretation as a mechanistic, overly rational, and circumscribed activity persists within the Jungian community.

As a result of his agenda to differentiate Analytical Psychology from Freudian psychoanalysis, Jung placed more emphasis on the differences, rather than the similarities, between his perspective and the Freudian perspective.[8] Despite this emphasis, Jung recurrently endorsed the need for "reductive analysis" before proceeding to a "synthetic process;" for example, "So long as one is moving in the sphere of genuine neuroses one cannot dispense with the use of either Freud or Adler" (Jung, 1954b, para. 24). Jung (1965) maintained this perspective throughout his life, asserting in *Memories, Dreams, Reflections*, "In dealing with individuals, only individual understanding will do. We need a different language for every patient. In one analysis I can be heard talking the Adlerian dialect, in another the Freudian" (p. 131). Elsewhere, Jung (1953a, para. 96) underscores the importance of analyzing the infantile neurosis of the patient: "In the transference all kinds of infantile fantasies are projected. They must be cauterized, i.e., resolved by reductive analysis, and this is generally known as 'resolving the transference'."

While Jung (1954b) is not often specific about how to proceed during an analysis, he does outline four stages or aims of analysis: "catharsis, elucidation, education, and transformation" (para. 122). Jung associates the elucidation stage with Freud and reductive analysis, in particular, the resolution of the transference through interpretation. While Jung cautions about lingering too long in a reductive approach, he indicates that interpretation is an essential element of the analytic process, for example, "the transference relationship is in especial need of elucidation" (para. 144).

Determining Jung's position regarding analytic interpretation is further complicated by the context of his statements about the interpretive process. In most instances, when Jung speaks about interpretation, he is referring to the interpretation of dreams rather than the interpretation of the analytic interaction. Therefore, it is necessary to make certain assumptions about Jung's approach to interpretation, namely that his perspective on the process of dream interpretation also generalizes to the interpretation of the analytic interaction. In terms of dream interpretation, the three primary areas of emphasis for Jung include: 1) the juxtaposition of "reductive" and "synthetic" approaches, 2) the delineation of "objective" versus "subjective" modes of interpretation, and 3) the utilization of a hermeneutic approach to dream interpretation. These areas of interpretative focus are briefly summarized below.

The primary distinction Jung makes in his model of dream interpretation is the juxtaposition of a reductive approach to interpretation as opposed to a synthetic approach. For Jung, a reductive approach looks to the patient's history searching for experiences which explain or give meaning to the content and configuration of a dream. Jung associated the reductive approach with Freud's model of dream interpretation and used the term "reductive" synonymously with the terms "causal," "regressive," and "analytical." Jung utilized the term "synthetic" to refer to a method of dream interpretation that seeks to understand dream material from a forward-looking or prospective position. The synthetic method asks the question, "What is emerging from the patient's psyche, and how is it guiding the patient?" This approach is closely tied to Jung's concept of individuation.

Jung (1917) proposed that synthetic interpretation, which he also referred to as the "constructive," "progressive," or "hermeneutic" approach, creates the greatest receptivity to symbols appearing in patients' dreams:

> The significance of a symbol is not that it is a disguised indication of something that is generally known but that it is an endeavour to elucidate by analogy what is as yet completely unknown and only in the process of formation. The phantasy represents to us that which is just developing under the form of a more or less apposite analogy. By analytical reduction to something universally known, we destroy the actual value of the symbol; but it is appropriate to its value and meaning to give it a hermeneutical interpretation.
>
> (p. 468)

It is clear that Jung (1954a) believed that the synthetic interpretive stance was superior to, and provided a broader perspective than, the reductive stance:

> Thus we apply a largely reductive point of view in all cases where it is a question of illusions, fictions, and exaggerated attitudes. On the other hand, a constructive point of view must be considered for all cases where the conscious attitude is more or less normal, but capable of greater development and refinement, or where unconscious tendencies, also capable of development, are being misunderstood and kept under by the conscious mind. The reductive standpoint is the distinguishing feature of Freudian interpretation. It always leads back to the primitive and elementary. The constructive standpoint, on the other hand, tries to synthesize, to build up, to direct one's gaze forwards.
>
> (para. 195)

However, elsewhere, Jung (1953a) also indicates that both reductive and synthetic interpretive processes have a place in the analytic process:

> When the analytical or causal-reductive interpretation ceases to bring to light anything new, but only the same thing in different variations, the moment has come to look out for possible archetypal motifs. If such a motive comes clearly to the forefront, it is high time to change the interpretive procedure.
>
> (para. 129)

Despite his position that the synthetic approach to interpretation is superior to the reductive approach, Jung (1954b) acknowledges that, during the course of an analysis, it is difficult to determine whether to utilize a reductive or a synthetic approach:

> The dialectical procedure has another source . . . that is the *multiple significance of symbolic contents* . . . I distinguish between the analytical-reductive and the synthetic-hermeneutic interpretation . . . Both interpretations can be shown to be correct . . . But it makes an enormous difference in practice whether we interpret something regressively or progressively. It is no easy matter to decide aright in a given case.
>
> (para. 9, italics in original)

According to Jung (1953a), the reductive and synthetic approaches to interpretation are interwoven with subjective and objective levels of dream interpretation:

> I call every interpretation which equates the dream images with real objects as an interpretation on the objective level. In contrast to this is the interpretation which refers to every part of the dream and all the actors in it back to the dreamer himself. This I call interpretation on the subjective level . . . Thus the synthetic or constructive process of interpretation is interpretation on the subjective level.
>
> (para. 130–131)

In other words, in Jung's method of dream interpretation, a dream can potentially be interpreted as pertaining to the dreamer's outer life experiences (i.e., objective) or the dynamic interactions of the patient's interior world (i.e., subjective). In the subjective mode of interpretation, interactions between various dream elements are interpreted as reflecting the dramatic engagement between various aspects of the patient's psychological structures and processes. Therefore, Jung equated subjective dream interpretation, focused on the patient's interior world, with his synthetic approach.

The final characteristic feature of Jung's approach to dream interpretation is the application of a hermeneutic methodology modeled after the interpretation of scriptures and alchemical texts. Jung came to see dream interpretation as a fundamentally hermeneutic process in which associations and amplifications can be utilized to deepen the meaning and experience of the dream. According to Jung (1953a):

> The essence of hermeneutics, an art widely practiced in former times, consists in adding further analogies to the one already supplied by the symbol: in the first place subjective analogies produced at random by the patient, then objective analogies provided by the analyst out of his general knowledge . . . Certain lines of psychological development then stand out that are at once individual and collective . . . Their validity is proved by their intensive value for life.
>
> (para. 493)

In this passage, "subjective analogies" refer to the patient's personal associations to the dream elements and "objective analogies" refer to amplifications of the dream elements drawn from the analyst's knowledge of archetypal images or motifs, such as those contained in mythology, fairytales, religions, and alchemy. In his study of alchemy, Jung noted that it was quite difficult to understand alchemical texts in isolation. It was only after he had studied a large number of texts that he began to recognize that there were lexical patterns used in the alchemical texts and that the alchemical authors often made reference to other alchemical works in their writing. It was primarily through this process of alchemical exploration that Jung came to recognize that similar patterns, when incorporated into dream interpretation, frequently led to deeper understanding of the patient's dreams.

While Jung offers little guidance regarding interpretation of the analytic interaction, he provides several perspectives on dream interpretation. Those familiar with Jung's opus are left to decide whether it is reasonable to assume that Jung would follow similar lines of thought in approaching other forms of unconscious communication during the analytic interaction. For myself, I find Jung's perspective on dream interpretation to be readily applicable to the interpretation of the analytic interaction.

Trends in post-Jungian perspectives on interpretation

With Michael Fordham's introduction of a new model of individuation (Fordham, 1958), which proposes that individuation begins *in utero* and continues throughout life, the reductive–synthetic dichotomy in interpretation began to be re-evaluated. As the concept of individuation was expanded into a life-long developmental model, it necessitated the analyst cultivate both "backward-" and "forward-" looking perspectives. Fordham (1978) argues that there are few occasions when a sharp contrast between reductive and synthetic approaches can be maintained. Like Janus, the two-faced god of the Greeks, it became necessary to look backward to resolve aspects of experience interfering with individuation, and to look forward, discerning the direction of psychological progression or movement. Based upon new understandings of synchronicity, infant development, and lifespan development, a contemporary Jungian position has emerged arguing that the maintenance of a reductive–synthetic dichotomy is no longer viable in the analytic setting (e.g., Siegelman, 1994; Jacoby, 1996; Connolly, 2015). This shift has also been accompanied by ideas emerging in the psychoanalytic world that have greater compatibility with Jungian concepts. As Jacoby (1996) frames the issue: "As far as the question of reductive analysis is concerned, I find it less and less meaningful to set 'reductive' against 'symbolic', 'clinical' against 'archetypal', etc." (p. 396). Similarly, Siegelman (1994, p. 494) advocates for the adoption of the term "developmental analysis" to take into account the retrospective, contemporaneous, and prospective lenses which are inextricably interwoven throughout any analysis.

A position has also emerged that argues against the bifurcation of experience into the personal and archetypal (i.e., collective) domains as Jung advocated in his work. As an example of Jung's (1953a) position, he states:

> When the collective psyche is conceived as a personal appendage of the individual, the result is distortion of the personality which it is almost impossible to deal with. That is why one is so strongly recommended to establish a very clear distinction between the personal psyche and the collective psyche.
>
> (para. 462)

For Williams (1963), Zinkin (1969, 1979), and Whitmont (1987), the distinction between experiences of the personal unconscious and elements of the collective unconscious have significance and utility on a theoretical level, but in practice they argue that these experiences are indivisible. As Williams (1963) points out, one of the potential dangers of this dichotomization is the reinforcement of splitting tendencies of the psyche: "In Jungian psychology, the conceptual split, though necessary for purposes of exposition, is considered to be undesirable in practice, since it may add to the splitting tendencies already operative in the psyche" (p. 49).

Despite these developments, a well-developed model of interpretation has not emerged in Analytical Psychology. Only a handful of authors have attempted to articulate a theory or method for interpretation. As previously mentioned, Fordham (1978, 1991a) was instrumental in incorporating aspects of psychoanalytic technique, in particular interpretation, into the field of Analytical Psychology. Much of Fordham's material on interpretation parallels the model developed by psychoanalytic practitioners. Fordham elaborates on the use of interpretation in the analysis of primitive mental states, articulates a model of interpretation that shifts the focus from the reductive–synthetic comparison to a model emphasizing the differentiation of self and not-self experiences, and describes the modifications of the interpretative method when encountering defenses of the self.[9] Quite illuminating and thought-provoking is a debate that occurred in print between Fordham (1991a, 1991b) and Schwartz-Salant (1991a) regarding the nature of interpretation, the effectiveness of interpretation in the engagement of primitive mental states, the analyst's use of their own experience in formulating interpretations, and the impact of the "analytic third" on the process of interpretation. Their debate serves as a useful introduction to the concept of interpretation and the diverse possibilities or positions inherent in the interpretive process, as well as providing the reader an opportunity for vicarious evaluation of their own perspective on interpretation.

In addition to the positions articulated in the Fordham and Schwartz-Salant debate, Dieckmann (1991) provides a useful introductory chapter on interpretation. His articulation of the relationship between interpretation and the working-through of the patient's complexes is particularly useful, as is his focus on the importance of reductive interpretation for the integration of the personal shadow. The central role of metaphor in Jungian analysis and interpretation is developed effectively by Siegelmen (1990). Her metaphoric approach is likely to provide a more familiar and comfortable transition into interpretation for Jungians working from a more classical perspective. Covington (1995) provides an articulate examination of the relationship between interpretation, the construction of the patient's personal narrative, and the development of the patient's identity.

Ledermann (1995) surveys the potential pitfalls of interpretation. She highlights the potential contra-indications for interpretation with patients with weak ego structure, the danger of premature interpretation, and the impact of the analyst's countertransference on the interpretive process. In terms of countertransference issues, Ledermann addresses the tendency for some analysts to resist interpretation out of fear of damaging the patient and the problems that arise when the analyst's need to interpret is motivated by their own psychopathology. Like Ledermann, von der Tann (1999) provides a cautionary examination of interpretation. Rather than falling into the myth that there is one correct interpretation for each analytic moment, von der Tann emphasizes the multiplicity of possible interpretations, each of which may articulate some essential facet of the various psychological dimensions present in every analytic moment. He proposes that "every interpretation is influenced by countertransference, however unconscious or unidentified this might be" (p. 62). Instead of searching for the mythical "correct" interpretation, he invokes Winnicott's concept of the "good enough" experience as applied to the process of interpretation.

More recently, Astor (2011) and Bisagni (2013) have continued the exploration of interpretation in Analytical Psychology. Astor (2011) focuses on the language used for interpretation, how interpretations are delivered, the affective component of interpretations, and conceptualizing the level of experience on which the interpretation is focused. He also emphasizes the importance of the listening process during the interpretive process, that is, during the formulation, articulation, and reception phases of interpretation. Astor proposes that the use of language in interpretation potentially becomes more nuanced when Bion's (1970) concepts of alpha function, dream thoughts, beta elements and alpha elements are paired with Jung's concept of the transcendent function. Bisagni (2013) reviews the interaction between mental representation, empathy, somatic experience, and the language of interpretation. More specifically, he examines word choice as an expression of intentionality and action in the analytic setting. Bisagni also reviews some of the potential hypotheses regarding interpretation that emerge from findings in contemporary neuroscience.

Summary

The preceding review of the history of technique and interpretation in Analytical Psychology highlights the Jungian ambivalence regarding these aspects of the analytic experience. The total available literature on interpretation in Jungian analysis consists of a couple of book chapters and a handful of articles. While the authors cited have contributed valuable insights into the interpretive process in Analytical Psychology, there has not been an in-depth exploration of the interpretive process from a Jungian perspective. This volume seeks to address this regrettable lacuna: historically, theoretically, and methodologically. My aim is to present an amalgam that integrates the best of the psychoanalytic and Jungian viewpoints.

Notes

1 Some Jungian programs also include the technique of picture interpretation, sand tray work, and active imagination in the training curriculum.
2 The analytic frame refers to general guidelines that shape how the analytic interaction will unfold, that is, a) whether free association (speaking whatever comes to mind without censoring thoughts) will be encouraged; b) whether the patient will utilize the couch or the chair; c) the time, frequency, and duration of sessions; d) how communication between sessions will be addressed; e) the establishment of the analytic fee and how analysis will be paid for; f) agreement upon arrangements for rescheduled, missed, or canceled sessions as well as vacations; g) the issue of physical contact; h) the physical set-up of the consulting room; i) confidentiality; j) and contact with outside parties. The purpose of the analytic frame is to create a relationship and setting that maximizes the unfolding and understanding of unconscious material. Within Jungian circles, this is often referred to in alchemical terms, such as the creation of the *vas hermeticum* or the *vas bene clausum*.
3 Also referred to as the working relationship or analytic alliance. The therapeutic alliance refers to the capacity of the analytic couple to develop a sufficient level of mutual trust, intimacy, and curiosity for analytic work to proceed.
4 For example, Fordham (1974a, 1978), Lambert (1981), Dieckmann (1991), and Sedgwick (2001).
5 Led by Harry Stack Sullivan, Eric Fromm, Karen Horney, Clara Thompson, and Frieda Fromm-Reichmann.

6 The progressive movement of the individual personality towards wholeness and expression of that wholeness.
7 See Blue and Harrang (2016), Hooberman (2007), Rubovits-Seitz (2001), and Stark (1999) for more detailed descriptions of the breadth and diversity of focus in contemporary psychoanalysis.
8 As a number of authors have pointed out, many of these differences have become much less pronounced, particularly within the past forty years, as ideas have emerged in psychoanalytic theory which parallel concepts cultivated by Jung, for example, Roazen (1976), Samuels (1996), Siegelman (1994), Winborn (2018).
9 A more primitive class of defenses identified by Fordham that focus on the protection of the self-structure against threat rather than the more commonly encountered defenses of the ego as articulated by Anna Freud (1967).

Chapter 2

Foundations of transformational discourse

Language, metaphor, and poetics in interpretation

Interpretation and language

Before venturing further into the exploration of interpretation, theoretical issues involved with the use of language in the analytic process will be examined. Psychoanalysis has long been referred to as the "talking cure,"[1] and the interpretive process is intimately tied with language and dialogue. According to Schermer (2011), "Freud viewed interpretation as the uncovering of a hidden set of predetermined meanings and structures" (p. 822). The characterization of psychoanalysis as a cure undertaken by talking, primarily through interpretation alone, persisted for decades. As a result, there is a tendency to think of the interpretation as a means of disseminating information from the analyst to the patient and attention has been overly focused on the content of the interpretation. Gill (1954) provides a characteristic example of this position which saw catharsis, insight, and working through as the primary modes of therapeutic change in analysis: "Psychoanalysis is that technique which. . . results in the development of a regressive transference neurosis and the ultimate resolution of this neurosis by techniques of interpretation alone" (p. 775). An outcome of this orthodoxy, and the ensuing backlash against such orthodoxy, has been the tendency to dismiss or overlook the potential and multiple layers of meaning associated with the interpretive experience.

Over time, the conceptualization of therapeutic change evolved. One of the first steps in that evolution was Franz Alexander's (Alexander & French, 1946) concept of the "corrective emotional experience" which suggests that the transference relationship is not just a repetition of the patient's past patterns, replicated with the analyst, but that the analytic situation also provides opportunities for new experiences with the figure of the analyst. It is important to note that similar themes were concurrently articulated by Jung (1946) in *The Psychology of the Transference* utilizing the lens of alchemy. Conceptual thinking about the mechanism of therapeutic change continued to evolve with the emergence of Kleinian analysis, object relations, archetypal psychology, self psychology, intersubjectivity, and the relational school of analysis.

The introduction of the intersubjective and relational perspectives into contemporary analytic thinking has resulted in increased attention to the interactive aspects of the analytic relationship. Mitchell (1998) characterizes the shift in this way:

In the relational-conflict model, both the informational content and the affective tone are regarded as crucial, but their effects are understood somewhat differently in terms of their role in positioning the analyst relative to the analysand. An interpretation is a *complex relational event*, not primarily because it alters something inside the analysand, not because it releases a stalled developmental process, but because it says something very important about where the analyst stands vis-à-vis the analysand, about what sort of relatedness is possible between the two of them.

> (pp. 294–295, italics in original)

While our understanding of the therapeutic action of interpretation has evolved since Freud, Vivona (2003) indicates, "Mutative moments in the therapeutic hour, then, must always involve embracing figures of speech" (p. 64).

Questioning the interpretive mode

While this shift has introduced a more nuanced view of the relational field, the shift has also been accompanied by a diminished focus on the art and craft of interpretation. Hillman (1975) called attention to this shift decades ago:

Even psychotherapy, which began as a "talking cure" – the rediscovery of the oral tradition of telling one's story – is abandoning language for touch, cry, and gesture. We dare not be eloquent. To be passionate, psychotherapy now says we must be physical or primitive. Such psychotherapy promotes a new barbarism. Our semantic anxiety has made us forget words, too, burn and become flesh as we speak. . . We need to recall the angel aspect of the word, recognizing words as independent carriers of soul between people. . . Words, like angels, are powers which have invisible power over us.

> (p. 9)

A facet of this shift has been the characterization of interpretation as a predominantly intellectual process. Various arguments and counter-arguments regarding interpretation have emerged in the analytic literature, resulting in an either/or dichotomization, or splitting, of the analytic process. The relational and interpretive aspects of analytic transformation have become conceptualized as opposed or operating along independent lines of influence.

The tendency to split or dichotomize these transformative processes has been influenced by infant observation studies and developmental research, which has resulted in increased focus on sensory, non-verbal, and pre-verbal experience. According to Vivona (2006), the new focus on infant and developmental research (e.g., Stern, 1985; Stern et al., 1998; Beebee & Lachmann, 2002) to inform understanding of non-verbal and unspoken aspects of experience, provided many useful insights, but has also resulted in a diminished emphasis on the language of analytic interaction. For Vivona (2006), Stern and his colleagues exaggerate the "abstract, orderly, and disembodied qualities of language, and consequently underestimate the degree to which lived interpersonal experience can be meaningfully verbalized" (p. 877) while creating a "radical" (p. 883) and artificial disconnection between the verbal and non-verbal realms:

> Because he conceives the nonverbal realm as organized preverbally, Stern forecloses the possibility that nonverbal experiences may be organized at other levels, or that meanings may be known and not spoken or spoken and not known. . . The belief that language is inherently unable to do justice to important felt experiences leads Stern and his colleagues to search for techniques that can; when found, techniques that mobilize affective interpersonal experiences are assumed to operate outside verbalization. . .
>
> (p. 894)

In contrast to Stern, Vivona (2006) argues:

> Language can and does evoke and even create mutative affective and interpersonal experiences; that is, the clinical data suggest that the verbal and nonverbal realms of experience are not inherently disconnected. Certainly these realms have different qualities and different communicative potentials; they are distinct; neither can subsume the other. Certainly some felt experiences are difficult to capture in words. Yet this difficulty need not be conceived as an inherent limitation of language. The fact that poets and novelists and even some psychoanalysts do paint pictures with words suggests that language offers this potential to us all.
>
> (p. 894)

As greater awareness about the non-verbal, relational, and implicit aspects of the analytic experience has developed, an unfortunate ramification has been a gradual diminishment of emphasis on the verbal interaction of analytic therapy and an associated decline in the appreciation of interpretation as a core competency for analytic work. At times, it appears the interpretive baby has unwittingly been thrown out with the bathwater.

Although fictive, the film *Arrival* (Villeneuve, 2016) captures the essential nature of language for communication. The movie follows linguist Louise Banks who is contracted by the United States military to establish communication with extraterrestrial beings who have appeared in several locations across the world. As anxiety and paranoia mount, Banks must discover a way to communicate with the aliens to discern why they have arrived on Earth before rising tensions lead to war. For a variety of reasons, spoken language is unavailable as a source of communication. The only communicative clues are fluid, inky, abstract images generated by the aliens into their atmosphere. Banks eventually realizes the images are logograms, is able to decipher them, and ultimately begins utilizing logograms to interact with the alien beings. The interactions depicted in the movie are informed by academic linguistic theories which address the function of language, both oral and written. How language influences or structures the subjective perception of reality is a particular focus. As vividly portrayed in the film, language is required to process experience and interact, whether the content of the communication is abstract, emotional, or relational.

Interpretation is a bridging experience in which insight and relationship are not in opposition but instead are two contributors to an underlying process – different avenues into a sense of connection – providing a sense of understanding and being understood that facilitates new growth and integration. The interactive and complementary qualities of interpretive, relational, symbolic, and implicit influences have been articulated in different ways from a variety of analytic orientations. Arlow (1979) states, "In the therapeutic interaction between patient and analyst, mutual understanding derives from the power of human speech to create states of mind in the listener akin to those of the speaker" (p. 364). Vivona (2006) indicates the "interactions between the implicit and verbal domains permits an expanded conceptualization of the mutative effects" during the analytic interaction (p. 887). Schermer (2011) proposes, "Hermeneutical perspectives, as distinct, say, from ideologies and scientific theories, are not contradictory ways of understanding and explaining phenomena but complementary vantage points for enhancing and deepening experience and establishing pathways to meaning" (pp. 837–838). From a Jungian perspective, Kugler (1982) argues that, "Language is always figurative, symbolic, and it remains a futile endeavor to try to separate the 'true' lexical sense from the figurative or metaphorical one" (p. 21). Schenk (2016) summarizes the central role that language plays in analysis and in mediating most other forms of experience:

> Clinical work, as all of consciousness, is steeped in and emerges out of language. Language is the medium of our knowing, and knowing the medium of our relating. Language has us; words dream us. . . Before any kind of distinction of thought, feeling, sensation or intuition comes language – language, not as "just words", but as image. Words are images, and images as encompassing worlds present themselves as and through language.
>
> (p. 676)

Even when expressive modalities (such as art, music, movement, or sand play) are incorporated into analytic therapy, these expressive experiences are ultimately discussed or interpreted in some way by the analyst and patient. To interpret in an emotionally impactful and transformative manner requires the analyst to be connected and present intellectually, emotionally, relationally, and symbolically. When viewed from a transformational perspective, "interpretation represents a revelatory 'presence' that transforms the patient and the analyst" (Schermer, 2011, p. 822).

This chapter examines the role of language and dialogue in analytic therapy, as well as the role of metaphor and poetics in interpretation. I maintain that interpretation remains one of the core modalities by which analytic therapy facilitates transformation and that the dichotomy set up between spoken and unspoken influences reflects a misunderstanding of language in general and interpretation in particular.

The qualities of language

One of the common criticisms sometimes directed at interpretive interventions is that language is abstract, logical, and not sufficiently affective to convey deeper emotions and bodily sensation. At times, this argument takes the form of, "Interpretation is too left-brained."[2] However, as Vivona (2013) indicates, words are not stored in purely abstract form: "Current neuroscience research. . . suggests that words are not stored in a purely abstract form, even in adulthood" (p. 1120).

Vivona's statement is consistent with other contemporary analytic viewpoints, such as Quinodoz (2003), who perceives verbal language as having more holistic qualities:

> The speaker is addressing his entire person, so implicitly giving rise to a form of listening that mobilizes affects and sensations, and arousing fantasies, including bodily fantasies. . . We can now more readily understand why the analyst needs to prioritize the incarnate aspect of language when addressing patients whose lack of internal cohesion makes them anxious: these patients need, precisely, to be heard by an analyst who can listen to them with the whole of his person – thought, feeling, and body combined in a unity – and who will speak to them in a manner that addresses the totality of their person.
> (pp. 36–37)

Similarly, Loewald (1980) emphasizes that language is not a passive collection of words; language is also an action and a potential when placed within the context of the patient's narrative: "Language is not merely a means of reporting action, it is itself action; narrative has a dramatic potential of its own" (p. 366).

Thinking and language

There are misperceptions regarding the relationship between language and thinking. Freud proposed two kinds of thinking – primary process and secondary process (Moore & Fine, 1990). Primary-process thinking, well illustrated by dreams, is non-linear, imagistic, less structured, and frequently characterized by an apparent disregard for logical connections or the realities of time. According to Freud, primary-process thinking is dominated by wishes, affects, conflict, and/ or unconscious fantasy. In contrast, secondary-process thinking is conceived as logical, primarily verbal, and reality-oriented. It is utilized in making judgments, problem-solving, or achievement of goals.

Jung (1956) put forth a similar organization of thinking in *Symbols of Transformation*. Like Freud, Jung proposed two kinds of thinking: directed and non-directed thinking. Directed thinking is verbally structured through language and associated with consciousness and logic. Non-directed thinking, also referred to by Jung as phantastic or subjective thinking, is associated with unconscious motives and relies more on archaic, imagistic processes. As Jung posits, imaging is a form of non-verbal thinking. Non-directed thinking and directed thinking are linked through the vehicle of metaphor.

Those questioning the value of language-based intervention often depict language as exclusively based on secondary-process thinking. However, Vivona (2003), incorporating research on language, neuroscience, and cognition, argues, "Language then is both a hallmark of secondary process and a bridge to primary process" (p. 54). She adds:

> Only language can bring together the conscious verbal knowing of secondary process and the doing, feeling, and being of primary process. . . Speech is both the intrapsychic and the interpersonal mechanism of transformation. It is due to the bridging potential of language that talking can cure.
>
> (p. 56)

Vivona concurs with Loewald's (1980) position that language, "ties together human beings and self and object world, and it binds abstract thought with the bodily concreteness and power of life. In the word primary and secondary process are reconciled" (p. 204). Rather than reinforcing abstract thinking, language and interpretation serve as bridges between primary-process/non-directed thinking and secondary-process/directed thinking. It is in this transitional area, between these two kinds of thinking, that the greatest potential for transformation exists.

Embodiment and language

Closely related to the issue of language and thinking is the issue of embodiment. In both psychoanalytic and Jungian circles, embodiment has taken on greater significance of late (e.g., Fast, 1992; Meissner, 1998; Muller & Tillman, 2006; Jones, 2011; Connolly, 2013). Embodiment theories hypothesize that psychological processes are strongly influenced by and processed through the body, including motor systems, somatically experienced affects, and sensory-perceptual processes. Embodiment theory also addresses body image, body schema, and body self, as well as addressing mind–body dualism.

Therapeutically, embodiment theory emphasizes greater awareness of the body during therapeutic sessions, including bodily focused interventions and utilization of language that creates space for the discussion of somatic experience. The recent emphasis on embodiment, while laudatory and necessary, overlooks the nature of the existing relationship between the body and language; language is already embodied. A simple example of this is the experience of physical motion through space. The bodily sensation of physical motion is "scaffolded" onto mental concepts of geographic space and chronological motion through time (Geary, 2011, p. 96).

In other words, the sensation of physical movement is the impetus for the activation of metaphors used to translate the sensation of movement into other domains of experience while retaining elements of the original stimulus experience. In Western culture, movement is often spoken about directionally, for example, forward or backward, yet these word concepts are also used to refer to past and future. While the experience of movement by the human body is relatively universal, it will be processed differently, both metaphorically and linguistically, by different cultures because of variation in language usage within each culture.

Contemporary research in the neurological and cognitive sciences (Varla, Thompson, & Rosch, 1991; Damasio, 1994; Johnson, 1987, 2007, 2017; Lakoff & Johnson, 1999; Pecher & Zwaan, 2005; Vivona, 2009; Saxbe et al., 2013) demonstrates the reciprocal influence of words on brain, mind, and body. Language itself is shown to be grounded in sensorimotor processes and personal memories: "This conception of words as entwined with aspects of lived experience is consistent with the contemporary view of language as embodied. . . which allows that language can have somatic and experiential concomitants, consequences, or both" (Vivona, 2013, p. 1123). Such studies demonstrate that cognition and language are grounded in embodied experience and that sensory perception and motor action support human understanding of words and concepts.

Understanding of both abstract and emotional concepts is shown to rely on embodied experience. A simple example of this is the tendency to associate emotion with bodily spatial position. "I'm up today" or "I'm on top of the world" are used to refer to a state of feeling happy, while "I'm down in the dumps today" is used to express a feeling of sadness or unhappiness. Similarly, a color perception – blue – is also used to express sadness. The emotion of envy is also expressed utilizing color – "I'm green with envy." Love is frequently referred to in terms of physical force or sensation, for example, "there were sparks flying," or "it was electric." Johnson (2007) indicates that cognitive research is "consonant with our theory of how language and image schemas emerge from bodily processes involving cross-modal perception" (p. 149).

Lakoff and Johnson (1999) provide evidence that Western conceptions of reason and language are incorrect; namely, that reason is conscious and passionless and that language is autonomous, developing separately from the body. These misconceptions originated with the philosophy of René Descartes. Lakoff and Johnson (1999) conclude that reason and language largely develop unconsciously, strongly influenced and shaped by perception, emotion, motion, and other bodily capacities. Working along similar lines, Vivona (2009) cites research documenting that verbs, nouns, and adjectives activate specific responses in relevant motor networks of the brain. Similarly, eye movement studies demonstrate that the verbal description of physical objects activates related neural perceptual processes. Research from neuroscience also documents that the mirror neuron system, closely associated with the capacity for empathy in interpersonal interactions, is as strongly activated in response to verbally described actions (e.g., "he is digging with a shovel") as it is in response to observed physical actions (Vivona, 2009).

Vivona (2013) describes the experiential linkages between embodiment, lived experience, and language acquisition found in mother–infant interactions:

> Words are by nature embodied, having grown out of sensuous lived experiences... Word meanings are not inherently abstract but potentially experiential... Language, in the form of the sounds of mother's speech, imbues the infant's lived experience from the beginning of life. The sounds of mother's speech are part of the infant's experience of interacting with the mother, and over time those sounds become differentiated from other sensations of the lived world as a special kind of sound; these special sounds grow into words... the word is neither wholly separate from its experiential foundations nor wholly merged in it.
>
> (p. 1121)

Quinodoz (2003) carries similar themes into the realm of the therapeutic encounter:

> I define a *language that touches* as one that does not confine itself to imparting thoughts verbally, but also conveys feelings and the sensations that accompany those feelings... If the words I pronounce as an analyst awaken, or reawaken, bodily fantasies in the patient, these words may enable him to find an emotional meaning in forgotten sensory or bodily experiences, which may then become a starting point for his work of thinking – and of symbolization.
>
> (p. 35, italics in original)

In summary, words and language are embodied from the beginning of the human developmental process. While there is value and utility in deepening awareness of somatic experience in analytic therapy, it is inaccurate to portray language and embodiment as operating dichotomously rather than as cohesive and interrelated elements of experience.

Relational aspects of language

A similar argument can be made regarding the relational aspects of language acquisition and the use of language in analysis. As language is acquired, words become grounded in a relational matrix:

> the word is grounded in experience in the world and within the relationship with the person from whom words are learned... The experiential context of language development is unique for each person, and that context imbues words with a personal sense, along with a consensual meaning.
>
> (Vivona, 2013, p. 1118)

The same interactive relational matrix also applies to interpretation in the analytic setting:

> Interpretation is the outgrowth of the collaborative process of these two
> people speaking and making meaning together. Interpretation is part of this
> process, indicates the process, and moves the process along. . . for the inter-
> pretation to do its work, the meanings active in the shared relational moment
> must be articulated by the speaker in language whose precise content, tone,
> and form creates resonance in the listener and thus is experienced as some-
> thing valuable and true. Moreover, for the words to foster change, the enacted
> meaning must be communicated by the person with whom it has been expe-
> rienced. It is the immediacy and specificity of the experience, and of shared
> understanding, that help us bypass defenses that would otherwise undermine
> the therapeutic moment. . . such moments involve the patient and analyst
> experiencing something meaningful together.
>
> (Vivona, 2013, pp. 1132–1133)

The relational aspect of interpretation is echoed by Tubert-Oklander (2006), "This
evolution, referred to as the interpretive process, includes both parties and is not
fully controllable by either of them" (p. 199).

Ornstein (2009) captures the nuanced relational movement that underlies
contemporary analytic practice by articulating the interaction between listening,
experiencing, understanding, and interpreting:

> The empathic mode of listening and responding radically changed our view
> of the manner in which interpretive comments participate in the process of
> treatment. We no longer think of interpretations as statements analysts give
> to their patients. . . In self psychology, with the emphasis on empathic immer-
> sion in the patient's inner world, the focus of the analyst's attention is on the
> patient's subjective experiences, and patient and therapist are jointly engaged
> in the exploration and in an ever better understanding of the patient's emo-
> tional life. Our aim is to interpretively encompass the patient's experiences so
> that he or she can feel understood in depth. This means that our words have to
> approximate as closely as possible what is being experienced.
>
> (pp. 469–470)

The relational matrix supports effective interpretation, and effective interpretation
deepens the relational matrix. Language use and relational experience are not disparate activities; indeed, they should be seen as inextricably interwoven elements
of the analytic experience.

Archetypal basis of language

Jung (1959b) asserts that there is an archetypal basis to language that extends to
interpretation: "Interpretations make use of certain linguistic matrices that are
themselves derived from primordial images" (para. 67). Kugler (1982) arrives
at a similar conclusion, "It is this shift in the linguistic mode that opens the

personality to the archetypal meaning-patterns poetically collated in language" (p. 24). Speaking of the poet, Jung (1966) observes that there is an archetypal foundation that infuses the poet's language with unique power:

> Whoever speaks in primordial images speaks with a thousand voices; he enthralls and overpowers, while at the same time he lifts the idea he is seeking to express out of the occasional and the transitory into the realm of the ever-enduring. He transmutes our personal destiny into the destiny of mankind, and evokes in us all those beneficent forces that ever and anon have enabled humanity to find a refuge from every peril and to outlive the longest night.
>
> (para. 129)

Cognitive research by Tettamanti et al. (2005) provides support for Jung's position. They conclude that language activity and the sensorimotor system are intimately interwoven: "In this domain, language does not appear to be detached from the evolutionarily ancient sensorimotor system, but rather strictly linked to it" (p. 278). Similarly, the conceptual work of developmental linguistic theorists Jean Piaget (e.g., "schemata") and Noam Chomsky (e.g., "universal grammar" and "deep linguistic structure") provide additional support for innate patterns in language acquisition and development (Piattelli-Palmarini, 1980).

Archetypal allusions to language and "gifts of speech" are found repeatedly in the mythological references to Hermes. Kerényi (1986) refers to him as the *Guide of Souls*, the navigator between life and death, a messenger for the gods, and the inventor of language. According to Kerényi, "meeting and finding are revelations of Hermes' essence" (p. 23). Both the field of hermeneutics and Herms, the revered square pillars placed at crossroads throughout ancient Greece to oversee our journeys, are named after him. The strong connection between Hermes and speech is readily observed in one of the Orphic Hymns:

> Hermes . . . prophet of discourse . . . Of various speech, whose aid in works we find, and in necessities to mortal kind. Dire weapon of the tongue, which men revere, be present, Hermes, and thy suppliant hear; assist my works, conclude my life with peace, give graceful speech, and memory's increase.
>
> (Taylor, 1792, p. 152)

Language and transformation

The language of analysis interacts with the imagination and psychological structure of the individuals involved in analytic therapy. The therapeutic action of language underpins the process of interpretation. The transformational possibilities inherent in language begin with the incarnation of the patient in the analyst's mind; an incarnation contextualized in the relationship between analyst and analysand:

The analyst's mind functions so that his interpretation can act as an agent of transformation: it starts from a current context situated between two histories, the one brought by the patient and the one that is constructed during the process.

(Baranger, 1993, p. 23)

Kugler (1982) posits that the transformative power of language lies in the psyche's associative mode of operation and in the interplay between logos and image: "Jung's association work. . . suggests a fundamental law of imagination, that its mode of operation is sonorous, acoustic, phonetic, that there is an innate connection between logos and image, between word and fantasy, that words are fantasies in sound!" (Kugler, 1982, p. 17). Kugler's position is echoed by Quinodoz (2003):

A *language that touches* uses words that can be heard on different levels, words that act as a meeting point between different networks of associations, so that if one of these points is contacted vibrations are set up in a large number of spaces oriented in different directions.

(p. 193, italics in original)

According to Vivona (2009), the embodied elements of language also contribute to the transformational power of language: "The power of language for the meaningful communication of inner experience is a basic assumption of the verbal psychoanalytic method; embodied language models propose a mechanism by which language achieves that power" (p. 1341). Schermer (2011) is more specific about the mechanism by which language transforms:

An interpretation does not so much provide explanations as it expands the patient's awareness of what is already there but not yet "re-cognized." The work of analysis is, in this respect, an enlargement and rearrangement of the patient's own current perceptions and expressions, especially of his or her emotions, and also of the patient's "inner world" of what is going on within what the patient thinks he or she "knows" but which has already been reconfigured by his or her thoughts and conscience.

(p. 826)

Ultimately, transformational interpretation "evokes a 'presence' that transforms both patient and analyst" (Schermer, 2011, p. 817).

Summary

Research from the fields of language acquisition and cognitive neuroscience, accumulated clinical experience, and contemporary theories of analytic interpretation provide evidence of the transformational power of language in the analytic setting. The complex and multi-layered qualities of language bolster the capacity of interpretation to evoke archetypal, developmental, relational, and embodied experiences in the analytic setting.

Metaphor and interpretation

> To use metaphor well is to discern similarities.
>
> Aristotle, *Poetics*, 335 BC

Definitions of metaphor

Metaphor is defined as "a figure of speech in which a word or phrase literally denoting one kind of object or idea is used in place of another to suggest a likeness or analogy between them" (Merriam-Webster, n.d.). Metaphor derives from the Greek words for transfer or transference, to change by carrying. As with the experience of the analytic transference, the transformative potential of metaphor depends on the similarities and differences between its components. It involves the utilization of one conceptual or imaginal domain to map or articulate the experience of a different conceptual or imaginal domain. Therefore, it transfers meaning between domains of experience (e.g., conscious to unconscious, cognitive to somatic, somatic to affective, past to present, or present to future), linking realms in ways not previously seen, and transforming meaning by means of novel re-combinations between domains.

Consider the metaphor, "The snow blankets the ground." Crossing domains, the metaphor invokes the image of a blanket on a bed but also says something about the completeness and thickness with which the ground is covered by the snow. It may evoke something about warmth, protection, and slumber until a period of awakening. Such associations form the underpinnings of the way in which the snow covers the ground. From this emerges an image of the earth sleeping and protected by the snow cover until its awakening in the spring.

Lakoff and Turner (1989) describe metaphor as:

> a tool so ordinary that we use it unconsciously and automatically. . . It is omnipresent: metaphor suffuses our thoughts, no matter what we are thinking about. . . Metaphor allows us to understand ourselves and our world in ways that no other modes of thought can.
>
> (p. xi)

Metaphor is constantly utilized, both consciously and unconsciously, in everyday life and language (Lakoff & Johnson, 1980). Everyday speech is filled with metaphor: *I'm all tied up in knots, The weight of the world is on my shoulders, I feel trapped, It feels like somebody is standing on my chest, It feels like my head is in a vice, It is a real pain in my neck*, or *I've got my back against a wall*. This is the deep power of metaphor. It is a property of the mind, soul, psyche, and body that is uniquely human. Metaphors originate from in-between places; between body and spirit. Therefore metaphors have the capacity to engage and integrate, not only feeling and thought, but also soul. Metaphor bridges image and language. Metaphor brings experience alive.

It is important to note that metaphor is not merely linguistic. Arnold Modell (2009) refers to metaphor as the bridge between knowledge and feelings, and indicates that metaphor is fundamentally an embodied experience, not just language. Like language in general, metaphor is also embodied. Modell (1997) indicates that:

> Metaphor is now viewed as an emergent property of mind. Metaphor is rooted in the body in two senses: metaphor is used to organize bodily sensation cognitively, especially affects, and secondly, metaphor is rooted in the body as it rests on the border between mind and brain.
>
> (p. 105)

Later, Modell emphasizes the close relationship between metaphor and affect, "Metaphor and affects enjoy a privileged connection. Inchoate feelings, that are cognitively unspecified, require metaphors" (1997, p. 109).

At times, metaphorical experience may appeal to the intellect, but it reaches more deeply – making connections on emotional and imaginal levels – rather than solely cognitive. Metaphor is the process that allows sacred texts, music, art, poetry, dance, and film to move us, bringing our imaginations to life. As Borbely (1998) points out:

> A metaphor is a figure of speech, yet it is not limited to the linguistic realm. . . The fact that language, actions, art and religion can be metaphorical, points to the fundamental importance of the metaphorical function for the mind. Metaphor is not only a phenomenon of language, nor even one of thought but of mentation (which includes thought, desires, feelings).
>
> (p. 927)

Metaphor is closely linked with metonymy. With metaphor, similarity is established or highlighted between two disparate beings, objects, or activities. As Borbely (2009) puts it, "Metaphor signifies the discovery of the similar in the dissimilar" (p. 67). Vivona (2003) characterizes the activity of metaphor as joining, "the new with the known, lending a sense of familiarity to the unfamiliar" (p. 56). For example, "the ships prow plows the sea" is a metaphor that reveals the similarity between the prow of a ship passing through the water and a plow passing through the soil. In contrast, metonymy is a linguistic device in which some aspect or attribute of an object, person, or activity is substituted to refer to the whole of the object, person, or activity, for example a business executive might be referred to as a "suit," or a king might be referred to as "the crown." More simply, with metonymy, a part of the whole is utilized to signify the whole.

Metaphor also influences our perceptions, anticipations, and preparedness for action. Modell (2009) asserts that we: "unconsciously interpret our affective world by means of metaphor in preparation for action" (p. 8), which is similar to a definition Jung (1964) offers for the archetype and its function: "Archetypes are systems of readiness for action" (para. 53). Modell goes on to state, "As metaphor is the interpreter of feelings, our own and that of the other, we may preconsciously construct simulated interactions that may or may not actually occur. An unconscious metaphoric process constructs a simulated anticipatory reality" (p. 9), hence metaphor is a pattern detector that recognizes similarities and differences, applying them to past, present, and future.

Language itself originates from metaphoric processes, as Civitarese (2015) points out, "All language is woven out of the transferences of primary metaphors" (p. 9). Civitarese also indicates, "The most important tropes of language, metaphor and metonymy. . . express the elementary modes of psychic functioning and the creation of meaning" (p. 23).

Metaphor and analytic therapy

The emphasis on metaphor is a characteristic of analytic therapy that distinguishes it from other forms of therapy. Metaphor is uniquely powerful and integrative because it has the capacity to evoke affective, imaginal, experiential, embodied, relational, and somatic states, as well as action (Arlow, 1979; Siegelman, 1990; Shengold, 1981; Vivona, 2003; Modell, 2003, 2009). During analytic therapy, metaphor, "fuses sense experience and thought in language" (Sharpe, 1940, p. 201), while also evoking "the construction of imagined possibilities" (Modell, 2009, p. 10).

Analytical Psychology, of all the analytic therapies, has the most highly refined relationship with metaphor. Analytical Psychology is a mythopoetic, imaginally based, metaphorically centered model of the psyche. This deep connection with metaphor is one of the greatest assets of Analytical Psychology. Jung asserts that the psyche is mythopoetic, meaning that the psyche creates myths, and myths are metaphors for ways of perceiving, experiencing, understanding, and being in the world. Concepts like myth, symbol, image, imaginal, and mythopoesis are all based on the notion of metaphor. Ultimately, it is not image that mediates the psyche, as Hillman attests, nor the symbol, as Jung asserts; it is metaphor. Image and symbol are powerful psychic influences because they convey metaphoric properties.

Analytical psychologists often think of myths, fairytales, religious motifs, and alchemy as representations of the collective unconscious and potential symbols but, on the most fundamental level, all of these systems serve as metaphors. For example, the study of alchemy is not useful for the analytic process because it reveals some kind of secret knowledge. It is useful primarily because an immersion in alchemical texts shapes the psyche of the analyst, teaching the analyst to swim in the arcane metaphorical world created by the ancient alchemists. The analyst immersed in alchemical texts over time begins to move more fluidly in the world of metaphor.

The centrality of metaphor for Analytical Psychology is clearly stated by Jung (1959b):

> An archetypal content expresses itself. . . in metaphors. If such a content should speak of the sun and identify with it the lion, the king, the hoard of gold guarded by the dragon, or the power that makes for the life and health of man, it is neither the one thing nor the other, but the unknown third thing that finds more or less adequate expression in all these similes, yet – to the perpetual vexation of the intellect – remains unknown and not to be fitted into a formula. . . Not for a moment dare we succumb to the illusion that an archetype can be finally explained and disposed of. Even the best attempts at explanation are only more or less successful translations into another meta-phorical language.
>
> (para. 267, 271)

However, all schools of analytic therapy have particular metaphors that are central to their systems of thought. For example, traditional Freudian psychoanalysis is built around the central organizing metaphor of the Oedipus myth. For the Kleinian school, the metaphor of the mother–infant dyad, as well as the metaphor of the good–bad breast, are given significant priority. The mother–infant dyad is a metaphor for thinking about experience; a metaphor that suggests, "It is *as if* what is going on inside of you, or what is going on between you and me, is like what transpires between mother and infant." Metaphors are "true" from the standpoint of "psychic reality." Even theories are metaphors (Colman, 2009; Levine, 2009). For example, Jung's concept of the shadow complex is not a thing, it is a metaphor. The shadow complex is a metaphor for a particular range of self-experiences that are sufficiently predictable and universal that a label can be associated with those patterns. The label itself, the shadow, implies something of the qualities associated with the pattern, thus creating a metaphoric relationship between the concept of the shadow complex and the pattern of psychological experience being described. The gift of metaphor is that it allows us to see, feel, and speak about a living connection between elements of experience. But, as Modell (1997) points out, the subject of metaphor has often been overshadowed in the analytic literature and training by the concept of symbol.

Metaphor and the process of transformation

From a Jungian perspective, Edinger (1991) emphasizes that metaphor is at the heart of the analytic process:

> The importance of analogy for realization of the psyche can hardly be over-estimated. It gives form and visibility to that which was previously invisible, intangible, not yet coagulated. Concepts and *abstractions* don't coagulate. . . .
> The images of dreams and active imagination do coagulate. They connect the outer world with the inner world by means of proportional or analogous images and thus coagulate soul-stuff.
>
> (p. 100)

The transformative potential of metaphoric experience is activated in analytic therapy when "a word, phrase, gesture, image, or story invites, triggers, or stimulates affect-laden associations by patient and therapist that move treatment forward" (Lichtenberg, 2009, p. 48). For Borbely (1998), this forward movement is associated with growth, learning, creativity, and a release from internal constrictions:

> It is generally assumed that most psychological changes occur unconsciously, via the primary process, involving the secondary process only peripherally. . . As such growth, entailing learning and creativity with new category searching and new priority setting, is impossible without the metaphorical function. . . To relate metaphorically to the demands of life means to live creatively, to be free of compulsions and obsessions stemming from earlier, unresolved conflicts.
>
> (p. 929)

It is primarily the metaphoric interpretation of experience in the here-and-now that provides an avenue for restoring the lost metaphorical potential of the patient:

> The cure is seen here as resulting from helping the analysand regain blocked creativity or metaphorical potential by linking transferentially coloured present experience with sequestered past experience. In the course of the analytic process the analysand learns to understand, rearrange and accept what was known and not known previously. Subsequently, motivations, inhibitions, demands and prohibitions, obsessions and compulsions all undergo change. . .
> *Therefore, interpretations, in principle, aim at kindling growth-promoting metaphors in the analysand by linking emotionally charged, isolated images of past and present to each other. The interpretation helps bringing them into metaphorical alignment.*
>
> (Borbely, 1998, p. 931, italics in original)

Metaphor, metonymy, and trauma

An understanding of metaphoric process is essential to working with trauma. Schwartz-Salant (1991b) asserts that trauma is internalized as myth; a process that is inherently rooted in metaphor. Traumatic memories evoke similarities, based in the emotion of fear, between past and present. However, in conditions of safety, metaphoric play can occur between similarities and difference and can be used to explore and create meaning. Modell (2009) articulates more fully the metaphoric process as it relates to trauma:

> Metaphor *can* be thought of as a pattern detector that recognizes similarities and differences across a nearly infinite variety of domains. When traumatic memories are activated, metaphor recognizes only similarities. However, in conditions of safety, the mode of cognition shifts and affective memory evokes

a metaphoric play of similarity and difference and meaning is expanded. . . This unconscious metaphoric process *interprets* or *judges* what is similar or different. In health, metaphor retains its complexity, generating a multiplicity of meanings; in interpreting the memory of trauma, metaphor loses its play of similarity and difference and becomes frozen, involuntary and invariant, and recognizes only similarities.

(p. 8, italics in original)

In the psychological fallout from traumatic situations, similarities between past and present events are typically used to identify danger and therefore operate as a metonymy rather than as metaphor – for example, "I was sexually assaulted when I was left *alone* as a child with a *male* neighbor. That was a dangerous situation. I'm now *alone* with a *male* co-worker. This situation is dangerous as well." *Male* and *alone* become the signifiers for the metonymy. As Modell (2009) emphasizes, the "oppositional relation between metaphor and metonymy in cases of trauma, where metonymy acts as a trigger that constricts the imaginative expansion of metaphor. Instead of generating a complex multiplicity of meaning, in cases of trauma, metaphor establishes only similarities" (p. 9).

The neuroscience of metaphor

Recent research demonstrates that the brain reacts strongly when encountering metaphor (Honan, 2011). These findings underscore the power of words and therefore interpretation. Shakespeare reminds us that it is not the subject matter that invests words with power but how those words are formed. In literature, neither the subject matter nor the underlying unconscious content of a work is sufficient to imbue a work with aesthetic qualities. Hamlet would not live so powerfully in our souls if he had said "I have a conflict" instead of "To be, or not to be." It is the particular composition of Shakespeare's language choices and use of metaphor, rather than stark linguistic meaning, that bring Hamlet's statement to life, allowing it to inhabit our imaginations. The sentence relies on six simple one-syllable words that initially sound almost childlike yet it communicates at great depth about the fragile line separating life and death. With the ensuing declaration "That is the question," Hamlet pulls us into deeper water – narrowing down all questions into one existential choice, one universal predicament with which we are all confronted.

Neuroscience demonstrates the power of Shakespeare's words and offers a hypothesis regarding the effect of his language. Using functional magnetic resonance imaging and electroencephalogram technologies, researchers (Thierry et al., 2008) studied functional shifts in brain activity when exposed to metaphor. They demonstrate how Shakespeare's metaphorical use of language creates shifts in mental pathways and opens new possibilities of thought, self-reflection, and associative connections. Volunteers in the study were recruited to read challenging prose, such as passages from Shakespeare's

King Lear or *Macbeth*, while their neural activity was monitored. Participants were also asked to read passages of modern texts. Passages from Shakespeare significantly increased neural complexity and activity in the volunteers. The metaphorical passages, associated with Shakespeare, resulted in a distribution of activity bi-laterally, across both hemispheres of the brain; a state of brain activity also associated with increased creativity and complex neural engagement. The metaphoric passages also resulted in more involvement of emotional centers of the brain. Ordinary modern prose, such as found in newspapers or non-fiction material, did not elicit these patterns of neural arousal in the subjects. The researchers conclude that the human brain is optimized to respond powerfully to metaphor.

How is the metaphoric language of Shakespeare different from normal language? Davis, a professor of English literature and one of the researchers involved in the Thierry et al. (2008) study, indicates that Shakespeare often introduced grammatical oddities or wordplay, creating numerous metaphors within his texts. Some examples (Davis, 2007, pp. 77–78) of these grammatical shifts include making an adjective into a verb: "thick my blood" (*The Winter's Tale*) or "A father and a gracious aged man: him have you madded" (*King Lear*); a pronoun made into a noun: "the cruellest she alive" (*Twelfth Night*); or a noun made into a verb: "He childed as I fathered" (*King Lear*).

Another study (Lacey, Stilla, & Sathian, 2012) found similar results using simple textural metaphors. Using a functional magnetic resonance imaging protocol, the researchers contrasted the responses to two simple sentences with similar meanings: "I had a bad day" versus "I had a rough day." With the second sentence, a simple textural metaphor is introduced as a statement of psychological experience. The somatosensory cortex, the part of the brain that is involved in processing texture during touch, was activated when processing the second sentence but not with the first sentence. This study provides further evidence that the brain moves out of its typical response patterns when metaphor is introduced.

These studies underscore why it is critical for analytic therapists to listen below the surface communications of our patients for the metaphors hidden within their stories and demonstrate why it is critical for the analytic therapist to frame interpretations in metaphorical language. As Colman (2005) describes the relationship between metaphor and interpretation:

> If interpretations are regarded as being metaphorical, this is hardly surprising. We do not judge a metaphor in terms of whether it is "correct"; far less do we expect things to be represented by only one metaphor. Metaphors are to be judged by whether they are apposite and illuminating and this would also seem to be a useful criterion for psychoanalytic interpretations. No matter how persuasive such interpretations are, they remain interpretations – figurative descriptions of unknown unconscious processes. To paraphrase Freud, it is simply impossible to free ourselves from the language of our metaphors.
>
> (p. 658)

Metaphoric interpretation – Charles

Charles had experienced life-long feelings of anxiety, insecurity, and inadequacy. He had compensated for these feelings through hard work, being compliant with requests, and rigorous self-scrutiny. Although Charles is quite successful in his field, he routinely worries about what others think of him, especially when he is unable to fulfill colleagues' requests for assistance. In a recent session, he commented, "During the last session, you said I sounded worried, but I realize I'm worn out. My whole career I've evaluated my worth by how busy I am, how productive I am, and how much money I've made." As Charles spoke, a well-known metaphor came into my mind, "people who live in glass houses shouldn't throw stones." As it stood, the metaphor did not fit Charles' psychological situation, but there was an element of transparency in the image that spoke to his sense of vulnerability. I replied, "You seem to feel you live in a glass house in which everyone can see your numbers and you think they will do the same thing you do; look at your numbers and always find them lacking. A constant refrain of never enough." In the interpretation, I use the word "numbers" to refer to his number of hours worked, the number of units produced, and the amount of income generated. Charles replied to the interpretation, "Yes! You're right about my living in a glass house. But I'm beginning to realize I have respect at work and I generally get the things I ask for from the administration. But I still get worried when I have free time at work." In response, I reply, "You have often equated money with security. In your internal formulas, free time and income are inversely related; if you have free time, you interpret it to mean you aren't earning money and therefore have no significance." In the next session, Charles continued with the metaphor of the glass house, "I've been thinking about the glass house. I try to behave in a way that makes me feel better about myself. But most of it is associated with external metrics. I realize my sense of deficiency and need comes from my childhood but I went off to college forty-two years ago with all those feelings still in place and I developed my current patterns of behavior. I used all these external markers then, good grades, graduate school, fellowships, and promotions. It takes time to change that: the fear of failure in my career, as a father, as a husband. I've just begun to realize that the realistic possibility of failure is actually quite small at this point of life." Changing metaphors, I reply, "Yes, it's as though you've been using a life preserver, barely keeping your head above water. Now you're learning to swim without the life preserver."

Metaphoric interpretation – Jamie

Jamie was describing memories of being tied down, initially in reference to memories of childhood abuse. Then, in a more metaphorical mode, she made reference to the expectations of her husband, during their former marriage, as being like ropes that constrained her. As I listened, I reflected on the contrast between literal experiences versus narrative experience. In reference to the expectations of her ex-husband, Jamie said, "The ropes are all gone but I'm still fighting them now." I understood her to be equating the constraints of her marital relationship with the ropes she continued to associate with memories of childhood abuse. Utilizing her metaphor, I said, "If you live in the present as though it is the past, the ropes will always be there." Introducing new associative material, she replied, "That comes up with money too. I charge money that I don't have so I won't feel contained or powerless." Jamie's introduction of new associative material signals the mutative impact of the interpretation, that is, that a link was established between her memories of childhood abuse, the constraining elements of her previous marital relationship, and her efforts to defend against feelings of powerlessness through her patterns of spending.

Summary

Many of the interpretive examples provided in the following chapters make explicit use of metaphor. Effective interpretation is metaphoric because it is making a translation from one domain of experience to another. It is critical to listen for the embedded metaphors and speak fluently in the language of metaphor. While some metaphors can be impersonal, conventional, and fixed in their meaning, as analytic therapists we are most interested in the personal, idiosyncratic, private meanings that emerge during the analytic interaction. Whether an interpretation incorporates archetypal imagery, elements of the patient's personal narrative, or references from the cultural landscape, at the most fundamental level the effective interpretation is always metaphorical. When the analytic session is experienced as a dream, as Ogden (2017) suggests, it becomes possible to consider all interaction and communication as potentially symbolic, thus permitting rich metaphorical and associative linkages to emerge.

The poetics of interpretation

Everywhere I go I find that a poet has been there before me.

Sigmund Freud[3]

When reflecting on the interpretive process, I find much affinity with poets – not just their poems – but in how poets speak about their craft, process, and art. In listening to poets speak with other poets about poetry, I am struck by the deep value they find in words and the careful consideration they give to the crafting of words into sentences. I am inspired by the imagination and creativity of an unexpected juxtaposition of two words; a juxtaposition that reveals facets or possibilities of experience not previously recognized. It is the spirit, curiosity, and creativity inherent in the work of the poet that is most closely akin to the process of analytic interpretation done well. When done poetically, analytic interpretations are not dry and mechanical pronouncements couched in theory; interpretation done well is generative. It reveals, engages, embodies, and opens new vistas. Well-crafted interpretations have the ring of poetry. Not in terms of sounding pretty, although at times interpretations may possess a certain beauty of sound and construction, but in terms of linking words together in a novel manner that permits the listener to experience and perceive in a new way. A good interpretation, like a good poem, often begins with the familiar but along the way reveals something previously unseen or unthought, while also forging something new in the psyche of the patient. That is the poetic basis of interpretation.

Effective interpretation requires listening to the patient as we listen to poems or songs – that is, listening for how the words lay together (the syntax in addition to the semantic meaning), how the metaphors are turned and played with, and how the poems and songs that capture us are the ones that do not just speak to us but also surprise us in some way. Consider the poem "Nothing Gold Can Stay" by Robert Frost (1923):

> Nature's first green is gold,
> Her hardest hue to hold.
> Her early leaf's a flower;
> But only so an hour.
> Then leaf subsides to leaf.
> So Eden sank to grief,
> So dawn goes down to day.
> Nothing gold can stay.

In this brief but dense meditation on the transitory nature of beauty, Frost introduces a captivating twist in the sixth line, "So Eden sank to grief." At first glance, this line seems out of place; moving along a different trajectory than the other lines. Employing a more indirect use of metaphor than the other lines, it is a line that requires more of the reader. The images of *Eden*, *sinking*, and *grief* emerge from a different realm – asking the reader to recall the theme of paradise lost, to imagine the grief of Adam and Eve upon their expulsion from the garden, and to experience the embodied feeling associated with the downward pull of *sinking*. There is an ineffable element of the line that draws attention, captures curiosity, and possesses inner coherence. It obliquely offers up a statement of the tenuous nature of beauty, being, and experience that is difficult to ignore. Well-crafted but spontaneous interpretations have the potential to capture the patient's attention and curiosity in the same way as lines of well-crafted poetry do.

Without a creative focus on the use of language, especially in relationship with the technique of interpretation, appreciation for the metaphoric possibilities of these interventions will languish and old patterns of interpreting, out of a position of perceived truth or correctness, will be perpetuated. Vivona (2013) describes the pitfalls when the analyst fails to observe, think, and feel as a poet:

> Lacking the poet's knowledge of these potentials in words, and his gift for mobilizing them, we may miss the experiential contributions of words to therapeutic action. This is perhaps all the more likely when we ascribe to a conceptualization of words as abstract, disembodied, emotionally neutral symbols whose connections are primarily with other symbols.
>
> (p. 1116)

The fundamental stance of the poet, like the analyst or analytic therapist, is in the simultaneous activities of observing, experiencing, and articulating. The poet must be impacted by what he is observing in order to constellate a moment he will communicate solely through language in order to reveal something previously unnoticed or forgotten. Like Proust's madeleine cake in *Remembrance of the Things Past*, the poet uses words, often in the form of metaphor, as points of entry into feeling states, memories, thoughts, and sensations. Poet Mark Doty (2008) describes the task of poetry thus:

> Poetry's work is to make people real to us through the agency of the voice. . . Meanwhile, poetry does what it does, inscribing individual presence, making a system of words and sounds to mark the place where one human being stood, bound in time, reporting on what it is to be one.
>
> (para. 31)

Cooper (1949) suggests that poetry's agenda is a conscious confrontation with our own being and the world surrounding us:

> Why is poetry feared? Because it demands full consciousness; it asks us to feel and it asks us to respond. Through poetry we are brought face to face with our world and we plunge deeply into ourselves, to a place where we sense.
>
> (first para.)

Robert Bly, in his book *Leaping Poetry* (1975), writes that fear of experience and "a pedestrian movement of the mind" results in "blocked love-energy, boredom, envy and joylessness" (pp. 2–3). Bly indicates that art has at its center a "long floating leap" which invokes risk and moves into experience. He goes on to say that some works, especially poetry, may have several leaps inside a single work.

> A poet who is "leaping" makes a jump from an object soaked in unconscious substance to an object or idea soaked in conscious psychic substance. . . some arc of association which corresponds to the inner life of the objects; so that anyone sensitive to the inner life of objects can ride with him. The links are not private, but somehow bound in nature. . . leaping is the ability to associate fast.
>
> (p. 4)

The leaps referred to by Bly are the connections made between domains utilizing the similarities and differences between those domains.

Such leaping can be found in the first line of John Keats' "Ode on a Grecian Urn" (1820): "Thou still unravished bride of quietness!" In this line, Keats *marries* an image of *quietness* with the image of an as yet untouched *bride*. The meaning of the line and its relationship to the Grecian urn, the subject of the poem, is not readily revealed, and yet there is a felt, unseen relationship between quietness and the unravished bridge that merges with the stillness or fixity of the urn. The listener's mind is pulled into a state of wonder or curiosity about this evocative but ephemeral relationship.

In a similar fashion, Oscar Wilde, in his poem "A Vision" (1881), sets the opening scene utilizing the metaphor of monarchy: "Two crowned Kings, and One that stood alone / With no green weight of laurels round his head, / But with sad eyes as one uncomforted." Wilde uses the metaphor of the laurel wreath to create a feeling of separation for one of the three kings. He implies that there is sadness associated with being the outsider or outcast. Yet Wilde does not directly reveal the source of the third king's sadness or reason for his exclusion. However, some hint is provided in the last line of the poem in which Wilde names the great playwrights of ancient Greece: Aeschylus, Sophocles, and Euripides. Curiously, in the last line, it is Euripides who is associated with a "wide stream of tears," perhaps playing on his reputation as the playwright with the greatest sympathy for those victimized and least powerful in the society of ancient Greece. It remains open to interpretation whether Wilde is making reference to himself through an association with the uncrowned king and the tearful Euripides. In this way, the function of leaping poetry is similar to the function of the symbol as defined by Jung (1960b), "A symbol does not define or explain; it points beyond itself to a meaning that is darkly divined yet still beyond our grasp, and cannot be adequately expressed in the familiar words of our language" (para. 644).

Highlighting the close relationship between poetry and analytic interpretation, Rose (2004) writes:

> The plasticity of words is seen in the fact that their separate aspects of physical sound, intellectual content and affective weight may be elaborated almost independently. Poetry recombines their physical attributes, emotional overtones and semantic meanings. In poetry, words are the plastic, malleable media, just as spatial forms are in painting and time is in music. The aesthetic plasticity of words that makes for dubious science can also make for effective interpretation.
>
> (p. 39)

Mann (2010) directly equates the experience of hearing a moving poem and the experience of hearing an empathic and well-crafted interpretation:

> The actual language through which patient and therapist meet, engage, and transform each other bears no resemblance whatsoever to the psychosurgical metaphors of Freud. In my experience, the language of clinical encounter sounds and feels much more like poetry – so much so, that I have come to regard clinical work all-in-all as a form of poetic action. . . Treatment is practical and poetic, not merely in ornamentation, but in its very substance. The whole form and content of treatment approaches that of poetry, and its purpose is intensely practical.
>
> (pp. 718–719, 725)

Along the same lines, Vivona (2013) indicates that, "The work of the analyst is to create language that mobilizes the experiential, memorial, and relational potentials of words, and in so doing to make a poet out of the patient so that she too can create such language" (p. 1109).

A close examination of the relationships between language, poetry, and psychoanalysis is found in the work of Thomas Ogden (1997, 2001). Ogden speaks to the importance of aesthetic themes in the way we listen and interact in analysis. In his exploration of poetry, Ogden uses poetry as a way of learning to listen, perceive, appreciate, and speak differently: "Prose states; poetry merely suggests. Poetry suggests because *what* it suggests cannot be stated" (Ogden, 2001, p. 177). He seeks to connect to the poet's use of language, timing, and tone in a way that brings out the complexity, richness, and movement of human existence as fully as possible into the consulting room. By listening in this way, the point of engagement shifts from the effort to unearth what lies "behind" the words and symbols of a poem or "beneath" the patient's report of a dream or life event. Ogden's (1997) emphasis on the form and feeling of what is said moves us away from "What does this mean?" towards an aesthetic experience that helps us know whether an experience is alive or dead.

Summary

Vivona (2013) indicates, "Psychoanalysis mobilizes the potentials of language that we admire in poetry" (p. 1127). The language of the analytic encounter and the interpretive process forms a series of potential aesthetic moments created and shared by analyst and analysand (Winborn, 2015a, 2017b). As Schenk (1992) points out: "One can see the experience of beauty occurring through the presentational nature of language. In contemporary life, language is revealed as a mode for the reappearance of beauty, as talking becomes cure through psychotherapy" (p. 137). Language, like sound, aesthetics, image, emotion, and physicality, is deeply woven into the human experience. Working effectively as an analyst includes a deep appreciation for and sensitivity to the embodied, relational, metaphoric, and poetic aspects of language that emerge during the analytic encounter.

Exercises for the reader

1) Practice holding your use of language in awareness. Consider your attitude towards language. Choose a few words or sentences that characterize your attitude towards language – light, heavy, loose, tight, specific, vague, searching, cavalier, eloquent, poetic, artistic, and so on.

2) Set aside time during the week to reflect on a few of your patients. Bring to mind the metaphors that you and your patient have shared in analytic sessions. Are there metaphors that have come to mind but you found it difficult to utilize? What factors in you, in the patient, or in the analytic moment inhibited that sharing?

3) Read poetry as a means of sensitizing your ear and your imagination to the turns of phrase and images that subtly reveal the previously unseen, that articulate the previously unarticulated, that embody the previously disembodied, that connect realms of experience previously unconnected, and that bridge past and present, inner and outer, self and other.

4) Find poetic voices that appeal to you in an effort to identify elements of your own analytic interpretive voice. Ask yourself, "What is it about this poet's voice, this poet's use of language, this poet's use of image, this poet's way of perceiving the world, that appeals to me?"

Notes

1 The "talking cure" is a term first introduced by Josef Breuer's patient Bertha Pappenheim. She is seen historically as the first psychoanalytic patient and is referred to by Freud (1895) in *Studies on Hysteria* as Anna O.

2 See Winborn (2015b) for a fuller discussion of the "right brain – left brain" metaphor that persists among laypersons and therapists alike despite being discredited and reinterpreted in contemporary neuroscience.

3 Quoted by Nin (1976, p. 14).

Chapter 3

The interpretive cycle

When first pursuing a creative activity, we typically begin by the imitation of others whose work we admire. When I first began working on the interpretive process as an analytic skill, my primary model was Mel Marshak. However, despite many efforts to emulate her style, I never managed to develop the crisp, concise style that went right to the heart of the matter in one or two sentences. Initially, I found this discouraging, but over time I came to realize, through trial and error, that my interpretive voice and style would be different than Marshak's simply because our minds, personalities, and experiences were different. I often found I needed to "build" towards an interpretation over several exchanges with the patient and eventually found the necessary tools to arrive at my approach to interpretation. I came to recognize that there is no ideal interpretation and that there are many ways to arrive at effective, evocative interpretations. As Jung (1954b) points out, "For two personalities to meet is like mixing two different chemical substances: if there is any combination at all, both are transformed" (para. 163). Therefore, the interpretation process always reflects the unique combination of the personalities of the patient and the analyst. Jung (1956) also indicates that the approach to interpretation must be modified for each patient, "Interpretation in any given case depends as always on individual circumstances and must be modified accordingly" (para. 681).

To develop this theme further, Sullivan (2009) frames the issue of interpretation this way, "While there is certainly no right way, there are ways that are, if not simply wrong, deeply problematic" (p. 11). The interpretive process involves a number of contributing variables: analytic theory, intuition, feeling, unconscious influences, the personalities of the patient and the analyst, and the intersubjective field constellated by the analytic dyad. However, each of these variables requires a methodology to structure how they will be utilized. During my initial forays into the process of interpretation, I came to realize that there were many potential pitfalls that can lead to ineffectual, vague, and non-mutative interpretations. Levy (1990) summarizes these dangers in this way, "I have repeatedly observed that even the most serious, dedicated, and talented students, in the absence of direct instruction on how to interpret, resort to a very unnatural, cliché ridden, and often counterproductive mode of interpretation" (p. xiii).

The cycle of interpretation

While there are a number of methodologies for interpretation available, an approach I found particularly valuable was developed by Auld and Hyman (1991, pp. 162–164), developed from an earlier model of Fenichel (1941). In their model, Auld and Hyman demonstrate how interpretation can be broken down into four steps or phases: confrontation, clarification, interpretation, and construction. Part of the value of the model is that it helps to clarify and differentiate the functional aspects of interpretation. It is a model that can be used like building blocks – that is, steps leading to interpretation but steps which also function as independent interventions serving the overall purpose of making the unconscious conscious. Like the modification of Fenichel's (1941) model by Auld and Hyman (1991), I have modified the model provided by Auld and Hyman, which I now refer to as the "cycle of interpretation" – underscoring the cyclical and evolving nature of the interpretive process. The notion of a cycle of interpretation also underscores the idea that no interpretation exists in isolation. Each interpretation is one small piece of psychological work in the larger narrative context of an analysis; each potentially contributing to the progressive movement of the psyche in response to the analytic situation.

Confrontational observation

The first step in the Auld and Hyman model is "confrontation," to which I refer as "confrontational observation." At first glance, the word "confrontation" suggests something aggressive or conflictual, but the meaning described by Auld and Hyman (1991) "is simply a calling of attention to an act or utterance" (p. 162). Therefore, we can consider the confrontational aspect of this step to be the initial engagement with a particular aspect of the patient's unconscious activity. Viewing confrontation as engagement, rather than aggression or conflict, is consistent with Jung's (1965, pp. 170–199) analytic perspective, which valued the importance of confrontation to the analytic process, having referred to his own descent experience during the years from 1913 through 1917 as his "confrontation with the unconscious." I choose to refer to this phase as "confrontational observation" because the confrontation is occurring, not interpersonally with the patient, but with some aspect of the patient's observable patterns – that is, patterns of feeling, behavior, verbalization, or physiological state.

For example, a confrontational observation may involve something as simple as, "I notice that you consistently wait for me to initiate the interaction at the beginning of our sessions." The analyst likely has further hypotheses connected to this confrontational observation but limits the verbal content to an observation of the patient's pattern of behavior at the beginning of their sessions. A confrontational observation is focused on something that is potentially observable to both the patient and the analyst but which the patient may not have consciously noted or considered to be of significance. In some situations, the observation may be framed in the form of a question, such as "Have you noticed that you frequently apologize when you struggle to find words to express what you are experiencing?" In both of these examples, the analyst is not offering an explanation for the observable pattern or inferring that there could be meaning attributed to the observed pattern. Ideally, observations will be followed by clarifying inferences and interpretations that do create meaning, as well as providing the patient with an experience of being understood. When confrontational observations are not followed by inferential clarification or interpretation, it is often the case that the patient will internalize these observations as an injunction to alter the observed pattern of behavior, or as criticism.

The confrontational observation can be thought of as an implicit invitation to participate in a mutual reflective process that is at the heart of every analytic presence. Jung (1960b, para. 246) hypothesizes the existence of a reflective instinct, that is, the tendency to search for meaning, as one of five primary instincts for all human beings. The capacity for reflection is precursory to the development of a symbolic attitude.[1] While reflection may be an instinctive process, many patients come to analytic therapy with a poorly developed capacity for reflection. Often the capacity for reflection is undeveloped or disrupted as a result of trauma or impaired developmental experiences. With a patient I have been seeing for approximately six years, the capacity to reflect and utilize interpretations offered during the course of the analysis has been very limited. Although I continued to offer various interpretive inventions over the years, she did not appear to make use of them psychologically. Until recently, she had primarily utilized me as a warm, sustaining presence and a psychological refuge. However, within the past month, she has begun to remember interpretations I made that had significance for her. Additionally, she has been able to reflect on those interpretations during emotionally stressful interactions with her husband which has enabled her to respond differently to him than she might have in prior exchanges. Recently, she has also begun to comment on her patterns of interaction with me. For example, recently she said, "I realized sometimes I just talk the whole session and don't leave room for you at all." These developments illustrate a nascent reflective capacity that has required six years of incubation to emerge.

Fonagy (2000) uses the terms "mentalization" and "reflective function" to refer to the patient's capacity to reflect upon, understand, and make inferences about one's own experience and motivations, as well as the experience and motivations of others. Or to put it more simply, the capacity to "think about thinking" (Fonagy, 1991). Similarly, Bion (1962), in his model of the psyche, proposes a theory of thinking that focuses on the individual's capacity to digest experience; not only the capacity for reflection about experience but the capacity for the mental representation of experience as well. Bion refers frequently to "thinking" in his writing, but his concept of thinking is not synonymous with cognition or intellectual acts. He uses the term "thinking" as a shorthand for the capacity *for being* through the reflective, embodied experiencing of emotion. Hence, the capacity to process emotional experience is the foundation from which increasingly complex forms of reflection emerge, such as Jung's concept of the symbolic attitude.

While Jung's (1971) theory of typology posits thinking and feeling as opposites, in Bion's model there is no opposition between emotional experience and thinking. Therefore, confrontational observations by the analyst are not solely intended to create insight, expand consciousness, facilitate understanding, or create meaning; confrontational observation is also intended to facilitate the engagement and development of the patient's reflective function.

Inferential clarification

Auld and Hyman (1991) identify "clarification" as the second phase of interpretation. As with "confrontation," I found the term "clarification" not fully descriptive of the process being described, therefore I employ the phrase "inferential clarification." An inferential clarification combines a confrontational observation with an inference of a possible unconscious process. It reflects an effort by the analyst to present a more complex understanding to the patient; one that moves beyond simple confrontational observation but without reaching the full descriptive action of an interpretation. Often, with an inferential clarification, a feeling state is linked with an observable pattern, another aspect of the patient's history, or a dream.

An example of an inferential clarification arose in a case with a bright young man who consistently disparaged his own thoughts immediately after speaking them aloud, for example, "That was stupid" or "That made no sense." After observing this pattern for a period of time, I said, "You have a tendency to label things you say in here as dumb or irrelevant. Perhaps you fear what your thoughts might reveal about you so you label them as dumb so that neither of us will take them very seriously." The first sentence in this example is a confrontational observation. The second sentence provides an inference regarding the possible motive behind the patient's pattern of labeling his thoughts as dumb. However, the focus of the second sentence is the patient's fear; yet it does not provide an explanation as to why the fear exists, nor does it provide a hypothesis regarding what he fears would be revealed. An explanation for the existence of the fear, or a hypothesis about what the patient fears would be revealed by his words, would provide the necessary additional content for a full interpretation.

Intermediate psychological steps, such as those provided by inferential clarifications, cultivate the patient's reflective function but also facilitate the creation of psychological linkages between aspects of experience that have been disrupted through dissociation (Jung, 1973, para. 719) and internal attack (Bion, 1959). Jung's (1973) studies with the word-association experiment document the psychological disruption that occurs when an individual's internal associative network becomes compromised (Bovensiepen, 2006). Inferential clarifications are often especially useful with patients who have poorly developed ego functioning or who are heavily defended. They permit psychological space for the patient to progressively adapt to the unconscious processes being engaged.

The following example is taken from an analysis with a successful woman in her late thirties with several presenting issues. It was only during the course of analysis that a feeling of deadness in her marriage also emerged as a focal point. In this session, she was speaking about her sense of deadness in the marriage and the decisions she might be confronted with in regard to the marriage. This passage was selected to highlight the analyst's use of a series of questions *[Q]*, confrontational observations *[CO]*, and inferential clarifications *[IC]* which facilitate gradual movement towards increased insight and deeper emotional engagement:

P: I always do what it is that I perceive those who are smarter, older, or wiser think I should do – anything that makes them an authority figure, which can be any number of things.

A: Anything that makes them seem better than you in some quality. *[IC]*

P: Right, I do what those people tell me to do. I may not this time. Maybe I will be able to listen to myself.

A: Are you saying there is a shift in how you feel this week? *[Q]*

P: *(laughs)* Wouldn't that be a surprise? There's not a shift in how I feel, it's just that I'm not coming in here and going "OK, here's what I'm going to do, I'm going to try to make this marriage work." I'm just not going to go through that charade this week. . . I'm not going to say what I am going to do because I don't know. I'll admit to being as clueless as ever as to what I'm going to do, but I'm not going to make a conscious effort to try to do what I think I should do. . . It's not going to be something like I make a decision to run six miles today and I will stay in this marriage and make it work *(long pause)*. I've been trying to fast forward in my mind and think about where will I be this time next year? Where in the world? In a year I think it's going to be so hugely different. What if it's not? What if I'm just in the same place? But something tells me it's going to be hugely different next year *(pause)*. Maybe that's just hopeful thinking.

A: Perhaps thinking ahead is a way you stay out of your feelings of the moment. *[IC]*

P: I'm good at doing that. The feelings of the moment are just so. . . *(pause)*. . . what are they? They're just so *(sadness/fear enters her voice)* . . . *(pause)*. They're just something I'm avoiding because they're so huge. They're going to be such. . . *(pause)*. They have the potential to be the hugest sadness ever. It's like I can't let it happen during Christmas. I've got to get through the next three weeks and then I can burst if I need to. The next three weeks I just have to be. . . *(pause)*. I just have to get through the next three weeks without anybody knowing anything about what's going on. . . *(voice trails off)*.

A: Is that to protect your feelings or Tim's *[her husband's]* feelings? *[Q]*

P: Tim's, mine, Tim's parents, my mom. It's to protect everybody. It's just something that shouldn't have happened at Christmas. Because then forevermore people will always think of it as "gosh remember that horrible Christmas" because even if that's going on inside of me that's okay. It just can't come out yet. I can't imagine it.

A: It sounds like you can't imagine bearing the guilt that you would feel around it. *[CO]*

P: Right. Oh yes. There's going be a lot of guilt. *(Patient relates story of several unanticipated divorces on both sides of the family.)* These girls, for no reason known to anyone, just didn't want to be married any more. So I'm hoping that Christmas. . . *(pause).* I don't know – fifteen years – God!

A: So you're hoping that they won't be judgmental with you. *[IC]*

P: Right. They're going to be shocked. Maybe they won't think too badly of me. Maybe they will. When it comes right down to it, that's all it is – I just don't want to be married any more. That's all it is. I can't come up with anything else. I just don't. . . Is there anything wrong with not being married? I'm not saying I will but I'm open to the possibility that I could.

A: And you're wanting me to give some kind of moral confirmation that that's okay? *[Q]*

P: *(laughs)* Not really moral. Just confirmation that I'm not just psychologically totally. . . *(pause).* I think the whole thing is you grow up and find somebody of the opposite sex and you get with them and you stay with them. . . Maybe that's just because I've been with somebody for fifteen years that I didn't love, I don't know. All I'm saying is I don't know. I just don't want to be married and that's not a good enough reason to leave a marriage, but maybe this time next year it will be a good enough reason, or maybe this time next month it will be a good enough reason. It's the only one I have.

A: I think you're saying that you're just now becoming aware that you have feelings and desires and you don't know what to do with them yet. *[IC]*

P: I don't know what to do with them yet, but I know that. . . *(pause).* I hate to sound like I know something when you probably think I don't know anything at all, but I know that it's not with Tim *(sadness in her voice).* . . I know that they're not feelings that I want to share or have anything to do with him *(tearfulness).* It makes me sad. It would be so much easier if they were. . . *(voice trails off).*

A: Can you say more about the sadness? *[Q]*

P: Well, it doesn't really seem fair that I feel this way. I don't mean fair to me, I mean fair to Tim. I don't care what's fair to me. I don't expect fair for me. . . . It just doesn't seem fair. . . it's grief *(patient chokes out her words).* A lot of the sadness is just because it's such a waste that there have been so many years that are just gone.

A: I'm not clear about whether you're feeling grief for the years that you feel you wasted for Tim or whether you're feeling grief for years that you wasted with Tim? *[Q]*

P: Both. I feel it for both of us, but I feel it more for Tim right now. God that's a long time. Life is short. But I feel it more for Tim because I think I'm going to be alright. I think I'm going to go on to be. . . I mean I may be wrong. . . . I don't know where it's coming from but there's just some sense of. . . could I possibly have any peace? Is it peace? Is it tranquility? I don't know. There's just this little tiny something – you know. . . . It's like I'm hopeless about almost everything, so I would even say that there's this little glimmer of hope, that's beyond hope, that I'm going to be okay. It's beyond that, I know

I'm going to be okay. It's weird. How can I know that when everything is so bad? It's just when I wade through all of that, if I pole-vault over everything that is going to come between now and then *(becoming tearful again)*, like moving my stuff and having to tell Tim and the lawyers. . . but when I can mentally pole-vault over that, I know I'm going to be okay.

A: It seems shocking to you to have an experience of yourself. *[IC]*

P: It's a total shock *(sobbing)*. It's scary *(said in a soft, young voice)*.

In this passage, none of the interventions can be considered a full interpretation, although several can be thought of as partial interpretations. It is often the case that the progressive movement in analysis will be sustained by this mixture of questions, confrontational observations, and inferential clarifications until a more fully developed interpretation occurs to the analyst or until the patient is prepared to receive a more thorough interpretation.

Interpretation

An interpretation gives meaning to events, feelings, or experiences that previously had no meaning or for which the meaning was hidden. Essentially it is a way of communicating to the patient, "This is how I understand your interactions with me and how I understand how those patterns relate to your interior world." As we initially examined in Chapter 1, interpretation is a specific form of verbal communication which moves beyond the spoken words or observable behaviors to make an inference about sources of motivation that are unknown (i.e., unconscious) to the patient. A full interpretation links observable patterns of narrative, behavior, physiological state, emotion, or perception with a hypothesis about an unconscious process contributing to those patterns.

To illustrate the concept of interpretation, I draw again from a session with John, who was first mentioned in Chapter 1. In the session, John was focused on his girlfriend, Kelly, with whom he was obsessed, but he also harbored significant concerns about her emotional stability. He began the session in a state of fragmentation, indicating that he did not know where he just came from and that he was not thinking straight. John told me about meeting Kelly for lunch the previous day and how, after a few minutes, she began doodling on some napkins. He produced several of the napkins to show me. The napkins were filled with quirky little drawings and nonsense sentences. John went on to tell me a number of other behaviors exhibited by Kelly which concerned him, and also expressed concern about their sexual relationship. Eventually, I felt John could tolerate an interpretation focused on his feeling of ambivalence about Kelly, and I said:

A: In regard to Kelly, I think there is a conflict going on within you about her. I think there is a part of you that cares about her a great deal and yet I think the reason you save these napkins and pictures and writings, things that are examples of things she says and does, is that you're trying to do something with your awareness that there is something pretty ill about Kelly. So the conflict is between your awareness that there is something really wrong with her and the fact that you also really care about her. However, I think it's frightening for you to think about both of those emotions together because you experience your concerns about her emotional stability as a threat to your feelings of affection for her.

P: I really do care about her, and I really just haven't forgiven her for dropping out of therapy with Jane because I think had she stayed in. . . *(John doesn't complete this thought)*. . . but to her, she dismissed it as a mere money matter as if there is nothing we can do about it. How do I know what happened or transpired? All I know is that she's given up on that.

In this instance, the interpretation assisted John in bringing his feelings of caring for Kelly closer to the surface while also bringing to the surface a previously unacknowledged resentment he held towards Kelly for dropping out of her individual therapy – a process he hoped would make more likely the possibility of remaining in a relationship with her. In short, during the session, he is able to engage more directly with his ambivalence about Kelly rather than keeping those conflicting emotions separated.[2]

In another illustration, when Michael initially entered analytic therapy, I was struck by the sense of anxiety and impending devastation that permeated his being. Every breath and movement seemed labored. For months, his speech was fragmented, halting, and disrupted – often punctuated with deep sighs or self-directed curses muttered under his breath. His thoughts would begin to career tumultuously almost as soon as he began a sentence; the words he initiated frequently being overtaken by competing thoughts or efforts to suppress forbidden thoughts. It was often difficult to follow the semantic thread in Michael's efforts to verbalize his distress. The dissonance and rhythmic disruption of his speech communicated as much as, if not more than, the content of his speech. Michael perpetually existed in the realm of the "catastrophic chaos" (Bion, 1970) where "nameless dread" (Bion, 1962) predominates. From a Jungian perspective, a significant portion of Michael's dread was associated with his father complex. Michael immigrated with his parents to the United States as a child. He had childhood memories of his father constantly telling him how much danger there was in their country of origin. Later, he recalled his father frequently delivering dark monologues about the state of the world and the ongoing dangers for people of their race. After listening to Michael's recollections of his childhood experience of his father, I interpreted:

It is hard to differentiate between your experience of yourself and your father's narratives about *(country of origin)* and the world. I believe that you've taken in his anxieties and fears, especially his anxieties about what could happen to you in the world, and have always experienced them as truth. Now, as an adult, it is difficult to imagine that your fears about yourself and the fragility of your life in this world could be anything other than truth. It feels dangerous to you to begin experiencing yourself in a new way because it feels that doing so will make you vulnerable to a more catastrophic fate than the fates you already imagine.

Through this interpretation, I attempted to make linkages between his current experience of himself and his childhood experiences of his father. The interpretation also attempted to articulate how he has internalized his father's fears and anxieties and assimilated them as part of his father complex which distorts or alters his ego identity. Finally, this interpretation expressed his unconscious fear of change that holds fast in place his current perception of himself and the world.

In a final example of interpretation, I offer an extended passage with Stacey. She had a multiple-year history of childhood abuse by someone outside her family and a very conflicted relationship with her mother. Stacey's strong defenses against her own experiences and her perception of weakness featured prominently in her analysis. In this passage, we had been discussing the appearance of a childhood friend, Tammy, during an active imagination process she had engaged in. Her active imagination took place in a closet, an imaginary space where Stacey "put" all of the bad things that had happened to her while she was growing up, that is, a dissociative defense.

P: No, I just want to jump ahead past this part of the conversation.
A: What's making you uncomfortable about this part of the conversation? *[Q]*
P: *(sighs)* Nothing. I just feel like time is precious in these sessions and so it's like "okay, we've done that, so let's move ahead to something important."
A: Do you see how your urgency about time, about trying to preserve all of our time, takes you out of whatever it is you're experiencing in the moment – and it's in the moment that we have to stay? *[IC stated as a Q]*
P: . . . It's too late. I've already lost it. We have to make a new moment *(laughs)*.
A: What I'd like to do is come back to Tammy, if that's okay.
P: Okay.
A: Tammy was the one whom you made an attempt to tell about the abuse – an attempt that frightened you because of your fears about how your mother would react if she found out. Perhaps you withdrew from Tammy in the closet because you were afraid Tammy wouldn't believe you. *[partial interpretation]*
P: Yeah.
A: And you couldn't bear feeling alone any more with these feelings than you already felt. But you also felt abandoned by Tammy when you moved to Panama at a point when all of this stuff was in turmoil in you. And then you went into a horrendous year after your family moved to Panama and you desperately needed support. It was such a horrendous year that even now you can't talk about it with me. . . . *[partial interpretation]*
P: *(tears)*.

A: Don't you think that's why Tammy is appearing in the closet? To remind you of what she meant to you. She serves as a reminder of the fears you were going through at the same time you attempted to share your experience with her and the loss that you felt around Tammy when she didn't write back – at a time that you desperately needed her to write back so that you would know you were connected to someone else that cared. *[An example of an interpretation that is begun as a question. I interpret her closet fantasy as though it is a dream.]*

P: I don't know that I thought that deeply about it.

A: I don't think these were conscious thoughts for you. These are your feelings that I'm referring to.

P: I know that I – like if you can grasp what that was like – like take Mr. X *(her abuser)* out of it – assume that there never was a Mr. X – okay. And we'd been uprooted so much that that wasn't a big deal. But we moved to a place where no. . . *(voice trails off)*. . . we couldn't go to school on base because we were retired military, and we couldn't go to the Panamanian schools because we couldn't speak Spanish, and the church that we went to was so little and there were no kids and no television and there was nothing. That was a really difficult. . . I went from being a social butterfly at school – making straight A's the whole time – to being homeschooled, which was a joke. I missed Tammy. I missed her. I don't know that that had anything to do with Mr. X or how horrible that year was *(tearfully)*. She was the only friend I ever had. I remember waiting for mail. I remember . . . *(Stacey does not finish her thought)*. . . this is pointless.

A: You cast off all your deeper feelings as meaningless, or pointless, or stupid, or weak. Your vocabulary to minimize your experiences is enormous. . . you have a thousand different words by which you toss away all of the things you've felt in life. What do you imagine prevents you from just being sad that you lost Tammy? *[partial interpretation]*

P: Because it's. . . I don't know. . . it's ridiculous to be sad about that. I was 14 years old. I mean it was a long time ago.

A: So you tell yourself that these are childish things and throw them away in the closet like you locked Tammy away in the closet. *[partial interpretation]*

The interaction above highlights the manner in which a series of partial interpretations can be linked to form a fuller interpretation while leaving room for the patient's responses to guide the movement towards a fuller interpretive statement. This interpretive sequence seeks to integrate the emotional aspects of childhood experiences that have been dissociated; both the experiences of the abuse by Mr. X and the terrible loss of her childhood friend Tammy when the patient moved to Panama. The sequence also confronts the defensive processes that keep these experiences unavailable for transformation. It links together her present psychological patterns with her past experiences as well as working within her metaphor of "locking things the away in the closet." The last line of the excerpted passage emphasizes the psychic reality[3] of the act of "locking away."

Construction

A construction is a pattern of interpretations extending over time that gradually lead to the development of a different sense of self, a new life narrative, or the weaving together of previously unintegrated aspects of narrative and identity. In Jungian terms, this would be referred to as the creation, or discovery, of the personal myth. This was Jung's (1965) goal in *Memories, Dreams, Reflections*, "Thus it is that I have now undertaken, in my eighty-third year, to tell my personal myth" (p. 3). In contrast, in classical psychoanalysis, the construction has to do with resolving the infantile neurosis, while in self psychology[4] the emphasis is on the role of the construction for the cohesion of the self.

Covington (1995), Spence (1982), and Schafer (1993) emphasize the creation, or reworking, of the life narrative as central to the overall analytic process and indicate that interpretation is the primary analytic activity associated with that process. Before the patient has even arrived in analysis, they have already developed a narrative or personal myth which explains why they feel and act as they do; a narrative that is partially conscious and partially unconscious. Spence (1982) indicates that we are dealing with "narrative truth" rather than "historical truth." The analyst's role is to understand how that "narrative truth" is functioning within the patient and influencing the analytic relationship, rather than trying to figure out what happened to the patient. Spence argues that we should not think in terms of reconstructing the patient's history but instead focus on construction – which he sees as an act of discovery and creation. The construction is intimately linked with transformation, or as Covington (1995) puts it, "Story-making within analysis is seen as being at the heart of symbolic process and of psychic change" (p. 405). Analytic therapy seeks to make conscious the personal myth of the patient and to modify the personal myth through the interpretive, symbolic, and relational aspects of the analytic process. The creation of a construction is a collaborative process of transformation, not unlike the process of film-making. The patient, like the cinematographer, provides the raw film footage of their life, that is, the recording of the experience. However, it is not yet fully a film (i.e., a narrative construction) until the raw footage has been viewed (witnessed) by the cinematographer (patient) and edited by the cinematographer and film editor (analytic therapist); ultimately splicing together the raw footage to create a cohesive story.

It is difficult to capture the overall thrust of an analysis in a succinct manner. From a Jungian perspective, we might describe the movement out of a victim complex (as a psychological dominant of the patient's unconscious situation) as a construction that reconfigures the patient's overall narrative. Or, with another patient, we might facilitate, through interpretation and construction, the transition from an identification with the hero myth into a personal mythology better suited to a new stage of life.

Dieckmann (1991), in his description of the complete interpretation of a complex, also provides an eloquent and useful summary of the process of construction:

> A complete interpretation. . . never takes place in a single analytic hour but may often extend over long periods of time. I would understand this sort of complete and successful interpretation as a conscious, emotionally laden verbal act on the part of the analyst which leads to bringing to consciousness a previously unconscious complex as well as the resistance and the systems of defense that have held this complex fast in the unconscious. A complete and successful interpretation should embrace the three tenses – past, present, and future – and should describe both the contents and the emotional cathexes. Likewise, it should give information about the personal contents and the archetypal core of the complex. In this context, "past" signifies the genetic component of the complex, that is, answers the questions of when and under what conditions did the complex develop and why was it absolutely necessary in the development of this particular patient to suppress and repress the contents, feelings, and affects of precisely this complex. To the present belongs first and foremost the interpretation of the effects that these complex contents evoke within the transference and countertransference situation between analyst and patient, and beyond that, of course, also those distorted situations that arise through projection of the unconscious complex contents in the current life situation of the patient as well as in interpersonal relationships in general. "Future" refers to the "final" element contained in every unconscious complex that presses into consciousness. . . . The final component – i.e., the tendency toward meaning and purpose that arises when drive and image are linked and in which the possibilities of resolution and development are contained – must be brought to consciousness or made conscious, and consciousness must judge it, that is accept it or reject it.
>
> (p. 166)

An example of a relatively complete and broad construction arises with Kate, an older patient. Kate experienced an episodic paranoid process that was most powerfully activated during her interactions at church. While church was a source of community and social contact for Kate, it was also intermittently perceived as a source of threat, insinuation, and reprisal. It was not possible to offer to Kate the following interpretation in full. Elements of the interpretation were given to her at times when she was not in a delusional state. To offer such a full interpretation would have been both ineffectual and overwhelming. However, this hypothesized interpretation illustrates how multiple aspects of her experience could be understood and integrated:

> When you tell me about bad things being done to you at your church, what I hear you saying is that you've been very frightened for a very long time, that people around you were attempting to hurt you, but you didn't have the capacity to understand who was truly dangerous. So you came to feel that it was necessary to anticipate that everyone was dangerous. That makes you feel safer but also always under the possibility of attack. Somewhere inside,

you've made the determination that it is better to feel safer, even at the price of feeling under attack. It doesn't yet feel you have the capability to discern who is safe and who isn't, so my suggestion of alternative possibilities of what is happening at church feels like an abandonment and a betrayal of the thing that you feel has kept you safe all these years.

This hypothetical interpretive construction focuses on the origins of the patient's paranoia, the affective components of the constellated complex/psychological state, the outcomes anticipated by the patient when in the paranoid complex, the triggering situation for the patient's paranoia, the perceptual constrictions of the complexed state, the behavioral reactions to the perceived situation, and the psychological price paid by the patient when she is lost in the complex. The interpretation also focuses on the perception of time, the impact of the paranoid state on the transference field, and on the use of verbs (i.e., action language) rather than nouns to formulate the interpretation.

Summary

Building upon the work of Auld and Hyman (1991), these four seemingly simple steps – confrontational observation, inferential clarification, interpretation, and construction – serve to organize the process of interpretation in analysis. Through the analyst's questions, observations, and clarifications, a deepening occurs which allows an interpretation to emerge as a joint creation of both the analyst and patient. In turn, a mutually created interpretation also has the potential to increase the patient's capacity for symbolization, linking of psychic experience, and development of richer associative networks (itself a form of psychic linking). As a distillation of technique, these four steps seem simple, but as Jung (1961) rightly points out, "A complete and really exhaustive interpretation is very difficult indeed" (para. 537). In the chapters that follow, some of the complexities, nuances, and significant underpinnings of the interpretive process will be examined more closely.

Exercises for the reader

1) Cultivating a process of self-supervision is extremely helpful to the integration of the interpretive model outlined in this chapter. A starting place is to simply keep a notepad in your lap during analytic sessions. If you write detailed process notes during sessions, it is a relatively simple step to add the abbreviations (*CO* – confrontational observation, *IC* – inferential clarification, *I* – interpretation, *Q* – question) from this chapter to annotate your process notes. If there is sufficient record of the verbal interaction, this exercise could also be done after the conclusion of the session.

2) To expand the scope of the exercise, other interventions can be added to build awareness of the degree of supportive interventions being engaged

in (interventions that often interfere with the analytic process), for example making note of advice giving (*AG*), reassurance (*R*), encouragement (*E*), intellectualized/educational interventions (*IE*), or problem-solving (*PS*).

3) If you do not keep detailed process notes (and do not feel comfortable making extensive notes during sessions), you can still build your interpretive awareness by making a list of these interventional abbreviations on a notepad and placing a checkmark beside the appropriate interventional category after it is offered to the patient. While not quite as effective in terms of learning to frame interpretations, inferential clarifications, and confrontational observations, the exercise will still build increased awareness of these interventional possibilities.

Notes

1 "The attitude that takes a given phenomenon as symbolic may be called, for short, the *symbolic attitude*. It is only partially justified by the behaviour of things; for the rest, it is the outcome of a definite view of the world which *assigns meaning* to events, whether great or small, and attaches to this meaning a greater value than to bare facts" (Jung, 1971, para. 819, italics in original).
2 A psychological process consistent with Melanie Klein's (1946) "paranoid-schizoid" position in which the individual is primarily operating on a part-object rather than whole-object level of psychological functioning. The individual operating at the paranoid-schizoid level fears damage or destruction of their good feelings, toward self or others, by their bad feelings, towards self or others. Therefore, good and bad feelings are kept separated by the psychological defense of splitting.
3 Psychic reality – "If I shift my concept of reality on to the plane of the psyche – where alone it is valid – this puts an end to the conflict between mind and matter, spirit and nature, as contradictory explanatory principles. . . all immediate experience is psychic and that immediate reality can only be psychic. . . We could well point to the idea of psychic reality as the most important achievement of modern psychology" (Jung, 1960b, para. 681–683).
4 Self psychology is the branch of psychoanalysis that emerged from the work of Heinz Kohut and became a significant influence on the relational and intersubjective schools of psychoanalytic thought.

Chapter 4

The analytic attitude and its underlying principles

Before continuing with the process of interpretation, it is critical to outline the processes and attitude that support the interpretive process. In my experience, psychic reality, intersubjectivity, meaningful indeterminacy, narrative truth, avoidance of foreclosure, the dialectic of the unknown and known, and a focus on experience are the principles that form the foundation for the analytic attitude.

The analytic attitude

Cultivating an analytic attitude is essential to working effectively with the interpretive process. Without the development of this foundation to our work, analytic therapy becomes just another psychotherapy. Most other forms of psychotherapy can be practiced primarily via the application of theory and technique, without serious consideration of the therapist's attitude. The analytic attitude places the encounter with the unconscious and the unknown at the core of the analytic process, over and above other concerns or considerations. It is reflected in the way the analyst listens, behaves, thinks, feels, and engages during the analytic process. The analytic attitude essentially comprises an ethical attitude adopted towards the analytic process itself (Allphin, 2005). According to Schafer (1983), the analytic attitude:

> will be evident in the analyst's remaining curious, eager to find out, and open to surprise. It will be evident also in the analyst's taking nothing for granted. . . and remaining ready to revise conjectures or conclusions already arrived at, tolerate ambiguity or incomplete closure over extended periods of time, accept alternative points of view, and bear and contain the experiences of helplessness, confusion, and aloneness that not infrequently mark periods of analytic work with each analysand.
>
> (p. 7)

Wolkenfeld (1990) identifies the "internalization of the psychoanalytic attitude" (p. 103) as the primary objective of psychoanalytic education, over and above the teaching of theory or technique.

Jung does not specifically utilize the term "analytic attitude" in his writing, but we can imagine that his conception of an analytic attitude would necessarily also include the symbolic attitude (Jung, 1971, para. 819) as a subset of the analyst's overall analytic attitude. Jung (1954b) articulates a position similar to the analytic attitude regarding the outlook that both the analyst and the analysand should bring to the analytic endeavor, stating that both must:

> believe implicitly in the significance and value of conscious realization, whereby hitherto unconscious parts of the personality are brought to light and subjected to conscious discrimination and criticism. It is a process that requires the patient to face his problems and that taxes his powers of conscious judgment and decision. It is nothing less than a direct challenge to his ethical sense, a call to arms that must be answered by the whole personality.
>
> (para. 315)

Rothstein (1995) makes a close tie between the utilization of analytic technique and the analytic attitude: "What is essential in analytic technique is the analyst's

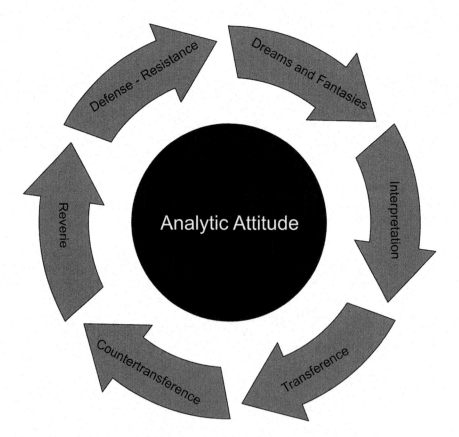

Figure 4.1 The analytic attitude as orienting compass

attitude. . . Other features of the analytic situation such as frequency of sessions and the use of the couch, though important, are not always and absolutely essential" (p. 45). Poland (2002) frames the issue even more succinctly, indicating that "technique is attitude actualized," and offers the phrase "the interpretative attitude" to capture the essence of the analytic attitude as applied to the interpretive process (p. 807).

Therefore, the analytic attitude is the analyst's primary orienting tool in conducting an analysis; the compass for the analytic process (see Figure 4.1). How the analyst is present in the session, what the analyst does, and how the analyst processes the experience of analysis will be guided by the orienting function of the analytic attitude. In addition, from a Jungian perspective, the analytic attitude will also be informed by the activity of the Self of the analyst (Ulanov, 1999).

The underlying principles

There are several basic concepts of psychic functioning essential to working within an analytic attitude: psychic reality, intersubjectivity, meaningful indeterminacy, narrative truth, avoidance of foreclosure, and a focus on experience.

Psychic reality

The principle most central to the maintenance of an analytic attitude is Jung's concept of psychic reality. Jung (1960b) defines psychic reality as follows:

> If I shift my concept of reality on to the plane of the psyche – where alone it is valid – this puts an end to the conflict between mind and matter, spirit and nature, as contradictory explanatory principles. . . all immediate experience is psychic and that immediate reality can only be psychic. . . We could well point to the idea of psychic reality as the most important achievement of modern psychology.
>
> (para. 681–683)

Elsewhere, Jung (1950) emphasizes the autonomous nature of psychic reality: "The unconscious is a living psychic entity which, it seems, is relatively autonomous, behaving *as if* it were a personality with intentions of its own" (para. 1418, italics mine). Analysts from other psychoanalytic perspectives have also come to recognize the essential nature of psychic reality for the analytic process, for example Quinodoz (2003): "The psychoanalyst is convinced of the presence and psychic reality of this world that transcends the limits of the measurable or the quantifiable" (p. 134).

The concept of psychic reality has great significance for the interpretive process because interpretations, as an attempt to engage and transform the patient's interior world, will frequently be framed to address an aspect of psychic experience that does not conform to the patient's conscious orientation and the ego's limited perspective. As such, interpretations grounded in psychic reality may even sound strange, illogical, bizarre, or disconnected from the "ordinary" reality of the patient's ego consciousness.

Intersubjectivity: Abandoning Archimedes

In philosophy, the Archimedean point (*Punctum Archimedis*) is the hypothetical vantage point from which an observer can objectively perceive the subject of inquiry. As analytic therapy has progressed over the past 118 years,[1] the field has necessarily relinquished the Archimedean point of the analytic therapist as the detached, objective observer-commentator on the patient's neurotic conflicts. The interpretive focus has shifted from the model of the objective observer to a model in which the analyst is in the analytic soup with the patient – not in terms of mutual self-revelation – but as subjective co-participant, co-experiencer, and co-creator of the analytic process. This shift in perspective is reflected most distinctly in the intersubjective and relational schools of psychoanalysis. These contemporary perspectives emerged out of the empathic-introspective mode of analytic interaction developed by Kohut (1959) as well as influences from object relations theory and the interpersonal school of psychoanalysis.[2] However Jung, by proposing a model of analysis that places the analyst's personality at the center of the analytic process, anticipated aspects of the intersubjective-relational development. In fact, Bovensiepen (2006) places complex theory squarely within the intersubjective paradigm: "I imagine then a complex to be a limited section, a sub-network from the entire fabric of intersubjective experiences" (p. 457).

The intersubjective-relational perspective can be discerned in Jung's conception of analysis via his references to the archetypal image of the wounded healer (Sedgwick, 1994). The myths of Asclepius and Chiron form the archetypal background for the wounded healer model (Groesbeck, 1975). In the wounded healer model, the analyst is open to being impacted by the suffering and experiences of the patient, while also drawing upon her own experiences of suffering as part of the healing process. Another example of Jung's (1954b) prescient anticipation of the intersubjective-relational movement can be seen in the following passage:

> In any effective psychological treatment the doctor is bound to influence the patient: But this influence can only take place if the patient has a reciprocal influence on the doctor. You can exert no influence if you are not susceptible to influence.
>
> (para. 163)

Although there is a shared subjectivity in the contemporary understanding of the analytic encounter, the analytic relationship remains fundamentally asymmetrical because it takes place in an analytic setting, which is powerfully defined by the relationship of the roles of analyst and analysand. As Ogden (2004) describes this inherent and unavoidable asymmetry:

As a result, the unconscious experience of the analysand is privileged in a specific way; i.e., it is the past and present experience of the analysand that is taken by the analytic pair as the principal (though not exclusive) subject of analytic discourse. The analyst's experience in and of the analytic third is (primarily) utilized as a vehicle for the understanding of the conscious and unconscious experience of the analysand.

(p. 186)

In most analytic situations, it is likely that the analyst will have a greater depth of experience in intersubjective fields and, hopefully, will have a greater awareness of how they respond in situations where mutually influential intersubjective forces are at work. Clearly, there has been a significant shift away from a model where the analyst possesses an objective perspective while the patient's perspective is completely subjective. The post-Archimedean recognition that both participants enter the situation from a subjective perspective has profound implications for the interpretive process.

Meaningful indeterminacy

Meaningful indeterminacy is a concept I introduce here as a vehicle for moving beyond the tension that existed between Jung and Freud (and continues to exist within the various perspectives on analytic therapy), that is, the tension between causal, biological determinism (of which Jung was critical in Freud's model) and the teleological model of the psyche proposed by Jung. This issue, which Jung addresses in *Symbols of Transformation* (1956), was the primary theoretical conflict that led to the schism between the two most significant figures in the history of psychoanalysis. However, as Horne, Sowa, and Isenman (2000) point out, there was intense debate within philosophy and science around the concepts of determinism and teleology at the end of the nineteenth century when psychoanalysis was initially emerging. Because this debate continues in contemporary schools of analytic thought, the field continues to be conceptually limited, remaining trapped in the philosophical dichotomization of causal attribution that does not reflect contemporary understanding of causality (Horne et al., 2000). Horne et al. (2000) point to Bion's model of the psyche as a model that transcends causality – whether it be deterministic or teleological causality. One example from Bion's model is his concept of the "selected fact." The selected fact is a transitory area of focus or attunement around which the analyst is likely to create an interpretation. According to Bion (1992), "The term, 'selected fact', I reserve for use in emotional experiences of thought about phenomena in which time is excluded" (p. 278). Elsewhere, Bion (1962) elaborates further on the selected fact, "The selected fact is the name of an emotional experience, the emotional experience of a sense of discovery of coherence; its significance is therefore epistemological and the relationship of selected facts must not be assumed to be logical" (p. 73). Clearly, Bion detaches the interpretation process from chronological time and ordinary modes of logic without denying the value of those vertices at other times. The causal transcendence that Horne et al. (2000) identify in Bion is suffused throughout his model. I introduce the term "meaningful indeterminacy" to bring greater focus to this aspect of contemporary analytic therapy.

Indeterminacy, as a general concept, was introduced by Heisenberg (1927) through his uncertainty principle in physics (which Heisenberg sometimes also referred to as the indeterminacy principle). In the simplest terms, it is a principle applicable to quantum mechanics in reference to the measurement of particles. It states that there is a fundamental limit in how well the position and momentum of a quantum particle can be measured simultaneously, that is, the more precisely the location of a particle is known, the more limited the knowledge of the momentum of the particle, and vice versa. As a general concept, indeterminacy has entered into the fields of philosophy, religious studies, literary criticism, sociology, music theory, semantic theory, neuroscience, and mathematics. However, it has not been adequately integrated into analytic therapy. Currently, most models of analytic therapy are conceptually rooted in the chronological metaphor of "looking backward" (reductively) or "looking forward" (progressively). As a result, the field is left without an adequate conceptual framework for "looking forward" and "looking backward" simultaneously, or remaining open to other non-linear, achronological ways of experiencing in the analytic moment. Psychoidal experience and synchronicity[3] are two Jungian concepts that can be thought of as foreshadowing the concept of meaningful indeterminacy. However, because they are also intimately tied to Jung's effort to articulate a teleological perspective of the psyche (in reaction to Freud), these concepts remain caught in the dichotomous reductive–progressive paradigm.

Meaningful indeterminacy, building on the work of Bion, seeks to constructively address the bifurcation that the reductive–synthetic debate has created in the Jungian community. Within the perspective of meaningful indeterminacy, the thoughts, behaviors, and feelings of the analytic dyad are not randomly generated; it is assumed that thought, behavior, and feeling are motivated by some conscious, unconscious, or intersubjective prompting. Therefore an assumption is made that all thought, behavior, and feeling is meaningful and communicative. However, the analyst and patient may not readily recognize that meaningful connection in the moment because the source of the meaning is often indeterminate; operating outside typical causal, chronological, and rational ways of conceptualizing experience. Furthermore, the meaningful "content" of the observed–experienced pattern requires a relational context and a moment of time in which to become incarnate. Therefore, interpretations are offered with the hope that the interpretation adds coherence to the moment, but with the recognition that the interpretation, as well as the understanding on which it is based, is subject to revision or reinterpretation as other possibilities emerge. It is a concept that holds open the possibility of creating meaningful linkages between varieties of experiences – whether explicit, implicit, or unconscious – while also holding open the possibility of multiple meanings emerging in relationship to any particular experience. In the face of what is emerging in the session, I attempt to keep this principle active by regularly asking myself, "What else might this be, other than (or in addition to) what it appears to be on the surface?"

Narrative truth

As touched upon in Chapter 3, the patient's personal narrative is the focus of analysis rather than the historical events (i.e., "historical truth") that occurred in the patient's life. Knowledge of historical events primarily serves to inform the analyst of the influences that have shaped the patient's narrative. The analytic attitude is one that focuses on the patient's "narrative truth" rather than attempting to decipher their "historical truth" (Spence, 1982). While Jung (1959b) does not refer explicitly to the concept of narrative truth, it is implicit in his writing, particularly the close link he makes between the interpretive process and the construction of meaning:

> When you come to think about it, nothing has any meaning, for when there was nobody to think, there was nobody to interpret what happened. Interpretations are only for those who don't understand; it is only the things we don't understand that have any meaning. Man woke up in a world he did not understand, and that is why he tries to interpret it.
>
> (para. 65)

As writer Aldous Huxley (1933) succinctly puts it, "Experience is not what happens to a man; it is what a man does with what happens to him" (p. 5). Schwartz-Salant (1991b) adopts a similar position, asserting that, "Trauma isn't stored as history. It is stored as myth." From a psychoanalytic perspective, a fuller explication of this principle is offered by Wolkenfeld (1990):

> As analysts, we are not concerned with defining reality, or pursuing the literal truth of the patient's perceptions, whatever that means, or even directly with the patient's life. Rather, our focus is on the immediate drive derivatives and defenses operative, the intrapsychic specificities of the patient-analyst interactions, and the functioning of the patient's mind.
>
> (p. 106)

Avoidance of foreclosure

Foreclosure, which can be carried out by the analyst or the patient, occurs when an interaction is structured in such a way as to prevent the emergence of unconscious communication, or when meaning is prematurely attributed to unconscious experience as it emerges. One could say that resistance to the analytic process by the patient is a form of foreclosure. However, in the context of interpretation and the analytic attitude, foreclosure primarily refers to situations in which the analytic therapist interacts in a way that prevents the patient's thoughts, feelings, and behaviors from emerging spontaneously. According to Connolly (2014), the analyst must "safeguard against the dangers of an over-eager search for understanding through premature or over-defined interpretations that risk foreclosing the teleological or aesthetic potentiality of the symbol" (p. 450). If the analyst has established an analytic attitude, the analyst endeavors to avoid foreclosing on the emergence of the patient's unconscious communications. Not only does foreclosure by the analyst result in a suppression of unconscious communication by the patient, it also may serve to close down the imagination of the patient by implicitly communicating that interaction with the patient's imagination is undesired by the analyst.

Foreclosure in the analytic setting results in what Bion (1970) termed a "minus K" situation in which experiential knowing (i.e., K = knowledge) is not just interfered with but sets into motion a process by which knowledge is under attack, damaged, or destroyed. Parsons (2000) summarizes Bion's concept in this way: "K is a function of all human beings, perhaps best described as a readiness to know. It is not simply the state of knowing, because there is also minus K (−K) and this is not just ignorance but the active avoidance of knowledge, or even the wish to destroy the capacity for it" (p. 49) as well as indicating that Bion was, "emphasising that knowledge is not a thing that we have, but a link between ourselves and what we know" (p. 67). Jung (1916) also implicitly cautions against foreclosure through the analyst's desire to understand, "The danger of wanting to understand the meaning is over-valuation of the content which is subjected to intellectual analysis and interpretation so that the essentially symbolic character of the product is lost" (para. 176).

In addition to the danger of foreclosure, there are related dangers in terms of the analyst setting the topic of discussion for the patient, avoiding sensitive subjects, moving too quickly past interactions that have the potential for analytic inquiry, or otherwise "leading" the patient during the session. For example, there is often an urge for the analytic therapist to set the opening theme for a session for the patient, such as, "How was your vacation?" or "How did your discussion go with your husband?" Another common form of foreclosure is the tendency for some therapists to "help" their patient avoid pitfalls, such as reminding the patient who has difficulty remembering to pay their balance to bring their checkbook to the next session, rather than analyzing the patient's difficulty in remembering. Such a reminder forecloses on what might be revealed about the patient's relationship to their analysis as expressed through their forgetfulness. Other examples of analyst foreclosure include the analyst's resumption of the dialogic thread for the patient when the patient has created a silence in the interaction, or verbally accepting a patient's apology without examining the reason behind the apology.

The dialectic of the unknown and known

The issue of interpretation in analysis brings up an inherent paradox for the analyst – the tension that exists between knowing and not knowing, known and

Figure 4.2 The analyst's paradox

unknown. I refer to the analyst's capacity to embrace the unknown and the capacity to know as *the analyst's paradox*. The dialectic tension between the unknown and known is essential to transformation in analysis.

The embrace of the unknown involves the avoidance of foreclosure, tolerating ambiguity and complexity, accepting the limitations of conscious understanding, and sustaining curiosity and wonder until the moment when some element of experience coagulates, allowing gnosis to emerge. This knowing is followed, once again, by a return to an attitudinal stance of unknowing.

Embrace of the unknown is a central aspect of the analytic process for both Jung and Bion.[4] Bion's emphasis on the unknown is best reflected in what he terms the analyst's "negative capability" (Bion, 1970). Negative capability is a term Bion borrowed from the English poet John Keats, who defined negative capability as the capacity to embrace uncertainty, live with mystery, and make peace with ambiguity "without any irritable reaching after fact and reason." This emphasis on negative capability is reflected in Bion's reliance on non-sensuous intuition, the use of reverie, and his recommendation to "approach every session without memory or desire" (1967, p. 272). It is also reflected in his selection of terms to describe his model of the psyche. Bion intentionally selected terms he felt were abstract, undefined, unsaturated by preconceived meanings, and open to interpretation in new ways. Bion felt that only by approaching the analytic session with this attitude and frame of mind would the analyst be able to discern what is emerging in the field rather than defaulting to a categorization of experience based on concepts, terms, and patterns previously experienced.

An embrace of the unknown is also strongly present in Jung's work but is more subtly stated, for example, "Doctor and patient thus find themselves in a relationship founded on mutual unconsciousness" (1954b, para. 364). Elsewhere, Jung addresses the unknown more specifically:

> The unconscious is not simply the unknown, it is rather the unknown psychic; and this we define on the one hand as all those things in us which, if they came to consciousness, would presumably differ in no respect from the known psychic contents, with the addition. . . of the psychoid system, of which nothing is known directly.
>
> (1960, para. 382)

Jung's (1960b) appreciation for the unknown is also reflected in his conception of symbols:

> By a symbol I do not mean an allegory or a sign, but an image that describes in the best possible way the dimly discerned nature of the spirit. A symbol does not define or explain; it points beyond itself to a meaning that is darkly divined yet still beyond our grasp, and cannot be adequately expressed in the familiar words of our language.
>
> (para. 644)

Often, there is difficulty for the analyst in being open to the unknown because this challenges the centrality of the analyst's ego when the analyst recognizes there is a locus of agency that exists beyond this. Jung refers to this transcendent agent as the Self, while Bion simply refers to it as "0."[5]

Just as there is fear associated with embracing and experiencing the unknown, for many analytic therapists there is also often a fear about "knowing" something about the patient with sufficient clarity to form an interpretation. This fear often arises as a defense of the analytic persona against being perceived as arrogant or omnipotent. The analyst's defense against knowing something may also reflect a fear that the patient will discover the therapist does not really know anything of significance; likely a manifestation of an imposter complex. In the face of these fears and defenses, the therapist can become trapped in comfortable murmurings of support and gently asked questions that have little hope of penetrating the patient's defenses strongly enough to constellate a transformative process.

In terms of the analytic attitude, the central issue is not a matter of choosing one end of the continuum or the other; knowing or not knowing. The issue is the analyst's awareness of both experiences, holding a true tension of opposites, holding the unknown and known in reciprocal dialogue, and creating openings for both to influence the unfolding of the analysis.

Focus on experience

In terms of the analytic attitude, the final principle to be addressed is the priority given to experience constellated in the analytic moment, particularly emotional experience. As Strachey emphasized in 1934, the analytic experience, especially the focus of the analytic interpretation, must be "emotionally immediate" and always be directed towards an experiential "point of urgency" (p. 150). Jung (1953a) made a similar statement in 1928, "I would not give priority to understanding. . . For the important thing is not to interpret and understand the fantasies, but primarily to experience them" (para. 342). Kohut (1971) introduced the term "experience-near" to address the dangers of reification[6] in psychoanalysis associated with the application of metapsychology during the interpretive process. Kohut underscores the importance of framing interpretations in experiential terms within an empathic-introspective mode of interaction. From a contemporary perspective, Ferro (2013) echoes the point originally articulated by Strachey: "It is necessary to interpret something the patient can touch and see, something that must be there. If there is no 'sensual' factor there is no point in interpreting" (p. 110).

Colman (2009) reminds us that theory is not fact, it is simply a metaphor that functions to make a translation from one form of experience into another form of experience. It is not uncommon in the Jungian community to incorporate Jungian concepts, such as shadow or anima, into interpretations as though these terms reflect actual psychological entities rather than theoretical constructs. In doing so, there is a very real danger of moving away from the patient's self-experience towards an intellectualized, theoretical understanding of their unconscious patterns, rather than creating an experiential knowing of these patterns.

Summary

The interpretive process is guided by and grounded in the analyst's overarching analytic attitude which is informed by several supporting principles: psychic reality, intersubjectivity, meaningful indeterminacy, narrative truth, avoidance of foreclosure, the dialectic of the unknown and known, and a focus on experience. The analytic attitude I propose is built on a foundation provided by Jung, but is one that has also been shaped by elements drawn from intersubjectivist theory, Bion, and Kohut. However, there is not a single, clearly defined analytic attitude, as only a general idea about an analytic attitude can be conveyed. It is incumbent on each analyst, analytic therapist, and analyst-in-training to cultivate their own understanding of an analytic attitude based on their analytic experiences, self-knowledge, theoretical orientation, and familiarity with the available literature on the subject (e.g., Gabbard & Ogden, 2009).

Exercise for the reader

Write a statement of your guiding analytic attitude based on your experiences of the analytic process. In crafting your statement, consider whether the supporting principles outlined in this chapter "fit" with your statement of your analytic attitude. Which of the supporting principles would you delete from your statement? Which principles would you add that might better articulate the analytic attitude you have cultivated?

Notes

1 The founding of psychoanalysis, the underlying basis of all later analytic therapies, is traditionally tied to the publication of Freud's *The Interpretation of Dreams* (*Die Traumdeutung*) in November 1899.
2 In the interpersonal approach to psychoanalysis, the focus in the psychoanalytic process shifts from a predominantly intrapsychic perspective to one that also includes the interpersonal interactions of the patient. Primary figures in interpersonal psychoanalysis included Harry Stack Sullivan, Erich Fromm, Frieda Fromm-Reichmann, Harold Searles, and Karen Horney.

3 Psychoidal experience and synchronicity are based on the idea that psyche has goals and aims – that is, that psyche is not just the product of causes, and there will always be experiences that cannot be known or understood from the historical-causal perspective. Synchronicity (Jung, 1958a, para. 816–997) is an acausal connecting principle that is a modification of the basic psychoanalytic hermeneutic. It proposes a meaning that exists *a priori* to human consciousness and that exists outside of man. Psychoid or psychoidal (Jung, 1958a, para. 353–442) refers to the space that exists between the instincts (soma-matter) and archetypes (psyche-spirit) as well as between inner and outer experience. Experiences in the psychoid realm may have characteristics of both matter and spirit. According to Jung, latent and unconscious meaning exists in all matter, not just the human psyche, or the conscious mind.

4 The relationship between the analytic approaches of C. G. Jung and Wilfred Bion is explored in more depth in Winborn (2017a, 2018).

5 Bion defines "O" as absolute truth, ultimate reality, the experience of the numinous, the fundamentally unknowable (Bion, 1965, 1970).

6 Reification is the fallacy of referring to concepts, such as ego, shadow, animus, or Self, as though they are material things rather than metaphors that serve a useful purpose in terms of theory (see Colman, 2009 for further discussion of this issue). For example, in terms of reification, there are psychological tendencies or processes in many individuals that seem focused on disowning or hiding aspects of self-experience from oneself and others. Jung introduced the term "shadow" as a conceptual short-hand for describing those patterns. When a concept is treated as an entity, the *as if* quality of it is lost and reification has ensued.

Chapter 5

The interpretive process

The *opus*

Having established a general conceptual structure for interpretation, as well as examining the analytic attitude that supports interpretation, we can now turn more specifically to the interpretive process. It is here that the alchemical emphasis on the work (*opus*) comes into focus. The consulting room of the analyst becomes both the alchemist's laboratory and the artist's atelier. Often during the study of alchemy, we can readily become transfixed by the unusual imagery and esoteric terminology which provides so many rich metaphors for the analytic process. However, in the alchemical literature, there is great emphasis on the methodology (*operatio*) used to carry out the alchemical experiments. There is also a focus on the attitude the alchemist must possess in relationship to the work: courage, conviction, faith in the work, close attention to what emerges during the *operatio*, perseverance in the face of uncertainty, and knowledge gained through experience in the laboratory. Jung (1953b) describes the alchemical method in this way, "The basis of alchemy is the work (*opus*). Part of this work is practical, the *operatio* itself, which is to be thought of as a series of experiments with chemical substances" (para. 401), and "The practice of the art is a hard road and the longest road. The art has no enemies except the ignorant" (para. 423). The often ordinary exchanges, both spoken and unspoken, that frequently occupy the space of the analytic consulting room – the words, glances, sighs, gestures, postures, tones, images, and interior states of the analytic field – are the *prima materia* for the *operatio* of the interpretive process. The psyche of the analyst, like the alchemists of days past, gathers the *prima materia*, engages the alchemical method via the interpretive process, and observantly waits to see what chemical transformation may occur.

Just as there are different stages to the alchemical *opus*, there are also several steps in the creation of an interpretation. Some steps are involved with every interpretive creation, while others will only apply intermittently. Stages in the interpretive process include listening, attending, gathering information and experiences, conceptualization, generating hypotheses, considering the frame of the interpretation, timing considerations, prioritizing what to interpret, crafting the language of the interpretation, offering the interpretation, and a return to listening and gathering. For the sake of explication, a schematized outline of the interpretive process is offered which can be helpful when first beginning to work interpretively. However, as interpretive experience grows, some aspects of the interpretive process begin to occur in the background of the analyst's process, just as the improvising jazz musician begins to respond unconsciously to the internalized musical structure of chords, scales, modes, harmony, melody, and rhythm.

Preparing for interpretation

Interpretation always begins with the analyst attending, listening, and experiencing. However, the interpreting analyst listens, attends, and experiences in a unique manner. To be able to make use of these observations and accompanying interpretations, the analyst's ego becomes divided into two parts: a participating aspect of the ego and an observing aspect (i.e., the aspect of the ego that can reflect on what the participating ego is experiencing). The experiencing aspect of the analyst is referred to as the analyst's participating ego even though some experiences may extend beyond the ego. Speaking to the essential nature of the participating ego for the interpretive process, Bolognini (2002) asserts that "The interpretive function of psychoanalysis cannot really be carried out without a partial experiential immersion in the patient's inner world" (p. 759). This shift reflects an intentional dissociation, or splitting, of the analyst's ego in the service of the analysis. This split is also referred to as the development of the analytic or working ego. The analytic ego, or working ego, attempts to maintain some

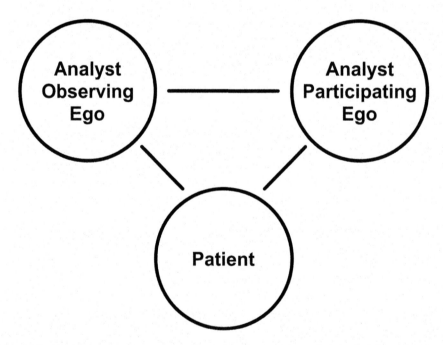

Figure 5.1 The analytic ego

separation from the immediate affective milieu of the patient–analyst interaction while still accessing the sensory-affective information being exchanged. Sterba (1934) first introduced the concept of the analytic ego and referred to this split as a "therapeutic dissociation" (p. 120).

The development of this capacity becomes especially important when working within the transference–countertransference matrix. The analytic ego is essential for the analyst's ability to maintain reflective capacity when the consulting room becomes charged with powerful emotional states, such as erotic, aggressive, avoidant, judging, shaming, demeaning, or idealizing states. In addition to enhancing the analyst's capacity for observing and conceptualizing what is occurring in the analytic session, the analytic ego also facilitates the development of the patient's introspection, self-insight, and autonomy by creating opportunities for the patient to internalize the analyst's capacity to reflect upon experience and create associative connections between bits of experience that were previously unconnected. Through this interaction, the patient has the potential to increase her capacity for reflection[1] by experiencing reflection through the analyst's working ego.

The pre-interpretive phase

Attending, listening, and experiencing are the three activities that precede any interpretation. These activities of the analyst are so interwoven it would be artificial to talk about them as separate processes. We can speak of these activities in connection with the sensory apparatus of the analyst: auditory, visual, olfactory, kinesthetic, tactile, affective, and intuitive. While the analyst is always listening at some level to the content of the patient's statements, if the analyst becomes overly focused on closely following the surface content of the patient's verbal statements, it becomes difficult for the analyst to leave space for observations about his own internal reactions. It also becomes difficult to have thoughts about the implicit communications inherent in the patient's statements and the underlying processes in which these statements are embedded. Therefore, the listening process is preferably held loosely – leaving room for the analyst's reflections beyond the storyline presented by the patient. We could also refer to this type of listening as "listening between the lines," or, as Reik (1948) puts it, "listening with the third ear."

As pre-interpretive thoughts begin to form around patterns observed, it is helpful to "hold" those thoughts before moving into interpretation. The period of holding varies widely depending on the patient and the focus of the observation. The decision about how long to hold a thought before transitioning to interpretation is informed by a mix of previous experiences, conscious discernment, and intuition. A holding period might last for a few seconds or stretch across weeks or months. Many possible considerations enter into the decision to hold an interpretation, such as the patient's level of psychological functioning, the types of defense mechanisms the patient is employing, the length of the analytic relationship, the level of rapport established, or the potential depth of the interpretation being considered.

As part of the holding process, I subject my own thoughts and impressions to a bit of suspicion, often asking myself, "What else might this be?" or "What else might be happening?" to avoid prematurely attaching undue significance to the initial appearance of something in the analytic field. This transitory self-query facilitates the process of peering beneath the surface to engage other levels of meaning or communication. Naturally, there also exists a risk of holding one's thoughts too long; allowing opportunities to pass or windows to close.

Throughout the pre-interpretive phase, it is essential for the analyst to create a permeable state of mind in which the network of attention is open to a broad range of experience.[2] As Freud (1912) put it, the analyst:

> must turn his own unconscious like a receptive organ towards the transmitting unconscious of the patient. He must adjust himself to the patient as a telephone receiver is adjusted to the transmitting microphone. Just as the receiver converts back into sound waves the electric oscillations in the telephone line which were set up by sound waves, so the doctor's unconscious is able, from the derivatives of the unconscious which are communicated to him, to reconstruct that unconscious, which has determined the patient's free associations.
>
> (pp. 115–116)

While listening to the patient's verbalizations, as well as the absence of verbalizations, the analyst remains open to abrupt shifts in the theme of the session, patient behaviors and gestures, emotions and affects, slips of the tongue, fantasies, shifts in the frame of the analysis (such as missed appointments, disruptions in payment for sessions, extending the time of sessions, late arrival for sessions, etc.), fantasies, physiological shifts (such as increased respiration, psychomotor agitation, flushing of skin, fidgeting), and shifts in the patient's reaction to the analyst. Recognizing the recurrence of these patterns, whether occurring during a single session or across time, involves the analyst's comparison of the analyst's current experience of the patient with her previous experiences of the patient. Just as in dreams, a repetition of pattern underscores the significance of the underlying process producing the pattern. It is also important to take notice of the temporal contiguity of events occurring during the analytic session. For example, temporal contiguity exists when a patient frequently begins coughing shortly after he speaks about his father.

In addition to the analyst's observations of the patient, the analyst also attends to shifts in her own inner states, including shifts in thought process, emotion, imagery, associations, and physiological state. Finally, the analyst makes note of shifts in the analytic field, such as the emergence of synchronicities, shifts in the energy of the room, or alterations in the tempo of the interaction. Collectively, these areas of attention form the ephemera of the analytic encounter; the fleeting but salient elements that serve as the faint markers of implicit and unconscious processes which often slip by unnoticed. Throughout the process, there is an ebb and flow of awareness between the foreground and background of experience.

There are a number of useful questions circulating through the analyst's reflections during sessions which serve to stretch the analyst's attention beyond the verbal exchange of the session: How do I feel when I am with this patient? How is this patient affecting me? What is constellated between the patient and me? Is my analytic activity moving the process forward or maintaining the *status quo* of the psychological situation? How is the patient utilizing me? What role am I being asked to play in the patient's psychic reality? What does my imagination or reverie tell me about the patient? By what means has this patient survived in his life? What am I reluctant to say to this patient, and why am I reluctant? What is occurring in my body when I am with this patient? Questions such as these keep the receptive function of the analyst's psyche open to a broad range of experience and encourage the analyst to attend at multiple levels.

Developing focus

From the many possible sources of input outlined above, the analytic therapist must temporarily narrow their focus in order for an interpretation to be created. Bion (1962, 1992) referred to this narrowing of focus as the emergence of "the selected fact." The selected fact is a transitory area of focus around an emotional experience from which an interpretation is likely to be formed. Bion is not making a statement about the accuracy of an observation or a statement of absolute truth by electing to use the word "fact." Instead, he is referring to a sense of emotional immediacy (or absence of emotional experience) that crystallizes, at least for the moment, some aspect of the patient's psychic reality or the shared experience of the analyst and analysand. From the perspective of the intersubjective field, the selected fact (we could also refer to "the selected scene" or "the selected character") is a production of the field rather than emerging solely from one participant in the field or the other. This should not be an unfamiliar way of thinking for most Jungians because we are frequently engaging in a similar process with dreams. In many ways, the selected fact has correspondences to the Jungian concept of symbol, but the function of the selected fact is less specific in Bion's model than the concept of symbol in Jung's model.

The process of arriving at the selected fact, like so many analytic activities, involves an amalgam of intuition, inspiration, emotional engagement, and conscious deliberation. There is no single rule of thumb, no guideline, to determine which of the many possible areas of focus to select. In many instances, there is a deliberate decision to interpret a particular pattern, perhaps a decision arrived at over a long period of reflection. At other times, an interpretation spills out like quicksilver, guided by some pre-conscious background processing or the Self. In the latter, the relevance of the interpretation is often only recognized in retrospect, after the interpretation has been offered. Ultimately, though, there should be some sense or resonance that an interpretation, built around a selected fact, will: deepen the patient's experience, engage unconscious processes, make an aspect of the patient's experience more salient, allow some sense of cohesion to emerge from chaos, permit some rigidity to become more fluid, reveal unrecognized meaning, or facilitate the confrontation of the patient's defenses.

Developing the capacity to utilize focal points is related to the development of the observing ego of the analyst. These points of focus assist the analyst in listening for themes that exist beyond the surface content of the patient's verbalizations. Becoming

engrossed in the surface content of the patient's communications is often a significant obstacle to the interpretive process. The tendency for the analyst to consistently
respond to the last words spoken by the patient is a signal that such a pattern has developed. Creating and maintaining a space for reverie (an inner place where the analyst's
thoughts, images, and emotions can emerge) is an analytic state that minimizes an
excessive focus on the patient's verbalized statements.

These focal points are also a way of holding the patient in the analyst's mind.
When the analyst has not developed tools for holding the patient in his mind, the
patient may experience a subtle but disruptive sense of abandonment. For example, it is not uncommon to hear a patient complain of a previous therapist, "He just
sat and listened; he rarely said anything," which likely reflects a therapist who has
not cultivated sufficient reflective space. Ogden (1996) has written eloquently of
the need for both the analyst and patient to maintain a degree of "privacy" during
sessions; providing space for reflection and reverie to occur.

Focal points can also be thought of as a way of operationalizing or conceptualizing the activity of complexes. With one patient, I needed to develop a deeper
understanding of a long-standing pattern of self-harm and self-mutilation that
had been resistant to transformation. As I attended closely to the links between
the observed shifts in her emotions, expectations, and behaviors, I was able to
identify a pattern that extended across time and a variety of situations. A schematic outline of her self-injury cycle gradually formed; presented here, in the
first person, as though the patient is thinking these thoughts consciously (even
though most of the cycle was operating as unconscious fantasy). Her internal
cycle was comprised of three main elements: 1) I feel angry, 2) I expect others
will hurt me or reject me, particularly if I am angry, and 3) In order to avoid
being hurt or rejected, I should hurt myself to express my anger. This schematic
outline was communicated to the patient as an interpretation: "I think you often
feel angry but feel frightened of expressing it because you feel you'll be hurt or
rejected if you do. On some level, you've come to feel that the only way it is
safe to express your anger is by injuring yourself. But because your anger feels
dangerous, you hide the knowledge of your anger from yourself and convince
yourself that hurting yourself is justified."

Incorporating theory

During the formulation process, it is frequently necessary to shift from a receptive-
attending-experiential mode to a conceptual mode in which the selected fact is
thought about from a theoretical perspective. This shift is less abrupt if we permit
ourselves to think of theories and concepts as simply part of the analyst's network of
possible associations in response to the patient – not unlike other personal associations, images, and archetypal motifs that float into the analyst's awareness during sessions. For Jungians, the conceptual focus will frequently involve complex theory. For
example, a Jungian therapist might consult complex theory in an effort to understand
a sudden shift in the patient's affect. Similarly, selfobject theory will be a reference
point for many self psychologists. A contemporary Kleinian will regularly consider

the selected fact through object relations theory or the conceptual framework of the autistic-contiguous, paranoid-schizoid and depressive positions. A classical Freudian analyst is likely to consult structural theory (id/ego/superego) or instinctual drive theory. Naturally, these examples are illustrative, not exhaustive.

At times, the analyst may shift out of their preferred theoretical orientation to consult theories or concepts from other psychoanalytic perspectives because other theoretical perspectives may be more articulate or useful in conceptualizing the selected fact at hand. Knox (2007) addresses the inherent limitations found in all analytic models:

> Each psychodynamic theory focuses on and highlights one or two particular aspects of unconsciousness, but no single model offers a complete picture of unconscious structure, content and processes, nor of the developmental pathways towards the achievement of internal object constancy, which itself depends on affect regulation, reflective function and the full experience of subjectivity achieved with the representational level of self-agency. These are the foundations on which the unique symbolic capacity of the human mind is constructed.
>
> (p. 334)

Connolly (2008) also addresses the necessity of varied approaches to the psyche, "Each Jungian should also be a potential Freudian, Kohutian, Kleinian, Winnicottian, Lacanian, Bionian, as each of these schools only reflects a certain limited analytical perspective" (p. 494). Jung (1950) frames the issue of plurality more succinctly, "Ultimate truth, if there be such a thing, requires the concert of many voices" (para. 1236).

A creative example of pluralistic conceptualization is Goodheart's (1980) integration of the psychoanalytic theories of Robert Langs and Harold Searles with Jung's theory of complexes to formulate a new Jungian conceptualization of the analytic field. Goodheart proposes a hybrid conceptualization that provides a fuller explanatory vehicle for the analytic field than could be articulated utilizing the theories of Jung, Langs, or Searles in isolation.

Interpretation

Developing a hypothesis

While the practice of analytic therapy is very much an art, it is rooted in science as well. According to Shamdasani (2003), "For Jung, psychology was the discipline to unite the circle of the sciences" (p. 18). In many respects, the process of interpretation follows the scientific method: a hypothesis is developed regarding the subject being studied, an experimental design is created to test the hypothesis, data are gathered in the experimental situation, and the hypothesis is evaluated based on the results of the experiment. In general, the hypothesis will be confirmed, disconfirmed, or modified based on the results of the experiment.

The interpretive process works in much the same way as the scientific: 1) experiential data are gathered by the analyst through observation, listening, and interpersonal experience with the patient; 2) a hypothesis is generated based on the experiential data and analytic theory; 3) an interpretation is offered to the patient (i.e., the experimental situation); and 4) the analyst returns to listening, observing, and experiencing in an effort to discern the patient's response to the interpretation. The patient's response (explicitly, implicitly, and unconsciously) will guide the analyst's evaluation as to whether the hypothesis underlying the interpretation was transformative, inert, or counter-productive. The patient's response may also lead to a modification or refinement of the interpretive hypothesis going forward. The pre-interpretive hypothesis loosely takes the form of, "Based on my observations and experiences, I believe the analysand feels (acts, thinks, or imagines) _____ because of _____ ". The analyst's task is to fill in the two blanks in the hypothesis in a way that clarifies, coheres, deepens, explains, or resonates with the patient's experience, ultimately providing the patient with a new perspective on their experience.

To illustrate the process outlined thus far, I recreate the interior process leading to an interpretation with a female patient who experienced a strong distrust of other women. This distrust left her frequently feeling on guard when around other women but also very lonely for the company of other women. As I listened to her describe a distrustful situation with another woman, I noticed myself focusing on her sense of loneliness. As I held that awareness, I also noticed a growing sense of emptiness within myself, as though something inside of me was being hollowed out by an unseen force. My thoughts turned to earlier sessions in which the patient recalled childhood experiences when she had felt her trust in her mother severely betrayed. The betrayal of trust was often followed by verbal attack. I recalled similar incidents stretching across the patient's adult life. Slowly bits of theory began to filter into my awareness – initially Klein's (1946) concept of projective identification and Jung's (1958a) concept of complexes. The concept of projective identification was useful as I reflected on my feeling of emptiness and wondered how my experience might relate to the patient's interior space. The utilization of complex theory[3] facilitated better understanding of the broad affective connections between the patient's past experiences with her mother, which had been internalized as part of the patient's mother complex, and her general reaction to women in the present. My memory of the patient's history with her mother and my experiences of the patient and myself were combined with a conceptual framework to arrive at an interpretation. I said, "Your distrust of women seems to leave you feeling safe but alone. I think your distrust of women is a way you've found to protect yourself from the possibility of being betrayed again, as you felt betrayed by your mother on so many occasions. The possibility of exposing yourself to that again must be quite frightening." After pausing a few moments to see whether she seemed to be able to tolerate and assimilate the first half of the interpretation, I continued, "It seems as though the loss of trust in your mother left you with a void inside that has yet to be filled, which perhaps can't be filled while this distrust of women exists." This interpretation relies on complex theory and projective identification as background structuring concepts, yet the interpretation does not introduce those conceptual terms to the patient. The introduction of the conceptual labels would have shifted the focus from engagement with her emotional experience to an intellectualization of experience. Edinger (1991) frames this issue in alchemical terms, "Concepts and abstractions don't coagulate" (p. 100).

Organizing templates

There are several useful templates to assist in organizing the experiential data gathered, conceptualizing initial hypotheses, and forming interpretations. One of the most helpful templates was developed by Malan (1995), a model he refers to as the triangles of insight. Malan (1995, pp. 90–91) describes two triangles of insight: the triangle of conflict and the triangle of relationship.[4]

Triangle of conflict

The triangle of conflict is based on psychoanalytic concept of signal anxiety[5] and the internal conflict underlying the anxiety. The three corners depicted in the triangle of conflict are: 1) a feeling or impulse that is hidden or repressed, 2) a defense used to prevent the expression of the hidden feeling, 3) and the anxiety associated with the possibility that the hidden impulse or feeling will be exposed

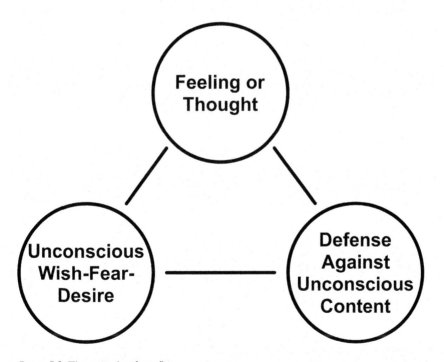

Figure 5.2 The triangle of conflict

despite the presence of the activated defense mechanism. The feeling of anxiety is typically the only element of the triangle of which the patient is conscious.

The triangle of conflict can be utilized in formulating interpretations that provide meaning to thoughts and feelings that otherwise lack meaning. For example, one patient, despite a variety of talents, experienced a fear of success and frequently became paralyzed when opportunities arose to create a positive impression at work or to progress in his career. After exploring his background and his concerns over several months, it emerged that he came from a working-class background and was the first from his family to go to college. Throughout his primary school education, he was constantly teased by his parents and siblings for being so dedicated to his studies and achieving high grades. Over time, he came to feel more and more like an outsider in his family. The teasing turned to outright ridicule, hostility, and ostracization when he announced a desire to leave their small town and go to college. He was accused of feeling superior to the other members of the family and thinking that their way of life was not good enough for him. Eventually, I interpreted, "I think the anxiety and paralysis you feel at work is related to the response you received from your family when you began to show a strong interest in academics, going away to college, and establishing a career rather than taking an hourly job. In some respects, your family was correct, you did want something more for yourself than what you saw was available around you; however, your family interpreted your desire as a rejection of them rather than as an urge to expand your life. Without realizing it, you came to believe there was a level of success you should not surpass because surpassing it would cause your family to reject you completely, leaving you feeling alone in the world. I believe you came to protect yourself from that possibility by finding ways to undermine the possibility of further career progress through paralysis." This interpretation relied on the triangle of conflict to provide the patient a way of understanding the origins of his anxiety and paralysis in terms of his family experiences and present patterns of behavior. The interpretation addressed his unconscious fear, the defense against the fear, and the anxiety associated with the potential emergence of his unconscious fear (i.e., that he would somehow confirm his family's accusations by becoming too successful). The interpretation also identified an obstacle to his individuation process. While no single interpretation transforms a complex or resolves a neurotic conflict, this interpretation provided the patient with a foothold in the face of his own fears which allowed him to begin taking on challenges at work that previously had carried too great a risk of success.

Triangle of relationship

The second triangle in Malan's model is the triangle of relationship. The three corners of the triangle of relationship refer to past relationships (primarily family of origin and significant figures of the distant past), current or recent relationships, and the analytic relationship (experienced primarily through the transference–countertransference matrix). The triangle of relationship facilitates the formulation of interpretations by creating links within the patient's network of significant relationships. These significant relationships can be thought of as existing in both

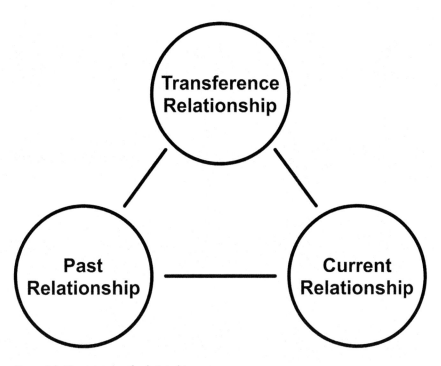

Figure 5.3 The triangle of relationship

the outer world and the inner world (i.e., relationship patterns that have become internalized as internal object relations or as complexes). Interpretive links can be established between any two corners of the triangle of relationship: between the analytic relationship and past relationships, current relationships and the analytic relationship, or between past relationships and current relationships. A full interpretation could include all three corners of the triangle of relationship. The two triangles of insight (conflict and relationship) frequently intersect, particularly with the triangle of relationship shaping interpretations formulated around the triangle of conflict, as occurs in the example in the paragraph above.

Another patient, one with an overbearing and critical father, would frequently withhold negative reactions she was experiencing toward me out of fear I would become angry and judgmental of her. This pattern became more apparent as the analysis progressed. Relying on the triangle of relationship as a template, I said to her, "I have the sense that your difficult experiences with your father have influenced the sort of interactions you anticipate with men, including me. You've come to anticipate that I will easily become angry and critical, like he was. However, you seem to protect against that possibility by never expressing your reservations about things that I say and do. In making that choice, you feel momentarily safer but, because your negative feelings

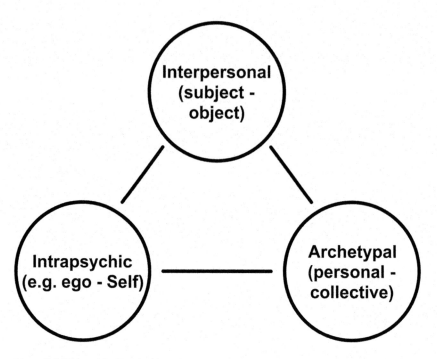

Figure 5.4 The symbolic triangle

are not expressed, you never have the opportunity to discover whether I will respond like your father as you anticipate. As a result, your short-term fear diminishes but your long-term fears of conflict, anger, and criticism remain intact in our relationship."

Symbolic triangle

In addition to Malan's (1995) two triangles of insight, I propose that the Jungian perspective encourages the addition of a third triangle of insight: the symbolic triangle. The symbolic triangle involves domains of experience commonly worked with by Jungian therapists but which may not be seen as dynamically interrelated. The three poles of the symbolic triangle are the interpersonal, intrapsychic, and archetypal. The interpersonal pole "locates" the focus of the patient's activated psychological material. That is, the patient's attention may be directed toward themselves (the subject), or their concern may be focused on the other, that is, the object (whether it be the analyst or other significant relationship from the past or present).

The intrapsychic pole identifies the intrapsychic dynamic currently active in the patient. For example, dynamic engagements often occur between ego and Self, shadow and persona, or between the parental complexes and the child complex. As Bovensiepen (2006) indicates, attachment theory, early childhood development research, and research on neural networks provide support for a contemporary model of complex theory that emphasizes the dynamic interplay of complex networks. A network model of complexes better reflects Jung's dissociative model of the psyche. Such a model moves away from models depicting complexes as rather monolithic and operating in isolation from one another. In other words, the analytic process is best served by considering the intrapsychic situation of the patient in terms of a matrix, network, or landscape of complexes rather than viewing complexes as individual centers of psychic activity operating in isolation (Bovensiepen, 2006, p. 455).

The final corner of the symbolic triangle is the archetypal pole. I conceptualize this pole as addressing the influence of archetypal-universal themes as well as representing the dynamic interaction between the collective aspects of human experience and the idiosyncratic or personal elements of the patient's psyche. As mentioned in the first chapter, Williams (1963), Zinkin (1969, 1979), and Whitmont (1987) have argued that the collective and personal dimensions of experiences are indivisible, outlining a continuum of experience. It is often an emerging symbol that serves as the vehicle for the movement of psychic energy along the personal–collective continuum. Utilizing the symbolic triangle as a conceptualization tool for interpretation, it could be asked, "Is there an archetypal aspect to this interaction?" "What is the interpersonal context in which the narrative drama (of the patient's network of complexes) is being staged?" or "What is the symbol that serves as a linking element between the personal and collective ends of the experiential continuum?" As with the other two triangles of insight, the utility of the symbolic triangle is enhanced when it is viewed as complementary to the triangles of conflict and relationship.

The therapeutic value of interpretation in general, particularly interpretations based on the three triangles of insight outlined above, involves a variety of transformative processes, for example, making the unconscious conscious, expanding consciousness, establishing narrative cohesion, discovering meaning, and facilitating moments of relational meeting. However, another function of interpretation is the creation of psychological linkages where linkages have been broken through dissociation, or where linkages have never been established. In a sense, one of the main tasks of the analytic therapist is to be a detector of patterns in the patient's varied experiences. Jung (1963) utilizes the term "bridging" to address the linking aspect of the interpretive process:

> The psychological interpretation (foreshadowed by the alchemists) points to the concept of human wholeness. This concept has primarily a therapeutic significance in that it attempts to portray the psychic state which results from bridging over a dissociation between conscious and unconscious.
>
> (para. 779)

The triangles of insight encourage the development of links between inner and outer experience, subject and object, archetypal and personal, and the known and unknown. Jung postulated a dissociative model of psychic functioning in which dissociation is the primary process underlying the development of neuroses (1950, para. 382) and psychoses (1960, para. 544). According to Jung (1973), dissociation is the process by which emotional experience is disrupted and kept separate by strong affects (para. 719). Jung's model of dissociation is conceptually similar to Kohut's (1971) concept of "vertical splitting."

Most contemporary trauma theories are conceptually rooted in the patient's use of dissociation to break up experience into component parts. In traumatic dissociative experiences, the connections between memory, somatic experience, affect, sensation, and chronology become ruptured. What was initially experienced as a whole becomes fragmented by the dissociative processes of the psyche in order to avoid its being overwhelmed by the intensity of the experience. Bion (1967b) proposes that there is another level of psychic organization even more disruptive than the effect of dissociation. Bion utilizes the term "beta elements" to refer to bits of experience that have never been integrated because of the absence of an integrating function of the psyche (referred to as the "alpha function"). Bion's description of beta elements has similarities with the impact of dissociative processes; however, beta elements do not arise from an original whole experience that has been shattered. At first glance, Bion's concept of beta elements can be difficult for Jungians to grasp because Jung's model of the psyche is based upon aspects of experience already represented in the psyche, particularly his theory of complexes. For example, a Jungian might interpret the lack of linking between elements of experience, as described by Bion, in terms of the annihilation associated with a negative mother complex. However, according to Bion's theory, beta elements accumulate at the pre-representational level of experience, meaning that these bits of proto-experience have not reached a level of consolidation sufficient for a mental representation to be formed in the psyche. Having available Jung's representational concept of dissociation (associated with complexes) and Bion's pre-representational concept of beta elements provides the analytic therapist with a wider range of theoretical tools to understand disruptions in the linking processes of their patients. Clearly, the repair or establishment of linkages between component aspects of experience is central to the transformation process for Jung and Bion. Bisagni (2013) indicates that "creating links" (p. 630) is central to repair in analysis, while Wilkinson (2005) underscores the importance of "undoing dissociation" (p. 485). The three triangles of insight assist the analyst in recognizing places where those links can be repaired or created.

Four W's of interpretation

Another organizing template I have found useful is the four W's – *what, where, when, why* – which is adapted from a model developed by Riesenberg-Malcolm (1995). She proposes three central factors for the analyst to consider during the interpretive process which can be summarized as the *what*, *where*, and *when* that form the rationale behind an interpretation. I find it beneficial to consider Riesenberg-Malcolm's model more broadly than she has presented it, and I have added an additional area of focus – namely *why*.

What refers to the focus of the interpretation, that is, *what* is being interpreted? For Riesenberg-Malcolm, the *what* is always focused on the transferential relationship, which she saw as the expression of past internal object relationships (or complexes) that are repeated (projected) within the analytic relationship along with the affective charge and behavioral patterns associated with the internal object relationship. I disagree with Riesenberg-Malcolm's position that the *what* of every interpretation needs to exclusively be focused on the patient's transference. However, it is quite useful to ask, "*What* is the focus of my interpretation?" This focus may be the patient's transference, but the focus may also be the analyst's countertransference, an internal object relationship, a complex, a defense process, the patient's resistance to analysis, an archetypal motif, a recurring dream symbol, or many other things. The utility of the *what* question is to assist the analyst in identifying more clearly the focus of the interpretation.

Where refers to the location of the patient's concern – that is, within themselves, within the analyst, or in the relationship between the analyst and patient. She notes that patients operating at an earlier developmental level, which Klein (1946) refers to as the paranoid-schizoid position in which splitting and projective defense mechanisms dominate, then the patient's concern will primarily focus on the person of the analyst. However, when the patient is functioning at a higher level, which Klein refers to as the depressive position and which Jung (1971) might refer to as possessing capacity for a symbolic attitude (para. 819), then the patient's concern will often focus on themselves because there is less pressure internally to project psychic contents onto others and introjection is better tolerated. The *where* of Riesenberg-Malcolm's model for interpretation closely parallels elements of the triangle of relationship and the interpersonal pole of the symbolic triangle.

I find Riesenberg-Malcolm's formulation of *where* extremely helpful in thinking through how an interpretation can be most effectively stated. Depending upon the subject of the interpretation, it can be worded from the patient's self-perspective, their perception of me, the patient's perception of some other significant person, or the patient's concern about what is transpiring in a relationship, including their relationship with me. For example, a patient who feels unattractive may be more concerned with their self-perception than whether I perceive them as unattractive. For an interpretation involving the patient's feeling of unattractiveness to be effective, it would be important to focus the interpretation only on the patient's self-perception and leave out other possible perspectives. Such an interpretation might focus on how the feeling of unattractiveness came into being or which factors hold that self-perception in place.

When refers to the issue of timing and the patient's readiness or receptivity to the interpretation. The timing of an interpretation is based on experience, judgment, intuition, knowledge of the patient, and connection to one's counter-transference. At times, the analyst may err on the side of conservatism and miss opportunities that may not be available again. At other times, the analyst may interpret prematurely, presenting material for which the patient is not ready, and thereby overwhelming the patient's defenses. Some interpretations will inevitably include the projection of elements of the analyst's psyche onto the patient. Finally, there are situations when an interpretation must be held for long periods of time, even for years, before the psychic conditions are appropriate for the interpretation.

Timing was a consideration with a male patient I had seen for approximately nine months. He was concerned with issues of sexual orientation and deliberating about whether to remain in his marriage. From the beginning, he spoke often about how much money he made, who supported him in the community, how he was perceived by others, invitations he had received, and who he knew in the community. I did not interpret this pattern during the initial months of the analysis; not having a sense that there was an opening where I could link my observations with something emerging in his material. Over several months, I noticed that the pattern had dropped off significantly, but I still experienced no insight that would allow me to address the shift. However, he eventually began to speak about his desire to get rid of some of the excess material possessions in his life. Then he said, "I know how to let go of that stuff, but I don't know how to let go of the internal stuff." I sensed an opening and replied, "I've noticed, for a number of months, when we began therapy, you would regularly mention things like the various people you knew, money that had been given to you, invitations you'd received, how successful you were in your business. However, that seems to have dropped off almost completely. Since then, you have seemed much more present and accessible. Perhaps that is the kind of letting go you're hoping for." He replied, "Yes, that's good to know about me. I think I'm motivated by safety but I'm tired of that. I wasn't aware I'd been doing that, but I think I do that to create a feeling of safety." His reaction signaled a shift in an underlying narcissistic process. In Jungian terms, we could also refer to this shift as the maturation of the Puer complex. In this instance, the interpretation served to consolidate psychological changes that were already in flux rather than serving to confront his narcissistic defenses as they were encountered during earlier sessions.

Similarly, a female patient who often experienced herself as the victim of those in her current life and in her past relationships was unable to tolerate or utilize interpretations that associated her feelings of victimization with her inner world. Therefore, most of my interpretations focused on her perceptions of others, how those perceptions developed, and how she felt limited in her capacity to respond differently to outer situations. However, over time, she became more receptive to interpretations focused on her interior states and how those states contributed to her feelings of victimization. This example also highlights the timing of interpretations, or the *when* of Riesenberg-Malcolm's three W's, which asks the question, "*When* is it appropriate to offer the interpretation, in terms of *when* it comes into the analyst's mind and *when* the patient may have receptivity for it?"

The issue of the timing of interpretations can be expanded to include priorities of interpretation. Prioritizing among the many possibilities available for interpretation in any session, or at any given moment in a session, is part of the process of arriving at the selected fact. It is useful to consider the relative salience and endurance of the various elements in the analytic interaction. Some aspects of the analytic encounter are more ephemeral than others, and it is beneficial to give first priority to the most ephemeral elements. As Baranger (1993) frames the issue: "What takes place in the analyst's mind between listening and interpretation could be described as the search for the point of urgency" (p. 18). In general, I work with what is happening in the room first before moving to subjects of analysis that exist psychologically outside the room. Often, the affect or emotion that is present in the room is the most ephemeral of all of the elements of the analytic encounter. Affect and emotion are frequently fleeting, for example, a glimmer of sadness in a patient's eyes, a flash of joy dancing swiftly across a face, or a dark cloud lingering in a furrowed brow. The manifestations of the transference–countertransference matrix are also quite fleeting, and patients will frequently defend against the emergence of transference feelings because of the feeling of vulnerability involved. Observable behaviors are somewhat less ephemeral, and the opportunity to interpret behavioral patterns will often be available later if an affect, emotion, or transference manifestation takes precedence in the moment. Images, once expressed, are also relatively stable elements in the analytic encounter. Concepts and intellectual ideas, because they often lack significant emotional charge, tend to be the most stable elements of the analytic session, and therefore can usually be addressed later in the session if other elements of a more ephemeral nature are present. In summary, I give the greatest priority to emotions and affects, followed by transference–countertransference phenomena, observable behaviors, images, and finally, intellectual ideas or concepts.

Why – in addition to the three W's offered by Riesenberg-Malcolm, I would also add the question *why?* Here, I am referring to the deepening of the analysis. In other words, I am asking *why* this interpretation is necessary in terms of the issues the patient brings to analysis, or *why* does this interpretation move the analysis forward? The *why* provides an explanatory aspect of an interpretation that ties together the other elements of the interpretation.

Post-interpretation

A delicate piece of the analytic work is developing the analyst's sensitivity for what is done with an interpretation. Following interpretation, there is a return to listening, observing, and experiencing. The analyst listens for, reflects on, and evaluates how the patient is responding, verbally and non-verbally, to the interpretive statement. Patient responses to interpretations will generally reflect some degree of transformative shift, a defense against the interpretation, or a neutral response. Naturally, the analyst must accept that there are times when the interpretation is off-base and must re-evaluate the underlying hypothesis of the interpretation. As Jung (1961) indicated, "If an interpretation is wrong, it cannot be forced on the patient; if it is right, the result is immediately visible and expresses itself very clearly in the patient's whole behaviour" (para. 40). Although there is a degree of clinical value in Jung's assessment, his position does not adequately take into account the patient's defenses and the frequent desire of the patient to hide negative responses from the analyst. Many patients will successfully hide or withhold negative reactions to interpretations in analysis, sometimes over several sessions, weeks, or months.

Often, the analyst's awareness of the developmental state constellated in the moment is typically the most significant influence in the decision about which analytic activity to engage in following an interpretation. There may be subtle, sometimes sudden, shifts or disconnections between the verbalizations and the patient's non-verbal developmental state. These shifts often occur following an interpretation. Attention to the space following the interpretation is where information is likely to emerge about the need to shift to a different kind of analytic activity, such as containment, playfulness, silence, or mirroring. This phase is also where the analyst's use of reverie would be essential in discerning whether to move forward along the same interpretive line, consolidate the work just done, or abandon that interpretive line completely in the face of heavy resistance and wait to see what emerges next.

In general, an effective interpretation results in some shift or opening up on the part of the patient. For example, the patient may reveal or remember something that is connected to the interpretation. Sometimes it will be reflected in an association, for example, "that makes me think of. . . ," or the patient will pause to reflect privately on the interpretation. In some instances, the patient's breathing, physical activity, or posture will shift. There may be a noticeable shift in affect, usually emotionally congruent with the focus of the interpretation, such as tears or anger. At times, there is verbal affirmation of the interpretation that has an affective congruity to it, or a sense of emotional release, relief, or "ah-ha" will enter the room. All of these are indications that the interpretation has impacted the patient.

When an interpretation is defended against, the patient will often actively disagree in a way that precludes further examination; however, it should be noted that an overtly negative reaction to an interpretation does not necessarily mean the interpretation was not effective. At times, a negative response may simply mean that the interpretation has activated the patient's network of complexes. Other indicators that an interpretation is being defended against might be a sudden shift of subject (avoidance) by the patient, a continuation by the patient with what they were saying before the interpretation (incorporation), or verbal agreement with the interpretation but with no felt sense of affective response to the interpretation.

When the patient's response to an interpretation is neutral, it is incumbent on the analyst to question the focus, hypothesis, or phrasing of the interpretation. In terms of negative or neutral responses, it is important for the analyst to resist the urge to justify the interpretation, shift to a more intellectual explanation of the interpretation, or become defensive when an interpretation is challenged or ignored by the patient.

Summary

Participatory observation, identification of a selected fact, generation of a hypothesis, organization and structuring of the available sources of information, incorporation of theory, crafting an interpretation, and evaluation of the patient response to interpretation form the basic building blocks of the interpretive process. Over time, the interpretive process outlined in the chapter can be integrated with the interpretive cycle of confrontational observation, inferential clarification, interpretation, and construction outlined in Chapter 3. The three triangles of insight and the four W's assist the analyst in organizing and developing focal points for interpretations, as well as deciding how to frame specific interpretations. These templates are the ones that I have adapted and found useful in the interpretive process. Naturally, the analytic literature contains other useful interpretive guidelines while others await creation.

Exercises for the reader

1) Begin moving into the interpretive process by simply making a mental note during sessions when you notice opportunities for interpretations.
2) Begin to ask yourself if you have gathered sufficient information to formulate a confrontational observation, inferential clarification, or interpretation.
3) Following sessions, take a few minutes to identify elements of the patient's experience between which you have attempted to create linkages. Articulate the pattern that has been detected or identified.
4) Following sessions, begin to identify places during the session where opportunities to interpret were overlooked.
5) Begin slowly. Simply attempt to craft and offer one interpretation per session.

Notes

1 Also previously referred to in terms of the capacity for mentalization, that is, the capacity to reflect upon one's experiences and the experiences of the other, both as the experiences are occurring and thereafter.
2 Bion (1962) refers to this state of mind in the analyst as "reverie." This concept is addressed more fully in Chapter 8 of this volume and is also closely examined in Winborn (2014, pp. 70–96).
3 Object relations theory, which has significant similarities with complex theory, could also have been called upon to conceptualize the information of the session. See Solomon (1991) for a fuller examination of the relationship between object relations theory and complex theory.
4 Malan (1995) used the "triangle of person" instead of the "triangle of relationship."
5 From a traditional psychoanalytic perspective, anxiety is a warning signal that a potential danger (real or imagined) is present, often leading to the person feeling overwhelmed and helpless. The danger may be perceived as arising from internal or external sources and is often associated with powerful unconscious fantasies.

Chapter 6

Categories of interpretation

Having outlined the analytic attitude, the interpretive cycle, and a general approach to interpretation, we will shift to differentiating among several specific categories of interpretations. While many elements of the interpretive process remain the same regardless of the focus of the interpretation, it is useful to consider different areas of focus for interpretations. When initially developing interpretive skills, it can be difficult to determine the focus of the interpretation. Having categories of interpretation to hold in mind is conducive to the learning process, much like the utility of learning underlying chord structures and scales when first learning to play music. In this chapter, the most frequently encountered areas of focus in the analytic setting are identified and discussed.

Frequently encountered areas of interpretive focus include: dreams, fantasies, behaviors, transference, countertransference, intrapsychic processes, interpersonal situations, situational–environmental events, defenses, resistance, and archetypal situations. Also included are trial interpretations offered at the beginning of an analysis. Confrontation, as a special category of interpretation, is addressed in Chapter 9. Because there are a large number of excellent texts on dream interpretation in the Jungian and psychoanalytic literature, dream interpretation will be addressed only briefly.

Trial interpretations

Trial interpretations are part of the analytic therapist's assessment process. They are utilized during initial sessions to assess the intensity of the patient's defenses and the patient's capacity to engage in psychological work. Rather than assessing "suitability" for analytic work, I am more interested in assessing the patient's current "capacity" for analytic work. This gives me some idea of where to begin with a particular patient rather than evaluating whether they are suitable candidates for analytic work. My experience is that most people can develop some capacity for affect regulation, reflection, and symbolic thought, but that these capacities are often lacking, or only minimally developed, at the beginning of an analytic process.

Trial interpretations deal with the most obvious elements of the patient's psychological dynamics that are evident in the patient's verbalizations and observable behaviors. In general, the goal of a trial interpretation is not the communication of significant unconscious material to the patient. Attempting to do so will likely constellate anxiety, create resistance to engaging in the analysis, and undermine the development of the therapeutic alliance. In addition to the needs of the initial assessment, when the therapist makes minimal trial interpretations, the patient experiences a sample of therapeutic work done from an analytic perspective. The trial interpretation also provides the patient with an experience of the therapist's capacity for understanding.

Because the goal is assessment rather than the communication of the unconscious situation of the patient, trial interpretations generally fall into the category of confrontational observation or inferential clarification as described in Chapter 3. For example, I might notice that a new patient seems uncertain or hesitant when entering my office for the first session. Noting some degree of discomfort, anxiety, or uncertainty in the patient, I might combine an observation with an inference, "You seemed somewhat hesitant when you came in, as though you have some anxiety about what might happen here." The goal of this inferential clarification is to observe the patient's reaction to the intervention, as well as communicating something about the nature of the analytic process, that is, that it will include a focus on the patient's feelings about the process and the therapeutic relationship. Another example is the patient who, over several sessions, consistently refers to the figures in their life generically rather than by name, such as "my mother," "my father," "my wife," or "my daughter." While there are many reasons someone might communicate in such a way, I would be curious about the pattern and would consider reflecting the pattern back to them, "I've noticed that you don't refer to the people in your life by name. Do you have any thoughts about that?" This intervention combines an observation with an invitation to the patient to share their associations. This allows an evaluation of the patient's reaction to the observation as well as an assessment of their current capacity to participate actively in the process.

Transference interpretations

The interpretation of the transference receives significantly more attention in the psychoanalytic literature than in the Jungian literature. Jung's most extensive statement regarding transference is found in *The Psychology of the Transference* (1946). However, Jung's focus is predominantly on the archetypal foundations of the transference relationship rather than personal aspects of the transference. Therefore, Jung offers little guidance about how to engage with the patient's transference to the analyst. Despite his archetypal focus, elsewhere Jung (1953a) does acknowledge the importance of interpreting the personal aspects of the transference:

The doctor has himself become the object of the unconscious libido. If the patient altogether refuses to recognize the fact of the transference, or if the doctor fails to understand it or interprets it falsely, vigorous resistances supervene, directed towards making the relation with the doctor completely impossible.

(para. 94)

Vivona (2003) also highlights the significance of transference interpretation in the analytic process:

This ability to capture and convey the emotional drama in words, to speak as both participant and observer, is essential for providing a context within which the patient may experience emotional insight. By linking the transference action, experienced interpersonally, with the conscious, verbally symbolized realm, interpretation potentiates transformation.

(p. 54)

For the purposes of this section, I refer to the transference as a multiplicity of experiences involving the patient's relationship with the therapist. From this perspective, transference refers to the whole of the patient's experience of the analyst, including: repeated patterns based on the patient's experiences in the past; needed experiences based on deficits in personality structure; needed experiences based on the requirements of the patient's individuation process; non-distorted perceptions/experiences of the analyst in the present; and archetypal influences on the transference.

In terms of transference interpretation, it is important not to try to dissolve or take away the distorted aspects of the transference too quickly. Often, the transference must be acknowledged and accepted by the analyst for long periods before beginning to identify the distortions/displacements in the transference, just as Jung indicates that the analyst must often carry projected elements of the Self of the patient for extended periods. As Mitrani (2001) puts it, the analyst must "take the transference" (p. 1085) of the patient in order to become a "containing object" for the patient. To do otherwise implicitly communicates that the analyst is not a safe container for the patient's shadow and unintegrated psychological material. Ponsi (1997) indicates that "Interpreting the transference is essentially that of making the interaction explicit" (p. 249). Davies (1994) uses the dual metaphor of magnet and architect to describe the subtleties of interpretation in the transference–countertransference matrix:

The analyst herself becomes both the magnet that draws out the reenactment of unconsciously internalized systems of self and object and the architect of the transitional arena where such self and object experiences become free to play and reconfigure themselves in more harmonious ways. Magnet and architect, as they volley between foreground of active interpretive work and background of containment and holding, bring into focus the necessity of discovering an optimal tension between interpreting the past and co-creating the new.

(p. 157)

Transference interpretation frequently begins with observations like "It seems as though you see me as _____," or "It strikes me that what you're saying about _____ might also reflect some of your feelings about me." The analyst's initial efforts involve acknowledging the observed pattern without making attributions about additional meaning as yet. The underlying or implicit meaning of such acknowledgment is, "This is a safe place to talk about your feelings about me directly without fears of reprisal, shame, or exploitation."

Over time, interpretive links between past or current relationships and the therapist can be initiated. Consider the transferential implications of a session in which a patient became angry as she related a difficult encounter with her husband but felt I was not adequately supportive of her perspective. In her history, the patient often felt unsupported by her parents during conflicts with her siblings. The patient angrily asked, "So you believe he was justified in talking to me that way?" In response, I interpreted: "You feel angry with me today because you want me to side with you against your husband, and it doesn't feel like I'm doing that in the way you wish I would. When you feel I'm not overtly taking your side, it also feels as though I've abandoned you." In order to bring a fuller interpretive perspective, I might have added, ". . . in the same way you felt abandoned by your parents during fights with your brothers and sisters."

Over time, through the interpretation of the transference, the analyst assists the patient in seeing how their inner landscape influences their perceptions and experience of their outer world, particularly the therapeutic relationship. Gradually, this creates new experiences and allows the patient's perceptual and experiential patterns to transform.

Transference derivatives

Often, the patient's transference response is not revealed or discussed directly but is instead communicated as a transference derivative or encoded message (Langs, 1992). A transference derivative or encoded message is a communication by the patient in which the surface or manifest content appears to be about something other than the analytic relationship but which, nonetheless, contains an unconsciously encoded (latent) message about the analytic relationship. The more difficult it is for the analyst to discern how the surface content of a communication is related to the patient's stated purpose for being in therapy, then the likelihood increases that it contains an unconscious communication related to the analytic relationship.

The following session excerpt is an example of a transference derivative. On the surface, in the interactions leading up to this intervention, I could not discern how the patient's focus on types of food was related to her reasons for being in analytic therapy. However, as I listened beneath the surface to what she might be communicating about her experience of me, an idea began to form that she was communicating an encoded message:

P: I don't ever remember being hungry. I don't ever remember eating in between meals. And I didn't eat much when I was little because I didn't like anything. I only liked mustard and catsup sandwiches.

T: Food with little sustenance to it.

P: I didn't like peanut butter and cheese sandwiches, I shoved them back in my desk.

T: I think sometimes the things I say to you feel like they have little sustenance for you.

P: *(laughs)* You're funny sometimes.

T: *(chuckle)* How so?

P: You're just saying things to see how I'll react to them.

T: I think I'm reflecting things that are implied in your words but which you don't feel comfortable saying directly to me.

Engaging patient transference derivatives can be difficult for the analytic therapist, especially for those relatively new to the interpretive process, because the interpretation of derivative communications frequently sounds and feels arrogant, or overly self-referential, to the therapist's ears when said aloud.

Countertransference interpretations

My working definition of countertransference parallels my broad definition of transference. Countertransference is the therapist's experience of the patient, including: the therapist's unresolved conflicts projected onto the patient; reactions to the patient based on the patient's projective identification processes; non-distorted perceptions/experiences of the patient in the present; and archetypal influences on the development of the countertransference.

The main issue in making countertransference interpretations is whether to speak directly from the analyst's countertransference (i.e., self-revelation). Speaking directly about the analyst's countertransference might sound like, "I find myself feeling sad about what you've just said." Speaking from, rather than about, the analyst's countertransference involves using the analyst's countertransference to inform what is said in an interpretation but without revealing directly the material that contributed to the interpretation. Both Ogden (1997) and Cwik (2011) generally encourage speaking from rather than about the analyst's countertransference.

For example, an analyst experiencing anger as a result of countertransference dynamics might bring it into the analytic dialogue in an exploratory manner, "I wonder if there's something you anticipate feeling angry about today?," or "I wonder if there's something about anger that feels difficult to discuss?" Both of these potential inquiries originate from the concept of projective identification. In projective identification, the patient unconsciously defends against unconsciously threatening material by projecting it onto the analyst and then subtly (and unconsciously) interacting with the analyst to evoke a response consistent with the projected element.

A second example of speaking from rather than about countertransference is taken from an analysis with Indra. With Indra, I experienced ongoing emotional whiplash in the transference–countertransference matrix. Each time I would begin to feel a sense of empathic understanding of Indra's psychic state, each time she would seem to be relating to me in a relatively consistent manner (whether positively or negatively), and each time she would seem to have established a consistent feeling tone about a significant other in her life, such as her husband or children, Indra would suddenly shift in her feelings toward herself, me, or her significant others. Her feeling about the situation or person involved would shift to the opposite extreme. Initially, this shift would take me by surprise, and I would feel confused about my own perceptions. Over time, I recognized this as a reflection of Indra's splitting defenses and her part-object way of relating to the world in a manner that was consistent with Melanie Klein's concept of the paranoid-schizoid position. In my sense of confusion, I recurrently experienced an image of quicksand, which I was eventually able to utilize in formulating an experiential interpretation of Indra's state shifts: "I sense it is confusing for you – not knowing what you want of yourself or of me. You seem to feel as if knowing is ever-shifting. The moment you feel you know something, it shifts, and you feel as if you know something else – like a quicksand of experience with no firm footing and no clear edge between your experience of yourself and of me." In formulating the interpretation in this way, I utilized my internal experience as a means of articulating something of the patient's interior experience that was being communicated to me through my countertransference. The analyst's use of reverie as a means of processing countertransference material is explored in greater depth in Chapter 8.

Interpersonal interpretations

As depicted in the triangle of relationship from Chapter 5, interpersonal interpretations focus on the patient's perceptions of, experiences in, and responses to relationships, current or past, rather than focusing exclusively on the transferential therapeutic relationship. Often, these interpretations link a pattern of experience in a current relationship with a pattern from a past relationship (sometimes referred to as a genetic relationship). In the psychoanalytic literature, these are also referred to as extra-transferential interpretations, while Jung refers to them as interpretations made on the objective level. While the interpretation is typically framed in terms of outer relationships, the analyst holds in mind that the interpersonal interpretation also reflects their understanding of a patient's network of complexes or internal object relationships. The following is an example of an interpersonal interpretation that creates a link between a past relationship and a current relationship: "I think you're feeling angry with your wife because you feel controlled by her just as you felt controlled by your mother." Another situation might link more directly an outer relationship with an interior response to the situation, for example, "I think you often feel in competition with other artists. When you feel that the work of other artists may be better than yours, you seem to feel that overt comparisons will be made and your work will always be found lacking. To avoid the risk of feeling inadequate, you find ways to divert attention from your work, but in doing so you lose the opportunity to experience having your art viewed in positive terms."

Defense interpretations

Traditionally, the concept of defense describes the ego's active struggle to protect against perceived dangers and limit anxiety, for example, the loss of a love object, rejection, disapproval, judgment, conflict, responsibility, or the experience of ambivalence (Freud, 1967). The fundamental split between conscious and unconscious realms of activity is maintained by defenses. However, defenses are unavoidable and necessary to healthy functioning in life and relationships.

The analyst's ongoing reflection on an individual's defense mechanisms focuses on the question: "By what means has this person survived?" An awareness of the individual's defenses in therapy sensitizes the analytic therapist to the way those survival strategies come into the therapy session and therapeutic relationship. When over-utilized or rigidly held, defenses limit choice, distort reality, and create patterns of perceptual, behavioral, affective, and cognitive rigidity. Much of the structure and technique of analytic therapy exists in order to address the presence of defenses. Working through defenses in analysis facilitates psychic flexibility and resilience, both necessary conditions for individuation to occur.

From a Jungian perspective, defenses are also utilized by complexes to maintain autonomy within the psyche. Defenses function unconsciously to avoid, cast away, or deny aspects of one's own experience in order to minimize internal discord. Therefore, defenses are directly related to the creation of the shadow complex. Fordham (1974b) added an additional category of defenses operating on a more primitive level that serve to protect the Self from being destroyed, overwhelmed, or fragmented in the face of further trauma. As opposed to ego defenses, these are referred to as "defenses of the Self," later elaborated further by Kalsched (1996, 2013) as "archetypal defenses of the personal spirit."

The interpretation of defense processes can often be conceptualized using the triangle of insight from Chapter 5. It is not uncommon for patients in analytic therapy to engage in self-censoring of their thoughts. For some patients, this is associated with a feeling of vulnerability that comes from the analyst offering interpretations related to their unconscious activity. An interpretation addressing that sense of vulnerability identifies the behavior as well as the feeling that motivates the behavior, for example, "I have noticed that after I make a comment, you frequently stop speaking from your thoughts and feelings and focus exclusively on the comment I have made. You may be doing this to avoid what you feel when I appear to know something about you that catches you off guard."

Dissociation is a defense that relies on the separation of overwhelming experiences into smaller elements to prevent being overwhelmed by the intensity of an experience. In operation, dissociation functions similarly to Kohut's concept of vertical splitting. Dissociation and vertical splitting stand in contrast to the horizontal split of the repression barrier between conscious and unconscious experience. A preliminary interpretive approach for a patient manifesting a dissociation between affect and intellect might begin, "As we talk about the abuse, you seem to have an intellectual knowledge of what happened but the emotional experience of it isn't available to you right now. I think it must feel dangerous to have the intellectual knowledge of what happened connected with the emotion of it – as though knowing about both at the same time would be overwhelming."

Resistance interpretations

Resistance refers to the ego's attempt to defend against anxieties stirred by the analysis. More specifically, resistance refers to the way the patient's defenses become activated to interfere with the analytic process, slowing or defeating the process of change in the analytic session despite conscious desire for change. Resistance includes all behavior, both conscious and unconscious, that stands in opposition to the therapeutic process: for example, silence, forgetting, lateness, failure to pay the bill, excessive verbalization; excessive production of dreams; or avoidance of certain subjects. Resistance to the development of a transference to the analyst is one of the most common forms of resistance. All of these responses stand in opposition to the patient's conscious desire to improve.

The following is a simple interpretive confrontation of a patient's resistance to the development of the transference, "I've noticed that you are silent every time I make reference to our relationship. You seem to feel that if you speak openly about your feelings about me that you will somehow be swallowed up by them and lose control of yourself." Another example involves a resistance interpretation that was offered to a patient who had difficulty receiving anything from the analyst: "Somewhere in your greatest need, someone goes away. If you take something from me, it feels like I'll go away too, so you wonder what the point is in receiving anything from me." This interpretation of resistance was linked to the patient's fears of abandonment. The patient resisted the introjection of any positive experiences of me because the assimilation of anything positive from a significant figure had become associated with the experience of abandonment.

Intrapsychic interpretations

Intrapsychic interpretations focus primarily on articulating the intrapsychic structures, processes, or conflicts of the patient. From a Jungian perspective, the structures would likely involve complexes, such as shadow, ego, or persona, or the Self. An object relations perspective would involve the interactions between internal object relations and the outer objects of the patient's life. A self psychologist would primarily conceptualize in terms of the interaction between selfobjects and the self-structure. The symbolic triangle figure from Chapter 5 provides a useful template for developing intrapsychic as well as archetypal interpretations.

As an example, a conflict-oriented interpretation might articulate an internal conflict between autonomy and a sense of security established through dependency, for example, "It seems there's a struggle within you between your desire for autonomy and your desire for security." Later interpretations would attempt to articulate the motivations associated with moving away from or towards each side of the conflict, while a Jungian interpretive perspective would emphasize holding the tension of opposites reflected in the conflict so that the transcendent function of the patient is activated. The following intrapsychic interpretation is focused on the father complex: "It seems like you begin to shrink back when you encounter men in authority that remind you of your father." This brief interpretation brings together the organizing core of the complex (father), the triggering stimulus for the complex (men in authority), and the behavioral response to the triggering stimulus (shrinking back).

Archetypal interpretations

Archetypal amplification is most often associated with dream interpretation; however, the incorporation of archetypal themes or motifs (i.e., mythologems) is also useful when making interpretations unrelated to dreams. Incorporating an archetypal motif into an interpretation is a way of saying to the patient, "This story is another lens for understanding yourself, your life, your thought patterns, your behaviors, or your feelings." Often, the archetypal interpretation utilizes only a small fragment of a larger archetypal narrative, that is, a mythologem.

Archetypal interpretations often link a pattern of behavior to a deeper understanding of the "purposiveness" of the behavior. For example, patients caught in an unrelenting pattern of repetition are often able to identify with the myth of Sisyphus who toils each day pushing his stone up the hill only to have it roll back down again each evening. However, many patients are unaware that the eternal task of Sisyphus was punishment for the hubris Sisyphus displayed in regard to Zeus. It is an understanding of the internal dynamic of the story that enables the patient to confront the interior cycle of punishment which results in the numbing pattern of repetition in their life. A fuller discussion of archetypal patterns in interpretation is provided in Chapter 7.

Situational–environmental interpretations

The main function of situational–environmental interpretations is to create links between events reported from the patient's life with the analyst's understanding of the primary internal conflicts and structures. Again, this is connected to the circumambulation or working-through process by which neuroses, complexes, and internal object relations are transformed through the engagement of the analytic process. An important factor in the working-through process is developing the patient's awareness of the way in which their interior landscape shapes their interactions with the world around them. A situational interpretation could involve a current event (e.g., the outcome of an election), with an affect (e.g., anger or hopelessness), and a past or current relationship: "You seem quite angry about the outcome of the elections and also seem to have a sense of hopelessness. I suspect that sense of hopelessness reminds you of those interactions with your father when it felt like you could never be heard by him."

Interpretation of fantasies and dreams

As I mentioned in the introduction to this chapter, dreams will be discussed in only the briefest terms. The tools of dream work are most pertinent when engaging patient fantasies. I inquire about and listen to fantasies from a perspective similar to the perspective used with dreams, that is, listening for the main characters, actions, shifts in action, and important emotional nodes of the fantasy. I also gather the patient's associations to salient elements of the fantasies, just as I would with dreams. While fantasies are often more circumscribed than dreams, but they frequently reveal the imagistic, non-directed thinking qualities of dreams. Additionally, as with dreams, I listen for the contrast between the patient's fantasy life and their waking, ego-oriented life.

Ultimately, both dreams and fantasies provide symbolic material that becomes part of the ongoing analytic dialogue. As an example, a patient with a powerful negative father complex reported a dream in which she was leaving a church. On the wall, there was a list of things she was supposed to do. Each time she would think she had done everything on the list and attempted to leave, an older man in a gray suit and glasses would stop her and say, "You're not clean. You haven't done it right. You've sinned. Go back and look at the list again." This pattern happened over and over again in the dream. While gathering the patient's associations to the dream, she indicated that the gray suit reminded her of the suits her father wore. The dream provided a powerful and evocative image that served as a symbol for her father complex. When her father complex was the focus of our interactions, I often made reference to "the man in the gray suit," such as, "It feels to you that I'm speaking to you like the man in the gray suit," or "It feels as though the man in the gray suit has come into the room and you feel compelled to follow the rules."

Interpretation of behaviors

The patient's behavioral patterns are often a useful focus for interpretive interventions. Often, the patient will recognize they are engaging in a particular pattern of behavior if it is called to their attention. Behaviors either can be public (i.e., observable by anyone in the visual field), or private (i.e., actions carried out privately in the patient's psyche and therefore not observable visually). Private actions can include thoughts, feelings, or actions carried out in fantasy, such as aggressive acts, acts of destruction, sexual acts, and so on. The analyst relies on the patient to report private acts as part of their associative dialogue during the session or makes inquiries about the patient's interiorized behaviors.

One patient routinely left her purse sitting in her lap during our initial sessions. After some degree of a therapeutic alliance had been established, I inquired, "Have you noticed how you always seem to hold your purse in your lap in front of you during our sessions?" She said, "No," and continued holding her purse in her lap. Several sessions later, after reflecting upon the function of her behavior, I interpreted: "You seem to feel it is necessary to find a way to protect yourself. I think you do that by keeping your purse between us as a sort of protective buffer, ensuring that it won't feel as though I'm getting too close. Perhaps you also hope that it may hide some of what you feel and what you want."

In another case scenario, Janet regularly fell into behavioral patterns of extreme responsibility. At one point, she called several days before a session and left a message saying she couldn't come to her session that week because she would be out of town, but also indicated that she would be there the following week. Janet had already mentioned, during the previous session, the possibility of being away at the time of her next appointment. Because the date of our next session seemed settled, I did not respond to her call. The night before the next scheduled appointment, she left an anxious-sounding message wondering if I had gotten her message and requesting that I call her with the next available opening in my schedule. I returned Janet's call, informing her that she was already on my schedule and that she could come in at that time. When Janet arrived, she said she had not remembered telling me she would be there the next session. Remembering her exaggerated patterns of responsibility originating from her lack of secure figures during her developmental years, I interpreted: "You became anxious about whether I would be responsible enough to hold your place open for you in my schedule, and you felt you had to step in and become responsible for reminding me in order to deal with your anxiety that I might fail you." She flashed an embarrassed smile which flowed into an obvious sense of relief. She realized I would be responsible for holding her place in my schedule and that she did not have to assume responsibility for that beyond normal patterns of communication.

Exercise for the reader

Using detailed process notes or a verbatim transcription from one of your sessions, someone else's session, or a published session transcription, identify and label the various categories of interpretation utilized during the session. Also, identify where opportunities arose for particular types of interpretations but were not acted upon.

Chapter 7

Jungian perspectives on interpretation

In this chapter, the focus shifts to interpretation from a Jungian perspective; examining how unique aspects of the Jungian orientation shape the content and focus of the interpretive process. In many respects, the technique of interpretation is trans-theoretical, that is, the theoretical orientation of the analytic therapist utilizing interpretation will shape the content and focus of the interpretation but the underlying interpretive method remains largely the same. Therefore, the material presented in the previous chapters is applicable to interpretation for all schools of analytic therapy. Regardless of their theoretical orientation, the analytic therapist will employ information-gathering questions, confrontational observations, inferential clarifications, partial interpretations, full interpretations, and constructions. As a result, a Jungian approach to interpretation will proceed in much the same manner as other schools of psychoanalysis, but the content and points of emphasis will be shaped by Jung's theories of complex, archetype, symbol, image, and metaphor.

Consciousness and insight

Traditionally, the goal of psychoanalysis has been the resolution of psychic conflicts through the use of interpretation; promoting affectively engaged insight, which in turn leads to lasting psychic structural change. According to Moore and Fine (1990), insight is the:

> capacity to apprehend the nature of a situation or one's own problems. . . understanding of the dynamic factors contributing to the conflict resolution. . . a product of the synthesizing aspects of the ego functions, that is, the location of insight is the ego. . . a gradual acquisition of self-knowledge results in psychic reorganization. . . insight has two significant components, affect as well as cognition, for cognitive awareness alone does not lead to therapeutic change.
>
> (p. 99)

The Jungian perspective creates a broader goal. For Jung, the transformational goal of analysis and of life is not limited to the development of insight and change on the ego level of functioning. Jung (1965) saw the creation of consciousness, which includes insight but is a more encompassing concept, as the goal of analysis: "Man's task is . . . to become conscious of the contents that press upward from the unconscious. . . . As far as we can discern the sole purpose of human existence is to kindle a light in the darkness of mere being" (p. 326). Summarizing Jung's position, Edinger (1984) states, "The purpose of human life is the creation of consciousness" (p. 57). Therefore, consciousness also includes elements of experience (such as facets of one's life purpose, meaning, and transcendence) that move beyond individual awareness.

Jung (1971) defines consciousness as, "the function of activity which maintains the relationship of psychic contents to the ego" (para. 700). Consciousness, in turn, is highly associated with the capacity for discrimination, reflection, and the differentiation of opposites: "The whole essence of consciousness is discrimination, distinguishing ego from non-ego, subject from object, positive from negative. . . The separation into pairs of opposites is entirely due to conscious differentiation . . . where no consciousness exists. . . there is not reflection" (para. 179). The development and deepening of consciousness is, therefore, the ultimate purpose of interpretation utilized in Jungian analysis.

Interpretation in Jungian analysis is utilized to facilitate openings in consciousness that permit the entry of unconscious contents. Doing this effectively requires the analyst's ongoing awareness of the patient's defenses, resistances, and network of complexes. From a Jungian perspective, interpretation serves to increase the tension of opposites between consciousness and the unconscious so that the transcendent function is activated. The activation of the transcendent function, in turn, generates symbols which ultimately foster the individuation process. As emphasized earlier, the transcendent function cannot perform its role without a degree of consciousness. Interpretation also facilitates the patient's assimilation and symbolic understanding of unconscious contents. Therefore, consciousness is both a goal of and a vehicle for the transformational aspects of analysis; interpretation serves the goal of consciousness.

Theory of complexes

A brief summary of Jungian complex theory will serve to highlight the aspects of complex theory that are particularly salient to the interpretive process. The psyche can be conceived of as a network of complexes possessing both adaptive, progressive aspects of the psyche as well as maladaptive, regressive aspects. In short, the network of complexes consists "of inner working models, affects and expectation patterns that are primarily saved in the implicit memory and are partially conscious but mostly unconscious" (Bovensiepen, 2006, p. 458). An adequately developed ego and the self-structure forms the core sub-network responsible for the cohesion and regulation of the psychological system (Dieckmann, 1999).

Jung refers to complexes in a number of different ways: as splinter psyches, miniature self-contained psyches, fragmentary personalities, dissociated personalities, and unconscious fantasy systems. He (1953a) highlights the autonomous nature of the complexes, which are often experienced as personified elements of the psyche, "Every autonomous or even relatively autonomous complex has the peculiarity of appearing as a personality, i.e., of being personified" (para. 312). Jung (1967) also points out that the complex will be experienced subjectively as something alien or other, "it also involves an experience of a special kind namely the recognition of an alien 'other' in oneself, or the objective presence of another will" (para. 481).

He conceptualizes complexes as having an archetypal core with a personal overlay or shell (see Figure 7.1). Jung also posits that archetypes tend to constellate around poles of experience, either positively or negatively, that is, the bipolarity of the archetype (Jung, 1959b). As a result of the bipolar archetypal core at the center, each complex will have a tendency to become valanced either positively or negatively. The personal shell of the complex is a patterned amalgam of experience impressions and response patterns made up of: images, memories,[1] feelings and affects, physiological states, thought patterns or cognitive sets, attitudes, defense mechanisms,[2] behavioral patterns, activating events, and patterns of object relatedness and attachment style. Bovensiepen (2006) understands the shell of the complex as, "a fall-out of later developmental, emotional and interpersonal experiences with significant others" (p. 452). Differentiating the elements of a complex is useful in terms of identifying which aspect of the complex to engage interpretively in an effort to create links between various aspects of experience.

Plaut (1974), Redfearn (1985), and Solomon (1991) highlight some of the parallels between Analytical Psychology (particularly complex theory) and object relations theory.[3] Complex theory and object relations theory both describe internal representational structures of the psyche which shape perception, response, and action. As Redfearn (1985) points out, while complexes often reflect an internalization of early object relations, a main conceptual difference between complex theory and object relations theory is that complexes are also frequently organized around *themes*, *things*, or *situations*, such as inferiority, money, sexuality, power, victimization, intimacy, success, failure, or avoidance. Redfearn (1985, p. xxii) collectively refers to complexes, internalized objects and part-objects, and elements of body image as "sub-personalities" that contribute to the making of our "many selves."

It is not uncommon for complexes to be discussed as though they operate in isolation. However, as mentioned in Chapter 5, a focus on the dynamic interplay within a complex network better reflects Jung's dissociative model of the psyche. In other words, the analytic process is best served by considering the intrapsychic situation of the patient in terms of a matrix, network, or a landscape of complexes rather than viewing complexes as individual centers of psychic activity operating in isolation. As Bovensiepen (2006) puts it, "I suggested that we should concentrate more on the relationship entanglement among the various complexes in the unconscious and not so much on how the pathogenic complexes influence the ego" (p. 451). For example, a child complex is typically co-activated with the mother and father complexes. Likewise, the mother and father complexes are linked within the psyche even if one side of the parental syzygy is activated more intensely at a particular moment. The identity structures of shadow, ego, and persona engage in an ongoing ballet of self-disavowal, identity maintenance, and

Personalistic Overlay
1. Patterns of Object Relatedness
2. Memories
3. Images
4. Feelings - Affects
5. Behavior Patterns
6. Defenses
7. Thought Patterns
8. Values - Attitudes
9. Physiological States

Personalistic Overlay

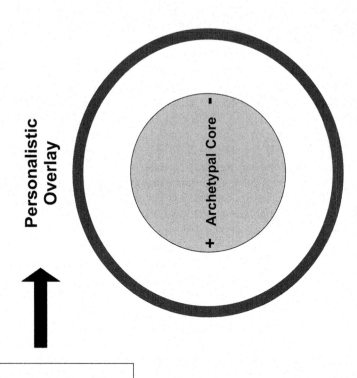

+ Archetypal Core -

Figure 7.1 Configuration of the complex

cultivation of outer impressions. The soul figures of anima and animus shuttle to and fro in their mediating role between ego and the unconscious. The interaction of Self, environment, culture, and the individual's network of complexes results in the narrative structure or personal myth being lived out, as well as in shaping the individual's path of individuation (Shalit, 2002).

In addition, the intrapsychic network of complexes and self-structure is also in ongoing interaction with the figures and environment of the outer world. As Fosshage (1994) puts it:

> The predominant ways in which we have come to see ourselves and ourselves in relation to others are the affect-laden thematic organisations that variably shape our experience. These affect-laden organising principles or schemas (I use the terms as equivalent) do not distort a supposed "objective reality", but are always contributing to the construction of a subjectively-experienced "reality".
>
> (p. 267)

Speaking with complexes

An essential element of interpretation, from a Jungian perspective, is the analyst's ability to hold in mind the aspect of the patient's psyche that is being engaged with. Bolognini (2002) frames his approach to interpretation as, "My intentional 'turning into' the feared object and giving it voice" (p. 758). I refer to this as *speaking with complexes*. In other words, an important aspect of effective interpretation is the capacity to frame interpretations so that the analyst is engaging or *speaking with* a particular complex, while also recognizing that the complex functions in relationship with other complexes. As an example, my interpretive activity might focus on the engagement of a patient's father complex; perhaps a father complex that is organized around overtaking or dominating the ego. Initially, I might be *speaking with* the father complex directly. At another point, my interpretation might be directed towards the ego complex of the patient, articulating the anxiety experienced by the ego threatened with being overtaken by another center of energy within the psyche – that is, *speaking with* the ego about the ego's perception of the father complex. Later, my interpretive focus might shift to assisting the ego in understanding the motivations associated with the activated father complex, that is, *speaking with* the ego about the function of father complex.

A brief illustration of *speaking with complexes* can be seen in an interaction with Bart, who grew up with little emotional support or acknowledgment and significant experiences of abandonment. Bart was voicing a recurring complaint that his partner, Sal, is dependent on him in terms of completing simple household or life tasks, for example, repeatedly asking Bart how to set the code on their household alarm system. Bart said, "Sal is so infantile. He's better than he used to be, but there are still so many things he asks me to do. It drives me crazy." Aware of the projective aspects of Bart's communication, my interpretive intervention was oriented towards the child complex activated in Bart's interior landscape, "You couldn't depend on anyone growing up, so anything Sal does that feels dependent or vulnerable angers you because it feels he's receiving something you've never had the opportunity to receive." While the interpretation addressed Bart's current situation with Sal, the emotional nexus of the interpretation centered on the feelings of deprivation and abandonment Bart experienced as a child which remain alive in the present through the organizing schema of the child complex.

Without the technique of *speaking with complexes* in mind, it is easy to fall into a pattern of interpretation primarily directed toward the patient's ego, as though the ego is the primary avenue of transformation. However, Jung (1967) states clearly that engagement of the dissociated aspects of the psyche is central to effective intervention:

> The treatment involves the integration of contents that have become disso-ciated from consciousness – not always as a result of repression, which is very often only a secondary phenomenon. . . The general rule is that the more negative the conscious attitude is, and the more it resists, devalues, and is afraid, the more repulsive, aggressive, and frightening is the face which the dissociated content assumes. *Every form of communication with the split off part of the psyche is therapeutically effective.*
>
> (para. 464–465, italics mine)

When we lapse into speaking only to the ego, there is a tendency to phrase interpretations in the language of rationality, about ego concerns, rather than in phrasing that speaks to the affective logic of the wounded aspects of the psyche. Additionally, interpretations focused only on ego concerns often reinforce the defenses associated with maintaining the conscious position of the patient.

At times, this interpretive approach may sound odd to the patient because the analyst's empathy, attention, and understanding are temporarily directed at a subset of the patient's experience which operates outside their conscious awareness (i.e., non-ego elements of experience) and is not consciously identified with. Another interpretive aspect that may strike the patient as odd or unfamiliar involves the subjective element of the time continuum; where past, present, and future have the potential to overlap in experience. Quinodoz (2003) highlights the confusion that can arise around the blurry subjectivity of time which, in turn, interacts with the spectrum of conscious, implicit, and unconscious elements of experience:

> At times the analyst has to put into words fantasies that could not be so expressed at the age from which they date. It may seem odd to verbalize childhood fantasies when the patient is an adult. Again, how can we know precisely what these fantasies were, given that the baby was not conscious of having them?
>
> (p. 67)

As with the indefinite and shifting perspective on time within an interpretation, there is also an overlap between personal and archetypal elements of experience

(Whitmont, 1987). The subtle but complex interaction between multiple interpretive vantage points is perhaps well summarized by the title of Grotstein's (2009) two-volume work – *But at the Same Time and on Another Level*.

The subjective–objective focus is another perspective to bear in mind in terms of the focus of an interpretation. Just as Jung (1953a)[4] indicates that all dreams can potentially be interpreted from a subjective or objective perspective, the analytic therapist must consider the directional focus of the interpretation. In other words, depending upon the psychological situation of the patient, the interpretation of a complex can be framed in terms of the patient's perception of their outer object world (i.e., outwardly oriented) or the patient's inner subjective world (i.e., inwardly oriented), or a combination of both. Riesenberg-Malcom (1995) highlights the importance of the patient's psychological position when formulating an interpretation. In Kleinian terms, a patient who (because of a strong reliance on the defense of splitting of the internal object, that is, into an experience of all good or all bad) experiences their internal object world primarily in terms of part-objects is referred to as functioning largely in the paranoid-schizoid state. In contrast, the patient who is capable of tolerating mixed or ambivalent feelings towards their internal objects is referred to as operating in the depressive state and is capable of whole-object relatedness. According to Riesenberg-Malcolm, the patient functioning in the paranoid-schizoid state relies heavily on the projection of threatening contents within their psyche, therefore interpretations that frame an experience as occurring in the patient are experienced intrusively. As a result, interpretations made to these patients should be framed in terms of their perception of the outside world until they begin to shift into whole-object functioning. Patients who are able to function within the depressive state (i.e., able to grieve loss and able to tolerate feelings of ambivalence towards others) are better able to tolerate interpretations intended to facilitate the withdrawal and integration of projected contents of the psyche. Riesenberg-Malcolm's perspective on interpretation is also useful when interpreting patient complexes. Interpretations are more effective when the analyst has considered the relationship between the ego and the dissociated complex or complexes. Often, a complex will feel quite alien for the patient when first introduced into the analytic dialogue. Therefore, it is useful to frame the interpretation in a way that takes that sense of alien-ness into account. Over time, as the circumambulation of the complex continues, it becomes possible to speak more directly with the dissociated element of the psyche. Rather than falling into the practice of speaking primarily with the ego of the patient, the analyst's task is to find a means of speaking with the complex directly as well as developing a sense of how the complex responds to the interpretation.

It is a delicate balance for the analytic therapist to maintain; speaking with the personifications of the psyche *as if* they are living beings while recognizing the danger of speaking of *concepts* as though they are *things* (i.e., reification[5]). Danielle Quinodoz (2003) outlines a similar balancing process, which she describes as "*Talking mad* while not forgetting that others do not speak this language" (p. 63, italics mine). By "others," she is referring to other aspects of the patient's psyche. Failure to recognize this tension results in a loss of experience and understanding. Maintaining this delicate balance, this tension of opposites, requires the analyst to simultaneously dwell on multiple levels of reality and subjectivity. Quinodoz (2003) goes on to articulate her interpretive position more fully:

> I should like to concentrate on the moment when, as an analyst, I directly address the "mad" part of my patient, feeling that if I want that part to understand me, I must speak its language – that is, I must "talk mad" to it. I feel that I am "talking mad" when I clearly interpret the archaic fantasies of my adult patients. . . However, I myself always take certain precautions before talking mad. In particular, I never forget that this mad part is not the totality of my patient's person, and that, although I may be addressing that part, I am also doing so with a view to finding the other part.
>
> (p. 63)

Harold Searles' capacity to speak with non-ego aspects of his patients was remarkable, particularly in his work with psychotic patients. This frequently took the form of working *inside* the delusional material of his patients.[6] An interaction between Searles and his patient Mrs. Douglas is illustrative of this approach (Langs & Searles, 1980, pp. 210–213). Mrs. Douglas asked Searles whether he thought she should bring her dog to the next session. Knowing from her history that she did not have a dog, Searles asked, "How large is it?" She replied with a gesture of her hands to indicate the size of the dog, and Searles responds, "About eight to ten inches. Well, you wonder if you should, huh?" In turn, Mrs. Douglas said, "Well, or take it to a hospital?" Searles, beginning to understand the nature of her inquiry more fully, makes a statement that is both a question and an oblique interpretation, "Well it does seem in need of some kind of treatment, doesn't it?" to which Mrs. Douglas softly agrees, "Yeah. Doesn't feel at all well once it's died, commit suicide." Searles responds gently with, "Hmm." In this exchange, Searles speaks *within* the concrete orientation of Mrs. Douglas who experiences the dog as a real dog, yet within himself, he maintains relationship with the *as if* aspect of the dog as a personification of the delusional psychological process that also carries Mrs. Douglas' suicidal impulses. While Searles is able to experience the dog at a symbolic representational level, Mrs. Douglas is not yet able to move from the concrete level to the symbolic level. Rather than making a direct interpretation about the meaning of the dog, Searles asked a series of questions which helped bring the dog into the room as a living presence without directly confronting Mrs. Douglas' reality orientation.

Patients with delusional processes often experience interpretations that directly confront the content of their delusions as a threat, often responding, "You don't believe me." However, interpretations that primarily focus on the affective and experiential qualities of the delusions are often more readily assimilated. For example, Ken was preoccupied with the idea that his adult son was sneaking into his house every day, sometimes several times per day, and taking his possessions.

In waking reality, this may have actually happened on occasion, but it would be physically impossible for it to occur with the frequency Ken was reporting. My initial interpretive response to Ken's delusional process formed over several months and ultimately consisted of four elements or ideas: "When you feel that you can't keep your son from coming into your house and taking your things, // there is also a sense that this is also happening inside of you as well. // It feels as if you can't keep the feelings and thoughts of others from invading your mind and stealing away with bits and pieces of you, // I think this reminds you of the situation you grew up in where there were no boundaries, no personal space, no sense of personal possessions, and no room to have your own thoughts." This was a single interpretation but I have separated the four elements of the interpretation with back-slashes. By accepting his delusional material at face value and then linking it with inner experiences and personal narrative history, Ken was able to take in my interpretation without feeling that I was trying to take away his view of reality. If I had offered the third and fourth pieces of the interpretation without the first and second elements, the interpretation would have been experienced as an invasion of his mind. I accepted Ken's delusional idea that his son was recurrently invading his house undetected to steal his possessions, but I understood the delusion as a metaphor for his sense that his mind was permeable and subject to invasion accompanied by the theft of bits of his identity structure. A number of similar interpretations have followed. Ken's delusion involving his son has dissipated, along with most of his other delusional fixations, permitting Ken to enjoy a comfortable relationship with his son.

For reasons stated earlier, the complex interpretation is formulated in experiential rather than conceptual terms to keep the interpretation aligned more closely with the patient's experience rather than their intellectual understanding. For example, with a patient with recurrent fears of abandonment, rather than speak to the patient directly about an abandonment complex, I might begin, "It seems that the part of you that feels abandoned. . . ." Similarly, when interpreting some aspect of a child complex, I will often preface my interpretation with, "The child-like part of you. . ." or "The part of you that doesn't feel fully grown. . . ." At other times, my interpretation engages the child complex directly without the additional preface that serves to locate the aspect of psyche I am speaking with. For example, if the patient is experiencing an intense feeling of abandonment in the transference field, I would be more likely to offer a here-and-now interpretation[7] such as, "I can see you're in great despair, as if I've left you alone with your fears, with little hope that I'll return to retrieve you from those feelings." As Bion (1992) indicates, "Psychoanalytic 'observation' is concerned neither with what has happened nor with what is going to happen, but with what is happening" (p. 380).

In terms of non-transference scenarios, I usually attempt to describe the pattern I am observing before making further attributions about the complex it is associated with. A patient with a controlling and condemning father complex often began sessions by chastising himself for things he felt he had "screwed up." I began our circumambulation of the complex with a confrontational observation followed by a clarifying inference and an invitation to reflect, "This seems to be an instance in which you behave towards yourself in a very domineering and aggressive way. You might wonder how this came to feel like a natural way for you to interact with yourself."

At times, it may be necessary to address two aspects of a complex simultaneously, particularly when those elements are in dynamic relationship within the psyche, as is sometimes the case in erotic constellations, for example, "The part of you that can seduce and the part of you which can be seduced. . . ." Ultimately, it is not sufficient to simply identify the existence of a complex. The origins and functioning of the complex must be sufficiently experienced and reflected on by the analyst so that these processes can then be communicated to the patient in experiential-affective-behavioral language.

Circumambulation of the complex

Often, when reflecting on the process of analysis, my mind often turns to a sculpture created by Zenos Frudakis titled *Freedom* (see Figure 7.2). The sculpture depicts a male figure in four movements, initially imprisoned in a bronze wall, but slowly extracting himself; ultimately breaking free of the entangling constraints. Frudakis (n.d.) describes the impulse behind his creation:

> I wanted to create a sculpture almost anyone, regardless of their background, could look at and instantly recognize that it is about the idea of struggling to break free. This sculpture is about the struggle for achievement of freedom through the creative process. Although for me, this feeling sprang from a particular personal situation, I was conscious that it was a universal desire with almost everyone; that need to escape from some situation – be it an internal struggle or an adversarial circumstance, and to be free from it.

Like the concept of circumambulation, the sculpture wonderfully captures the process of analysis, which is oriented to recognizing and breaking free from one's internal constraints and habitual patterns of being, so that one can live with greater freedom of choice in thought, feeling, perception, and behavior. Elements of the sculpture are left intentionally unfinished to convey the sense that we, as individuals, are always in progress, always coming into being, just as Jung conveys that individuation is an ongoing process rather than a destination to be arrived at.

The Frudakis sculpture *Freedom* provides a compelling visual metaphor for the process of transformation. According to Strachey (1934), a mutative (transformative) interpretation is one that allows the patient's ego to "become aware of a distinction between his archaic phantasy object and the real external object. The interpretation has now become a mutative one, since it has produced a breach in the neurotic vicious circle" (p. 143). Strachey's description of the differentiation between the archaic phantasy object and the external object is similar to Dieckmann's (1991) description of the interpretation and transformation of complexes:

Figure 7.2 *Freedom*, sculpture by Zenos Frudakis (2000)

The interpretation of the effects that these complex contents evoke within the transference and countertransference situation between analyst and patient, and beyond that, of course, also those distorted situations that arise through projection of the unconscious complex contents in the current life situation of the patient as well as in interpersonal relationships in general.

(p. 166)

In Freud's (1914) seminal article "Remembering, repeating and working-through," the phrase "working-through" refers to the working through of the patient's infantile neurosis.[8] In Freud's model, this is accomplished by the interpretation of each segment of the infantile neurosis. Through this cycle of interpretation, the patient comes to recognize and experience the impact of their neurotic conflict on various aspects of their life and in their relationships. Over time, the patient becomes increasingly familiar with the unconscious conflict as a theme that penetrates much of his or her behavior, thoughts, and feeling states; ultimately becoming less frightened of the wishes and feelings connected with the conflict.[9]

In contrast, the Jungian analyst conceptualizes the "working-through" aspect of analysis from the perspective of the complex rather than the infantile neurosis. From a Jungian perspective, an infantile neurosis would be understood as a manifestation of a child complex. The interpretive cycle associated with working through a complex is similar to that of the infantile neurosis. However, Jung (1953b) refers to the working-through process as the circumambulation of the complex, "If the life-mass is to be transformed a *circumambulatio* is necessary, i.e., exclusive concentration on the centre, the place of creative change" (para. 186). Essentially, the circumambulation of the complex is the process of coming back to the complex over and over again, revealing different facets of the complex, as well as observing and engaging the complex from different vantage points.

Calling the patient's attention to recurring patterns in their verbalizations, behaviors, relational patterns, feeling states, somatic states, fantasies, and dreams is the initial emphasis in the interpretation of complexes. As these recurrent patterns become identified, it is then possible to begin articulating the underlying schemas tying these patterns together – that is, the operation of the complex. Over time, the function of individual complexes can also be located within the patient's network of complexes. Unlike the traditional Freudian concept of infantile neurosis, which is conceptualized as a more overarching, monistic experience, the Jungian concept of complexes assumes the presence of several core complexes in each individual. Jung drew heavily upon his research with the association experiment (1973) in developing his theory of complexes (1958a). The results of the association experiments consistently demonstrated the existence of several complexes in Jung's subjects.

There are reductive and synthetic aspects to the *circumambulation* of a complex. At times, both elements are simultaneously present, while at other times the analyst moves back and forth between reductive and synthetic interpretations (Williams, 1963; Zinkin, 1969, 1979; Whitmont, 1987). Over time, the *circumambulation* of the complex comes to articulate the past, present, and future of the complex (Dieckmann, 1991, p. 166), that is, how the complex came into being (the past), how it operates in the present, and where it seems to be moving the individual (the future). As the circumambulation of a complex proceeds, the analyst moves back and forth in time, offering interpretations that address the various time frames through which the complex can be experienced.

Often, during the circumambulation of a complex, the analyst's task is to look for where a tension of opposites is constellated. The vignette that follows provides an example of a tension of opposites constellated in the transference. The patient, Zoe, was expressing her ambivalence and discomfort about continuing her analysis. Zoe experienced conflicted feelings – that is, that she was somehow betraying something in herself by continuing in the analysis but at the same time did not want to leave analysis. This ambivalence emerged during an extended period of erotic transference that paralleled a long-standing idealizing transference. Zoe was telling me about talking with her friends about her conflicted feelings and how it made her feel better to talk about her ambivalent feelings. But speaking with her friends about her ambivalence also intensified her feeling of internal conflict. Holding Zoe's two primary transferential patterns in mind, I attempted to articulate the unconscious contributors to her consciously experienced ambivalence while also heightening the tension between opposing desires to leave or stay. I interpreted, "There's a tension inside about needing to feel I'm above you so that you feel I can be helpful to you, but then you feel resentment about being my patient, which makes it feels as though we're not equals and therefore cannot be lovers." She replied, "With you, I think it's clear my boundaries aren't great. I need to remind myself that you're my therapist. And maybe remind you too – well, maybe I don't think you need that."

The circumambulation of the complex creates the conditions conducive to the transformation of a complex. The understanding, assimilation, and re-structuralization of complexes comes through repetition, that is, the circumambulation of the complexes that is ongoing during the course of the analysis. Naturally, a containing relational context is a necessary condition for this process. As Auld and Hyman (1991) point out:

> Principally, the therapist helps through making interpretations . . . The warm relationship is the necessary context for the interpretive actions of the therapist, because interpretations necessarily involve some narcissistic affront to the patient.
> (p. 35)

The interpretation is a narcissistic affront to the patient because it offers a different perspective on the patient's situation than the one they consciously hold. Reciprocally, accurate and empathic interpretations reinforce the patient's experience of being seen and understood, even if those experiences are uncomfortable or unfamiliar at times.

Through the ongoing circular movement around the complex, the patient has recurrent opportunities to:

- Gain insight into origins of the complex(es).
- Recognize cues and triggers associated with the activation of the complex(es).
- Recognize the capacity of the complex(es) to disrupt feeling, perception, thought, and behavior.
- Understand the relationship between the complex(es), self-perception, and self-experience.
- Understand the relationship between the complex(es) and interpersonal issues.
- Distinguish what the patient brings, via the complex(es), to relationship issues and what other people bring to those relationships.
- Understand the secondary gain aspects of the symptoms associated with the complex(es).
- Understand the symptoms of the complex(es) as an unconscious attempt at self-cure.
- Imagine the course of the future if the complex(es) remain unaltered.

Although some of these areas of understanding and integration will occur spontaneously, through self-awareness during the analytic process, most will be facilitated by the interpretations offered by the analyst. These interpretations will be further refined by the interaction between the analyst and patient. Ultimately, the goal of the process is the de-potentiation of the complex, that is, a reduction in the intensity associated with a complex and the acquisition of greater emotional, behavioral, and symbolic capacity.

Circumambulation and symptoms

In Analytical Psychology, perhaps more so than other schools of analytic therapy, symptoms are understood as conveyers of information regarding the organization of the patient's psyche, particularly the patient's network of complexes and associated defense mechanisms. The close relationship between symptoms (neuroses) and complexes is highlighted by Jung (1973), who proposes that, "Every psychogenic neurosis contains a complex. . . The complex, therefore, is the *causa morbi* [source of the illness]" (para. 665). Elsewhere, Jung (1950) indicates that, "A neurosis is a dissociation of personality due to the existence of complexes" (para. 382). Later, in the same passage, Jung proposes that the outbreak of a neurosis is an attempt by the psychic system at self-cure, "It is an attempt of the self-regulating psychic system to restore balance, in no way different from the function of dreams" (para. 389). Here, Jung indicates that the self-regulating mechanisms of the psyche will often occur through the process of compensation, that is, providing a compensatory position to the conscious situation of the analysand, just as dreams do. The symptom represents an attempt at adaptation and reflects the best the patient is able to do with their available psychic resources. Symptoms are not something to be rid of or fixed; symptoms are inherently symbolic of the underlying conflict. Therefore, symptoms are intimately associated with complex theory as well as the circumambulatory process. Interpretations of the patient's symptoms are framed to help the patient see that what they are unconsciously doing to protect themselves also has the effect of wounding themselves.

All symptoms (such as depression, anxiety, obsessions, compulsions, psychosomatic issues, or delusions) have the potential to carry symbolic information or meaning. The systemic effort to self-regulate through the implicit symbolic function of symptoms can readily be seen in the symptom cluster of a patient with obsessive-compulsive disorder. Linda had ongoing, significant experiences of trauma and abandonment while growing up. During that time, she began engaging in a variety of behavioral patterns consciously designed to minimize her exposure to traumatic situations and contain her anxiety. However, as an adult, those patterns became well established in her behavioral repertoire even though she was no longer exposed to the same traumatic situations. Her adult patterns centered on compulsive behaviors designed to establish her sense of personal security, such as repeatedly checking that doors and windows were secure. Linda had a long list of required security operations she used to manage her anxiety, particularly at night when she felt most vulnerable. In the morning, she would awaken feeling relieved that she had survived another night without being attacked. However, Linda's efforts to manage her anxiety through her obsessions and compulsions also resulted in the maintenance and reinforcement of the trauma complex generating the obsessions and compulsions in the first place. In other words, by undertaking the security operations, she reinforced her belief that the feared attack was not solely a result of events in her past but also a distinct likelihood in the present as well. It is as though there were a voice chiding her, "If there isn't a danger, then why are you taking all of this time to check the security of the doors and windows?" Therefore, the very behavioral patterns (symptoms) utilized to manage her anxiety also served to reinforce her anxiety, particularly when circumstances prevented her from taking the steps she felt were necessary to maintain her sense of security. Additionally, because she lacked sufficient psychological capacity for reflection, Linda made the implicit assumption every morning that she had remained safe during the night as a result of her behavioral security operations.

Linda was initially unable to entertain the possibility that she remained safe because there was not an immediate, impending threat waiting outside her home every night. In other words, Linda's capacity for making distinctions on an emotional level between past and present, or between inner threat and outer threat, was limited. My initial interpretive interventions focused on her difficulty in making those distinctions: "Each morning you wake up feeling relieved, taking that relief as confirmation that your repeated checking of the doors and windows was necessary. It's difficult for you to imagine that you may have remained safe during the night because there wasn't an impending danger. I suspect the possibility that the danger exists in the past, rather than the present, feels like a dangerous thought for you to take in when you hear me speak it aloud." Over a long period of time, Linda gradually relinquished many of her security rituals. While she still has the feeling that something bad could happen to herself, or someone she cares about, those fears have grown less intense and less specific, while the compulsions have diminished significantly.

Another example of the symbolic value of symptoms can be observed in an interaction with François. François was an intelligent, competent, and articulate graduate student who experienced significant writer's block and associated procrastination in completing assigned projects. This symptom pattern was a recurrent subject during his analysis. During a particular session, there was a breakthrough in the understanding of his procrastination and writer's block. Something in the way he was speaking about "difficult things" allowed me to see that François' procrastination was often an unconscious rebellion against the expectations of others. Also, I came to see that he was unable to value things unless completing them or attaining them was difficult. During the course of the session, I had shared with François an association to Aldous Huxley's statement "Experience isn't what happens to us. Experience is what we do with what happens to us." Following my mention of the Huxley reference, there seemed to be an affective shift, or opening, in François. A short time later, I interpreted, "You've created an illusion of control, thinking that you can discover yourself by attempting to avoid fulfilling the expectations of others." He responded enthusiastically, "That's what it is! How is it that I hadn't seen it before?" Hoping to invite his mutual reflection, I then asked, "You create these scenarios that are overwhelming to you – what's the value for you in being in this role of being the one who is overwhelmed? It's somewhat like the character Mendoza, played by De Niro in the movie *The Mission*, who makes his penance more arduous than the one assigned by the priest. Without making it more arduous, his penance had no significance to him." After several moments of silent reflection, I interpreted, "You take everything and make it arduous. Without it being arduous, you feel your tasks have no significance." It was obvious in François' face that the interpretation allowed François to see his symptoms of writer's block and procrastination in a new way. Interestingly, François came back to the next session with a memory of the feeling of the session, but an inability to remember the interpretation I had offered that led to that feeling. This suggested that his defense mechanisms were activated to avoid the mutative changes that might ensue following the interpretive sequence. François opened the next session, "Thank you for the great session we had last time. I felt many doors opened up; it was very intense and rewarding. Now, I was recalling the course of the session, but, curiously enough, perhaps making things difficult again, I can't recall your comment that motivated my statement, 'That's what it is! How is it that I hadn't seen it before?'" Remaining within the framework of the previous interpretation, I replied, "If you had remembered, it would have been too easy and not worth having." After making the interpretation, I then shared with François my recollection of the sequence of events that had led to his sense of insight.

Archetypes, archetypal theory, and the collective unconscious

In the contemporary Jungian world, it is no longer possible to speak of archetypes, archetypal theory, or the collective unconscious as universally accepted theoretical constructs. There is currently significant discussion within the Jungian community regarding the origin and transmission of archetypes. In recent years, several new conceptualizations have emerged that question or modify Jung's (1959b) original position regarding the pre-existent or innate qualities of archetypes and the collective unconscious.

Newer conceptualizations of archetypal theory include proposals that archetypes are primarily culturally determined and transmitted (e.g., Roesler, 2012) or are manifestations of emergent/developmental patterns resulting from the interaction of human systems (e.g., Knox, 2003; Hogenson, 2009; Cambray, 2009; Merchant, 2009). These early patterns form the "initial scaffolding" (Knox, 2003), "image schemas" (Knox, 2003), or "action patterns" (Hogenson, 20099) that structure how later experiences in life will be internalized and responded to. This perspective is similar to Stern's (1985) concept, emerging from infant developmental studies, of "representations of internalized experiences generalized" (RIGs) which shape how later experience is perceived, interpreted, and responded to. There is also similarity with Bowlby's (1969) concept of "internal working models" associated with attachment theory.

Adopting a pluralistic stance, Martin-Vallas (2013) proposes that archetypes possess both biological and emergent properties, that is, that archetypes have biological and transmissible origins interacting with cultural influences to determine the activation and expression of the archetype, "I am proposing that the archetype is an emergent structure, a by-product of the encounter between culture and instinct, in other words, a higher level of complexity" (p. 283). In contrast, Skar (2004) proposes that "we no longer need the 'archetype-as-such' to explain the formation of complexes. In fact, we could do without it altogether and still have the same basic psychological system that Jung proposed" (p. 245). Finally, Colman (2016), in his rigorously researched and articulated *Act and Image*, deconstructs Jung's reasoning that led to his theory of archetypes and the collective unconscious. Colman argues that Jung's concept of archetypes as innate experience has outlived its theoretical utility, and proposes a focal shift towards "symbolic imagination" as an emergent and unique phenomenon of the human species; "Mind is emergent from the symbols we use to imagine with; without symbols there can be no imagination and without imagination, there can be no human mind. Hence, imagination makes us human" (p. 168). Colman's redefinition of the Jungian focus has similarities with Bionian ideas of *dreaming oneself into existence* (Ogden, 2009) and *coming into being* which Bion (1962) associated with the patient's capacities for reflective thought and learning from experience.

Ultimately, the question regarding the nature and origin of archetypal patterns is more important from a theoretical perspective than in the context of how the analyst practices clinically. For the purposes of interpretation, it is the archetype as experience (i.e., the phenomenology of archetypal experience; descriptive of something occurring in the analytic session, or in life) that is most essential rather than archetype as theoretical construct. In the following passage, Jung (1950) highlights the emotional experience of the archetype as the most essential quality of archetypal phenomenon:

Not only is the existence of archetypes denied, but even those people who do admit their existence usually treat them as if they were mere images and forget that they are living entities that make up a great part of the human psyche. As soon as the interpreter strips them of their numinosity, they lose their life and become mere words. . . . It is true that the forms of archetypes are to a considerable extent interchangeable, but their numinosity is and remains a fact. It represents the value of an archetypal event. This emotional value must be kept in mind and allowed for throughout the whole intellectual process of interpretation. . . it forms the link between psychic events on the one hand, and meaning in life on the other.

(para. 596)

In other words, archetypal patterns can be utilized to describe or engage with experiences of the patient, and the analyst, that possess a "something more" than ordinary experience. A theoretical position regarding the origin of archetypes is not necessary for the use of the concept as a descriptive category of experience. Experiences having a ring of universality, inherent order, or transcendence can be engaged without necessitating an attribution about the "location" or origin of these experiences. In the clinical setting, the focus is on the immediacy and quality of the experience, just as Otto (1923) articulated numinosity and awe as qualities of religious experience. Similarly, the introduction of archetypal motifs into the analytic setting can be functionally effective and transformative regardless of the theoretical genesis of archetypal experience. In the sections that follow, I am referring to particular qualities of experience when I utilize the terms "archetype" and "archetypal."

Archetypal interpretation of the analytic dialogue

Those working from a Jungian perspective typically have a good grasp of archetypal material used to amplify and interpret patient dreams. However, the material used for archetypal amplification during dream work can also readily be used with the other forms of communication encountered in analysis. Interpretation is a means for the analyst to communicate to the patient – "This is the understanding I have about you, your life, your thought patterns, your behaviors, and your feelings." Archetypal amplification places the interpretive communication in the context of a story or image from sources outside the patient's personal experience, but which has relevance for the patient's personal experience. Interpretation from an archetypal perspective links a pattern observed in the patient to a deeper understanding of the purposiveness of the pattern based on the analyst's knowledge of archetypal patterns. Archetypal interpretation serves to broaden the patient's emotional experience of the analytic moment and may assist the patient in locating their particular experience within the broader panorama of human experience. At the most fundamental level, the incorporation of archetypal motifs moves the analytic interaction into the world of metaphor, thereby bridging image and concept. Archetypal motifs provide the analyst a means of communicating, in non-conceptual language, impressions of the patient's inner world and how their inner landscapes shape their experience of relationships and the world around them. Ultimately, archetypal patterns provide a third perspective on the analytic situation that originates beyond the ego consciousness of the two participants.

Contrasting personal and archetypal interpretation

Imagine a woman named Cynthia, who harbors a deep sense of inadequacy and who lacks a sense of efficacy. She has a sister, Nikki, who is rather overbearing, intrusive, and controlling. Nikki has insisted that Cynthia come to her home for an upcoming holiday. Cynthia does not want to acquiesce to Nikki's directive but feels powerless to decline. During a session, Cynthia asks if the analyst would call Nikki and explain to Nikki that her anxiety prevents her from traveling. The analyst can respond in a variety of ways to Cynthia's request. From a personal (non-archetypal) perspective, the analyst might choose to address the patient's difficulty in establishing boundaries as well as the transference implications of the request: for example, "I understand that setting boundaries with Nikki is difficult for you. There were few boundaries in your family growing up, so now you have trouble establishing boundaries with others. You would like me to do that for you so that you won't have to experience the discomfort of learning to set them yourself." However, the analyst could also choose to interpret from an archetypal perspective: "In the unfolding of your life, it doesn't appear that you had opportunities to experience yourself as a warrior, like Joan of Arc, able to take up shield and sword to protect yourself and your borders. That capacity was never nurtured. Now you hope I'll carry the role of the warrior for you, standing in for you to do battle with your sister. But in doing that, your opportunity to discover the warrior in yourself is lost."

Archetypal interpretation and mythologems

Mythology derives from the Greek words *mythos* – meaning report, tale, or story – and *logos* meaning word or speech. The mythological perspective informs by locating experience within a narrative; a narrative that has similarities with but is also different from the patient's personal narrative. Mythology, like the understanding of complexes, orients us to the past, present, and future. It helps the patient to identify their position within an archetypal narrative, that is, where they might be located or headed within that narrative and what role they might be playing. Mythology, and other systems of archetypal imagery, also facilitates the movement into reverie or non-directed thinking. By introducing metaphor into the analytic moment, archetypal motifs have the potential to shift the perspective from an intellectual to an experiential and trans-rational perspective.[10]

Despite the benefits of utilizing archetypal material during the interpretation of the analytic dialogue or dreams, there are also potential dangers. Fordham (1998) cautions about the possibility of losing analytic contact with the patient when introducing archetypal motifs. At times, patients may experience the analyst's introduction of a narrative that does not appear to be directly connected to their experience as an "empathic break" (Kohut, 1971) on the part of the analyst. At other times, the archetypal narrative presented by the analyst may be too emotionally evocative or contain too much information for the patient to assimilate, resulting in an "oversaturated" interpretation (Ferro, 1999). Ferro argues that the introduction of oversaturated interpretations is a result of the analyst's anxiety in the face of uncertainty rather than a reflection of accurate comprehension of the patient's conscious and unconscious situation. This raises the issue of whether the analyst is finding true correspondence between the patient's narrative and an archetypal narrative, that is, finding the archetypal arc within the patient's communications, or whether the analyst is forcing the patient's material into an archetypal template to create a sense of understanding in the face of uncertainty. Therefore, the analyst must remain sensitive to the patient's response to the material and be willing to move away from archetypal themes if the patient is unable to engage with the archetypal motifs. Often, such lack of engagement can be sensed as a shift in the feeling or energy of the analytic field, or experienced more overtly when the patient refers to the archetypal material introduced by the analyst as "your story."

In the analytic interaction, archetypal patterns do not often manifest fully represented, in Technicolor, accompanied by trumpet fanfare, as depicted in Peter Paul Rubens' painting *The Fall of the Phaeton*. In the analytic setting, the archetypal pattern often emerges in a more subtle way. When interpreting from an archetypal perspective, I find it more effective to focus on mythologems rather than entire archetypal narratives. Mythologems are the basic core elements, or themes, of larger mythic narratives. Mythologems are like the Legos or building blocks of myths, providing the underlying structure for the mythic narrative. The notion of archetypal building blocks can be expanded to include fairytales, religions, and alchemy, as well as sources of cultural amplification. Therefore, the term "mythologeme" can be utilized broadly to include smaller foundational elements of any archetypal system: mythology, religion, fairytale, alchemy, as well as manifestations from culture, such as film, literature, poetry, art, music, and so forth.

The term "mythologeme" was introduced to Analytical Psychology by Kerenyi in *Essays on a Science of Mythology* (Jung & Kerenyi, 1949). In the following passage, Jung (1960b) emphasizes that the primary rationale for recognizing and articulating these patterns is to aid in the understanding of the individual psyche:

> Since the meaning and substance of the typical individual forms are of the utmost importance in practice, and knowledge of them plays a considerable role in each individual case, it is inevitable that the mythologem and its content will also be drawn into the limelight. This is not to say that the purpose of the investigation is to interpret the mythologem. But, precisely in this connection, a widespread prejudice reigns that the psychology of unconscious processes is a sort of philosophy designed to explain mythologems.

(para. 436)

Some commonly encountered mythologems include: creation, death, the hero, sacrifice, the encounter with the monster, the descent, the dying and resurrecting god, the scapegoat, the witch, transformation, acquisition of knowledge, punishment, hubris, the golden child, the outcast, the villain, the necessary task, abduction, and the quest. Often, these mythologems materialize like small, verdant sprouts peeping up through the surface of the analytic interaction or dream. By recognizing these foundational mythologems, it becomes possible to move down through the associative networks of their root systems into the broader mythological panorama as manifested in the narrative arc of the patient's psyche.

Archetypal interpretation – Evelyn

Evelyn had lived much of her life coping with the residual effects of childhood trauma, two difficult marriages, and several psychiatric hospitalizations. Her chaotic emotional state eventually resulted in the loss of employment and her home as well as necessitating a period of psychiatric disability. She began treatment in a rather fragmented state immediately following one of her hospitalizations; a state that characterized the early part of her treatment. However, six months into our work, the fragmentary state of her psyche had sufficiently cohered that she was able to return to employment in her field. For the next several years, Evelyn continued to improve in terms of her overt depressive and dissociative symptoms; however, there was still a lack of vitality, a lack of engagement with life, which persisted despite improved stability, ego functioning, and affect regulation. She was dutifully trudging through the motions of life but with little affective engagement with life. At some point during this bleak period, an image appeared in my reverie of the burial tomb of Christ. After considering the implications of the image in terms of Evelyn's Christian belief system, I interpreted: "You seem to be in an in-between place, between one way of being and another, somewhat like Christ must have felt when he was lying in the tomb between crucifixion and resurrection." It was clear from Evelyn's face that the interpretation had deeply penetrated a previously impenetrable area of her psyche. Naturally, there was much work left to be done, but this archetypal interpretation initiated a new period of healing and transformation. Approximately a year following this interpretation, she came into a session and announced that we needed to conclude our work in about six months. Surprised by the abruptness of her announcement, I asked her why we needed to conclude the analysis. She said, "All of my life I've always wanted to live in New England but I was too afraid to move. I had too many fears and felt too uncertain about myself. Now those fears don't dominate me the way they used too. I don't want to go through the remainder of my life feeling I never tried, so I've contacted a friend who lives in New England and I'm moving in six months." At that moment, it became clear that Evelyn had emerged from her transitory tomb of half-living.

Archetypal interpretation – Abigail

Abigail was successful in her career but struggled with depression, anxiety, and body-related issues around weight and eating. During the first years of her life, she experienced significant maternal deprivation and indicated that her mother felt like a stranger to her when they were reunited. Abigail was frequently plagued with guilt for a variety of acts and perceived shortcomings. She would often appear for sessions with several bags of books in tow, the contents of which were always changing. When I inquired about her bags of books, she indicated that she wanted to read them but never managed to find the time. Abigail also had an entire spare bedroom and several closets filled with clothing and other merchandise that she purchased but never wore or used. Abigail's patterns could readily have been interpreted as obsessive-compulsive patterns used to manage her anxiety – that is, ritual behaviors and compulsive accumulation. However, during sessions with Abigail, I found my thoughts drawn to the Greek myth of Tantalus.

Tantalus was a son of Zeus and honored by the gods above all of Zeus' other mortal sons. He was invited to share in the banquet of nectar and ambrosia. Tantalus accepted their invitation but decided to demonstrate that the gods could be deceived. Tantalus had his son Pelops killed, boiled, and served to the gods. However, all of the Olympians recognized the deception and withdrew from the table, with the exception of Demeter who partook of the child's flesh. Tantalus was cast into the Underworld, where he remains forever in the middle of a waist-deep lake. Hanging over him are trees laden with pears, pomegranates, apples, and sweet figs. However, each time Tantalus attempts to satisfy his hunger, the winds toss the branches of the trees out of his reach, and each time he bends down to quench his thirst, the cool waters recede. Thus, he stands forever, in the midst of plenty, his desires never satisfied. The mythologems of hubris, deception, unfulfilled desire, and punishment provide the underlying structure for the Tantalus myth.

With Abigail, the archetypal interpretation felt more enlivening than an interpretation built on the psychological construct of obsessive-compulsive behaviors used to manage anxiety and ward off imagined catastrophes. I began to see the Tantalus myth as a depiction of the internal processes governing Abigail's outer behaviors as well as her feelings of guilt. I introduced Tantalus into the interpretive process by saying, "Many of the things you do and feel, as well as the ways you see the world and yourself, have some similarities with the Greek myth of Tantalus." She was unfamiliar with the myth, so I offered a brief overview of the story. Over time, I began to form smaller interpretations using bits and pieces from the Tantalus myth. One of the early interpretations dealt with her desire and her guilt: "I think you still feel a great deal of emptiness inside around your mother's absence during your early years which you attempt to fill by accumulating things such as books and clothing. But you feel undeserving of these things, so you rarely permit yourself to use them – always keeping them nearby but out of reach. It's as though you punish yourself for both your emptiness and your desire." Sometime later, I offered an interpretation centered on the mythologem of deception contained in the Tantalus myth. However, unlike Tantalus' deception of the gods, Abigail's deception was with herself rather than with others: "You deceive yourself by creating an outer appearance of things being okay despite the turmoil inside. You have convinced yourself that if you look okay and accumulate more things, then things must be okay inside, just as Demeter assumes when she unwittingly consumes the flesh of Pelops. But a part of you recognizes your deception and calls attention to the deception through your depression and anxiety."

Archetypal interpretation – Victoria

Prometheus, Sisyphus, Ixion, and Tantalus form a quaternity of suffering in Greek mythology with common mythologems tying these myths together. Each involves an offense or sin against the gods which constellates the anger of the gods. Each involves a perpetual punishment and hence perpetual suffering. Finally, each punishment takes place in the form of a cycle or circular process. The repetition can be felt viscerally if one identifies with Prometheus as his liver is plucked out each day only to grow back each night. One can imagine the psychic disorientation experienced by Ixion as he rolls endlessly across the sky on his fiery wheel. The repetition can be felt each time Tantalus stoops to drink or reaches out to eat, yet each time his desire goes unsatisfied. And certainly, repetitive suffering can be felt in the interminable struggle Sisyphus must endure as he pushes the stone up the mountain each day only to have it monotonously roll back down each evening. One can sense the leaden sigh escaping from his lips as he turns to trudge back down the mountain where the boulder awaits him after having come to rest at the bottom.

These common mythologems, eternally repeated in these four myths, also repetitiously occupied Victoria's psyche. Victoria was caught in a repetitive, eternal cycle of punishment like Prometheus, Tantalus, Ixion, and Sisyphus. Victoria's every waking moment was occupied with carrying out her punishment via compulsive behaviors, such as cleaning and eating rituals, as well as obsessive self-condemnation. The first myth that entered my reverie while working with Victoria was the myth of Sisyphus. During one session, she was speaking about the anxiety she experienced as she attempted to go to sleep each night. In discussing the source of her anxiety, she said, "I'm anxious about having to get up and perform again tomorrow because that is the only thing that matters. What I did today doesn't mean anything. I have to prove my worth all over again." At that point, the myth of Sisyphus came into my mind, and I briefly described the story to her. She connected affectively with the story and said, "Yes, that's exactly how I feel." A few sessions later, she indicated she had been thinking about that myth and said, "I realized it is my mother that I have to prove myself to each day." In this instance, the story alone, without additional interpretive refinement, provided the necessary stimulus for growth of consciousness.

Each evening, Victoria would stand in front of her garbage disposal carefully examining the portions of food she had placed on her plate. Almost always, her anxiety was elevated and she felt compelled to throw part of her food into the disposal. From an archetypal perspective, she had identified with Prometheus who decides which food belongs to the gods and what should be given to humankind. At the same time, she was also identified with Tantalus whose hunger can never be satisfied. Victoria's Zeus (manifesting in the form of self-condemnation and anxiety) never allowed her to relax and enjoy what food she had permitted herself to keep on her plate. Like Prometheus being devoured by the vulture each day, Victoria paid for her imagined offenses against the gods by becoming hollowed out, both physically and psychically. Her physical body came to reflect the emptiness that had been cultivated psychologically.

Yet Victoria's gods are not only condemning and punishing, they are also jealous gods. Ixion was condemned for his erotic urges and for constellating Zeus' jealousy over Hera. In a similar way, the gods of Victoria's interior landscape demanded exclusivity in the relationship with her. Each time Victoria entertained the possibility of relinquishing some element of her eating disorder, a voice inside loudly proclaimed, "If you let go of the eating disorder, you will have nothing. You won't have any friends. There will be no one to depend on, and then you won't have the eating disorder either."

Victoria's crimes were the crimes of other mortals. According to her gods, she had failed to live up to expectations. Like Sisyphus, who was punished for speaking what he saw, Victoria was punished for saying what she felt. Victoria's destructive network of complexes persecuted her each time she confided in me regarding her needs or desires. A brief vignette, one year into our work together, provides an example of the conflict Victoria experienced around her needs, as well as the self-punitive cutting off of relationship she engaged in, both with me and herself, in response to these needs. While my interventions during this interaction do not overtly refer to specific myths or mythologems, my interventions are influenced by an awareness of these archetypal patterns:

P: I'm struggling so hard. See you win if I tear up. No, you can't win.

A: So Victoria is it possible. . .

P: (*Victoria interrupts me*) Ugh, you did that on purpose.

A: Used your name?

P: See my usual game is to make you cry, to make you hurt more.

A: How are you trying to do that with me now?

P: I'm not.

A: But usually you would try to make me cry? Make me hurt more?

P: Look, I am hurting so bad that I don't really give a crap about you. You're just a man and you're not going to hurt me more. So I can't show you a thing. Then you'll see that I'm weaker than you. So I hold in the pain. I hate you right now.

A: You hate me right now.

P: I hate you right now.

A: Do you think you came in hating me?

P: No, I just came in tired.

A: I'm trying to understand what happened that started you hating me.

P: (*tearfully*). . . because I can't be responsible for pulling me out.

A: It's difficult for you to say you need my help.

P: (*pause*). . . . If I was playing a game as a child, you would win if I said that. . . . so there's the tug of war. I need your help and then you win and then my hands cut off.

A: So I wonder what would make it okay within you to ask for help.

P: I need your help. I can't do it. . . What? What? I can't go through another day like this. I don't like crying like this. No. No.

A: But you do seem to be letting yourself admit your need of me right now.

P: No, No. I need to go inside. No.

A: You feel vulnerable and don't want to be outside of yourself right now. Making connection feels dangerous, as though you'll be punished for making connection with me.

P: Just keep looking at me.

A: The connection is important.

P: No, leave me alone.

A: That's the feeling. I think why you've been hating me is because you feel like I've left you alone today.

P: I feel dirty.

A: For needing?

P: I can't need. Especially a man. I can't need (*looks up at me*). Ugh. Ugh.

A: You're having trouble stomaching me.

P: You're disgusting. You are totally intolerable. . .

A: (*I interject*) I'm intolerable to you because I remind you of your need that you try to kill off in order to feel safe. You can't tolerate your feeling of need for me.

P: I need no man.

A: Maybe it would be the same feeling even if I was a woman.

P: I don't need a woman.

A: But right now you are focused on not needing a man. You feel like you have to kill off any emotional needs or a relationship with me and punish yourself for those needs.

Summary

Jung's theories of complexes and archetypal phenomena are unique aspects of Analytical Psychology and central to the process of analysis from a Jungian perspective. As a result, these theories are also central to the process of interpretation. The effective circumambulation and interpretation of complexes, that is, *speaking with complexes*, goes well beyond the naming or labeling of complexes activated during sessions. It involves moving into relationship with the complex on an imaginal level while attempting to understand the unique characteristics that make up each complex. It also involves grasping the role of individual complexes within a larger network of complexes and the archetypal patterns that provide the deeper organizing structure for complexes. Similarly, working effectively with archetypally focused interpretation involves the recognition of the component parts, that is, the mythologems that are found in myths, fairytales, alchemy, religions, and culture. The explicit use of archetypal amplification is often powerful and transformative. However, in many interpretive situations, the archetypal amplification is used implicitly by the analyst, informing the shape and focus of the interpretation, without necessarily sharing with the patient the overt archetypal amplification, or associated mythologems. Ultimately, the determination whether to utilize archetypal amplifications implicitly or explicitly rests with the analyst's intuition, clinical judgment, and sense of timing.

Exercises for the reader

1) In working interpretively with complexes, it is often useful to create visual maps of the patient's network of complexes, somewhat like the associative maps created by Edinger (1985, p. 16) to illustrate the various alchemical processes and the interrelationships between them.

2) It is also a useful exercise to list the contents of the personal shell for the primary complexes of each patient, that is, the images, memories, feelings and affects, physiological states, thought patterns or cognitive sets, attitudes, defense mechanisms, behavioral patterns, activating events, and patterns of object relatedness and attachment style.

3) As an imaginal exercise, select a patient and write out a short narrative drama, that is, an interior play, using the patient's primary complexes, including the ego, as the characters of the play. As a follow-up exercise, write a second play introducing the analyst as a new character while paying close attention to the reactions of the original characters to the introduction of the analyst character into the dramatic interaction.

4) At the end of each session, or work day, review the archetypal amplifications that entered your reverie. Identify the primary mythologems that provide the foundation to those amplifications. Finally, identify the mythologemes that are recurring patterns in each patient's narrative.

Notes

1 Jung (1958, para. 202) asserts that each complex has its own separate memory.
2 Bovensiepen (2006) discusses the defense organization of complexes (p. 453) as well as referring to similar material in Knox (2003).
3 Object relations theory is an outgrowth of the theoretical model of Melanie Klein. Object relations is an inclusive technical term that spans the intrapsychic and interpersonal dimensions. According to Scharff and Scharff (1992), "An internal object is a piece of psychic structure that formed from the person's experience with the important caretaking person in earlier life, captured as a trace of that earlier relationship" (p. 5). An internal object relation, "Refers to the system of in-built parts of the personality in relationship to each other inside the self. . . . Internal objects and other parts of the self are reciprocal with outer parts so that, in any relationship, the personalities are mutually influenced by each other. Our external relationships are in interaction with our internal psychic structures" (p. 4).

4 Jung (1953a), "I call every interpretation which equates the dream images with real objects an *interpretation on the objective level*. In contrast to this is the interpretation which refers every part of the dream and all the actors in it back to the dreamer himself. This I call *interpretation on the subjective level*" (para. 130, italics in original).

5 See Chapter 4 of this volume for a fuller discussion of reification.

6 See Langs and Searles (1980) for a remarkable verbatim record of Searles' work with a schizophrenic patient along with the observations and discussion by Langs and Searles, in particular see Chapter 4: *Techniques of Therapy with a Schizophrenic Patient* (pp. 185–264) and *Appendix* to Chapter 4 (pp. 265–308).

7 Here-and-now interpretations (Bauer, 1993) focus on the experience of the patient, most often in relationship to their transference feelings towards the analyst, rather than "there-and-then" interpretations which focus on linking the patient's experience back to the historical origins of the symptoms being experienced in the present. For decades, the curative factor in analysis was thought to rest with uncovering repressed aspects of the psychic experience. While contemporary analytic perspectives continue to recognize the importance of historical antecedents to current experience, recovering repressed memories is typically no longer seen as the primary curative factor in analysis. It is most often the case that the curative or transformative element of the analytic process takes place through a re-organization or re-structuralization of the patient's psyche through new experiences with the analytic clinician (Stern et al., 1998). While here-and-now interpretations are now typically viewed as having precedence over there-and-then interpretations, this development does not eliminate the utility of, or need for, there-and-then interpretations in the full circumambulation of a complex and the overall course of the analysis (Busch, 2011).

8 Infantile neurosis is the term used by Freud (1918) to describe the patient's primary psychic conflict; originating in early childhood experience and expressed through various neurotic symptoms such as anxiety, depression, obsessions, compulsions, or psychosomatic issues. In analysis, according to Freud, the infantile neurosis will be expressed through the transference relationship with the analyst, that is, the transference neurosis.

9 New theoretical models of change have emerged from contemporary schools of psychoanalytic thought. For example, Kleinian and object relations analysts focus on increasing the patient's capacity to tolerate ambivalence in relationships and experience object constancy; Bionian analysts emphasize the creation of psychological structures for processing experience where such structures are missing; and self psychologists seek to fill in the deficits in the patient's self-structure, as well as increasing cohesion of the self.

10 Trans-rational is a term introduced to Analytical Psychology by Jerome Bernstein (2014) to identify a category of experience that moves beyond the dichotomy between "rational" and "supernatural." As Bernstein asserts, the trans-rational experience "transcends the binary Logos concept of rationality but poses no contradiction to the rational" (p. 175).

Chapter 8

Reverie and interpretation[1]

As the previous chapters illustrate, the technique of interpretation can be applied in a variety of ways. However, interpretation is most effective when closely linked with the "feel" of what is happening in the consulting room and when integrated as fully as possible with the analyst's conscious, preconscious, and unconscious processes. Reverie is a state of mind that facilitates the greatest openness to these processes and to the interactive field constellated between the two analytic participants. Reverie encourages the development of a more experience-near, organic interpretive process rather than one relying on intellectual understanding and the imposition of theory.

What is reverie?

Reverie is opening to one's own internal stream of consciousness – to ideas, thoughts, feelings, sensations, memories, images, urges, and fantasies. The subtle flow of conscious and preconscious thought, affect, and sensation associated with reverie is ephemeral and ambiguous; appearing on the periphery of experience and often eluding our efforts to hold or shape those fleeting impressions. French philosopher Raphaël Enthoven (2011) eloquently describes reverie as:

> Daughter of consciousness and sleep, reverie blends their realms. Like intoxication, reverie is lucidity without an object, an activity but one that's passive, a search that begins by giving up and lets itself be dazzled rather than looking. It remains, happily, somewhere between imagination and the ability to put it to use. . . Reverie is contemplation from within, letting the person who gives way to it feel change. . . Born of the desire – and not the need – to be directly involved in our surroundings, reverie strips the world of its utility. It borrows the power of narration from wakefulness and the power of divination from sleep, and keeps them vying to suspend the alternation of day and night. Reverie is how one arrives at immediacy. . . Reverie never rests. . . Because it generously accords the world the absentmindedness it deserves, reverie is light years distant from being a distraction, which does reality the considerable honor of turning its back on it. In fact, reverie celebrates the rediscovery of understanding and imagination, sets free the secret of disinterest which, because it lets you see beauty without your consent and see nature without ego, invests the world with intense interest.
>
> (para. 3–4, 7)

Analytic reverie involves being receptive on many levels to the experience and communication, both explicit and implicit, of the other person's presence in the room. It also includes a sensitivity to the emerging potentiality of the "analytic third" (Ogden, 1994) – the mutually constellated but indeterminate creation of the analytic dyad that comprises "something more" than the combined individual contributions of the analytic partners. The potential range of reverie stretches from the ordinary to the transcendent. For example, Ogden (1997) describes reverie as "an experience that takes the most mundane and yet most personal of shapes. . . They are our ruminations, daydreams, fantasies, bodily sensations, fleeting perceptions, images emerging from states of half-sleep, tunes, and phrases that run through our minds, and so on" (p. 158). Working from a different vantage point, Mathew (2005) articulates the connection between reverie and soul: "Reverie is both a process and a state of mind. . . it is reverie that extends psyche's vision beyond the door and windows of our minds into the cathedrals of our souls" (p. 391). The concept of reverie is quite compatible with Jungian theory and practice but enjoys wider recognition among other schools of psychoanalytic thought, particularly those engaged with the work of Wilfred Bion.

The concept of reverie

The term "reverie" was adopted by Wilfred Bion (1962) to refer to a state of mind that the infant requires of the mother – a state of calm receptiveness to take in the infant's feelings and give them meaning. Through this making sense of, or meaning-making, the mother digests feelings placed in her mind by the infant through projective identification that are felt by the infant to be intolerable, such as anxiety or terror, that is, beta elements. Optimally, the mother transforms them through her "alpha function" into tolerable bits of experience, that is, alpha elements.[2] Over time, the infant takes in (introjects) the receptive, understanding mother and eventually begins to develop the capacity for reflection on their own states of mind. In analytic situations, Bion refers to this process as the "container and the contained." Ferro (2013) links the analyst's use of interpretation with the development of alpha elements in the patient: "When the analyst gives the interpretation, this acts as a stimulus to the patient to form the α element, and he creates an emotional photogram of how he has experienced the analyst's interpretation" (p. 14).

The analyst serves as the "container" for the patient, whose emerging psychic material needs to be "contained." However, implicit in the notion of "container and contained" is the need for the analyst to be able to "contain" their own reverie and to find sources of containment themselves, for example, through peer consultation or self-consultation with theory. Gabbard and Ogden (2009) point out that the need for containment, which is an experience of "the other," is ever continuing in the ongoing development of the analyst.

Reverie and Analytical Psychology

Reverie is not simply allowing oneself to daydream, where there is no engagement with the flow of thoughts, ideas, and sensations. The stance adopted in reverie is similar to Jung's (1916) active imagination in which a relationship or stance is established with the internal flow. Active imagination, which has been described as "dreaming with open eyes" (Sharp, 1991, p. 13), is a technique developed by Jung to facilitate the engagement and assimilation of unconscious processes while in a relaxed but waking state. However, it is important to note that Jung saw active imagination as an activity primarily engaged in by the analysand which, at times, might be facilitated by the analyst. It does not appear that Jung saw active imagination as something that was engaged in with another person as reverie is typically conceptualized. The fundamental nature or quality of reverie also has close parallels with Jung's (1956) concept of non-directed thinking discussed in Chapter 2. Therefore, the analytic therapist is typically engaged in non-directed thinking when in a state of reverie.

Davidson's 1966 paper "Transference as a form of active imagination" provides a conceptual movement towards reverie by proposing that analysis and the patient's transference is a "form of lived-through active imagination" (p. 143). Schaverien (2007) builds on Davidson's offering by suggesting that active imagination is a method the analyst can use to understand countertransference. Schaverien proposes that active imagination can be thought of as nearly synonymous with reverie. However, active imagination as a concept has been predominately conceptualized from an intrapsychic, or one-person, perspective. In contrast, Ferro (2006) highlights the inherently reciprocal, dyadic nature of reverie:

> There is, I believe, a constant baseline activity of reverie. . . which is the way the analyst constantly receives, metabolizes, and transforms whatever reaches him or her from the patient in the form of verbal, paraverbal, or nonverbal stimuli. The same activity of reverie is at work in the patient in response to every interpretive or non-interpretive stimulus from the analyst. The purpose of analysis is first and foremost to develop this capacity to weave images (which remain not directly knowable). . . there is no communication that cannot be seen as having to do with and belonging to the field itself.
>
> (p. 1054)

Therefore, there are limitations and pitfalls in re-purposing active imagination as a dyadic (two-person) or triadic (i.e., the addition of the analytic third to the dyadic perspective) concept. Attempting to use active imagination as a concept to discuss the two-fold and three-fold influences of the analytic encounter evokes the biblical parable of putting new wine into old wineskins.

In contrast with active imagination, analytic reverie has been a dyadic concept since inception. Reverie has been referred to by Ogden (2017) as a "waking dream," (p. 5) but one that is dreamt with another person rather than alone. In this vein, Ogden (1997) sees reverie as both a personal/private event (i.e., intrapsychic) and an intersubjective one. To put it another way, he acknowledges the presence of two subjectivities who can experience their interaction as being both individual and collective (i.e., as an interconnected and emergent experience).

Reverie has parallels with other aspects of Analytical Psychology, for example, reverie can also be considered an experience of *participation mystique*.[3] The moderate blurring of subject–object boundaries in reverie, consistent with participation mystique, facilitates the deepening of the experience for both analyst and analysand, while at the same time increasing receptivity to the emergence of preconscious or unconscious material. Hence, in the case of reverie, it is desirable for there to be a blurring of subject–object boundaries. Colman (2010) highlights the close conceptual relationship between Bion's concept of reverie and Jung's concept of participation mystique. Additionally, Colman suggests that the analyst's reverie is a manifestation of the analyst's symbolic attitude; a point also emphasized by Bovensiepen (2002).

Dieckmann (1991, p. 160) provides a case example that richly captures the experiential overlap between participation mystique and reverie. Dieckmann describes his internal response to a patient speaking in an agitated and repetitious manner about a hallucinated image of a streetcar in a forest; according to the patient, a "terribly ruined sight." Dieckmann struggled to understand his patient's agitation until, "Her stereotyped repetition gradually induced in me a participation mystique in her image, and a memory arose in me." In that moment, Dieckmann recalled his own waking encounter with a scene that struck him as an "unexpected, grotesque image, so foreign and unadapted to the situation." The induced recall of his memory allowed him to shift his focus from the content of the patient's image to the feeling of strangeness and ruin in which the patient's image was embedded, thereby facilitating a shift in the patient's feeling of agitation and repetitious fixation. While Dieckmann does not use the term "reverie," his case description illustrates well the dyadic aspect of reverie.

Reverie has been addressed by several Jungian authors, including Mathew (2005), Bovensiepen (2002), and Cwik (2011) and Winborn (2014). In Cwik's work on reverie, he coins the term "associative dreaming" to refer to a broad continuum of "reverential-like" states that occur in the analytic setting. Reverie also features prominently in the work of Jungian analyst Nathan Schwartz-Salant, particularly in his understanding of the analyst–patient interaction. However, Schwartz-Salant has adopted his own terminology, such as "imaginal sight" (1989), "imaginal sight of the heart" (1991b), and "heart-center" (1998) to discuss the experience and manifestation of reverie in the interactions between the analyst and analysand.

A metaphor for reverie

The experience of watching a movie in a theater provides a metaphor for understanding reverie. Going to the theater is itself an experience of mild participation mystique. We walk in as strangers sitting side by side, mostly quietly, in the dark, waiting to be drawn into the same story or action. We are subtly different in the theater than we would be if we were watching at home – already shifting into a shared altered state of sorts. Once the movie begins, we often become oblivious to the passage of time or to the world existing outside the theater.

Now, imagine a theater that is somewhat different in configuration. It is a theater built for only two persons – an imaginal theater or theater of reverie (see Figure 8.1).

In this theater, the screen is not at the front of the room but, instead, it divides the room. Each half of the room has space for one person and a projector. The projectors are used to cast images onto each side of the screen. The screen itself is white, opaque or translucent. Images are projected onto both sides of the screen, but because it is also translucent, some of the light and form being projected from the other side will bleed through. Naturally, the light and images being projected from the other side of the screen will be discernible, but will be much less distinct than the images being projected from the same side as the viewer. Thus far, I have described a metaphor for the dyadic experience of reverie. If we expand the imaginal theater by adding a projector attached to the ceiling, which projects down onto the screen through the top, we have added the contribution of the analytic third, also referred to as the inter-subjective third. For Jungians, this influence can be referred to as the transcendent third, reflecting the archetypal influence of the objective psyche. The three sources of imagery all blend together as they are filtered through the translucent screen. However, the final imagery perceived will be different from each vantage point, even though the imagery originates from the same primary sources.

Reverie and neuroscience

It is likely that the capacity for reverie is correlated with the default mode network of the brain that has been identified in neuroscience. The default mode network is a network of brain regions that are active when the individual is not focused on

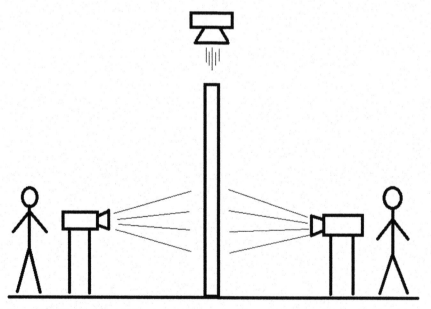

Figure 8.1 The theater of reverie

the outside world and the brain is at wakeful rest (Mars et al., 2012; Davey et al., 2016). During goal-oriented activity, the default mode network is deactivated and another network, the task-positive network, is activated. The default mode network is associated with task-independent introspection, or self-referential thought, while the task-positive network corresponds with taking action – whether physical, verbal, or cognitive. The full function of the default mode network remains unclear; however, activity in the default mode network negatively correlates with activity in regions involved in focused attention and executive function. Additionally, the default mode network has been hypothesized to be involved with generating spontaneous thoughts, associative linkages, creativity, and inferences about the mental states of others. Many of the characteristics associated with the activation of the default mode network are the same characteristics associated with states of reverie.

Multi-determinant nature of reverie

Freud (1900) asserts that dreams and symptoms are over-determined, that is, generated by and representing multiple unconscious sources. Like dreams, analytic reverie is also multi-determined; reflecting an amalgam of analytic ways of being and states that are typically discussed independently. The activity of reverie includes elements of Freud's (1912) "evenly suspended attention," and Heinz Kohut's (1959) "empathic attunement" via "vicarious introspection," as well as the previously discussed "container–contained" functions of Bion, and several Jungian concepts, that is, active imagination, participation mystique, and non-directed thinking. When reverie is possible for both analyst and patient, a "secured symbolizing field" (Goodheart, 1980) is created in which there is a potential for mutual exploration, speculative play, and symbolic transformation.

Several possibilities regarding the content of one's internal flow of reverie have been mentioned above. I also find it useful to think in terms of influences on the analyst's reverie. The categories I find generally useful include transference, countertransference, cognitions, images, somatic impressions, aesthetic responses, affective shifts, and archetypal patterns (see Figure 8.2).

Just as there are multiple contributors to reverie experiences, reverie can also be thought of as having multiple functions. One of the important functions of reverie, for both patient and analyst, is information-gathering. By opening to the flow of intrapsychic and intersubjective experience, reverie allows a shift from the more circumscribed perspective of the ego and facilitates the emergence of material that is unconscious or implicit.

In reverie states, there is often the felt experience of connection common to all participation mystique experiences. As Jung (1964) suggests, "Although the participation mystique is an unconscious fact to the person concerned, he nevertheless feels the change when it no longer exists" (para. 70). Reverie has the potential to deepen the sense of connection vital to any psychotherapeutic or analytic relationship.

The concept of reverie is directly tied to Bion's (1962) model of psychic functioning and introduces a metabolizing function to the analytic interaction. In this

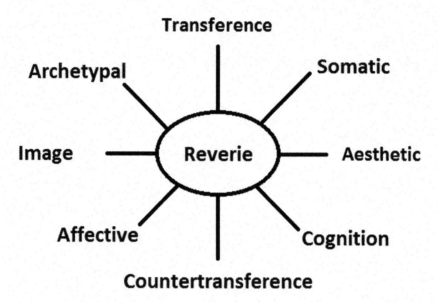

Figure 8.2 The components of reverie

function, the reverie of the analyst serves to digest the intolerable or unrepresented experiences of the patient and make them available for assimilation by the patient in a new experiential configuration. A similar process is proposed by Fordham (1976) in regard to the individuation process. In Fordham's model, potentialities of the infant are "deintegrated" from the developing self and matched with objects in the infant's outer world. If the fit between the "unpacked" potential and the outer world object is relatively good, that potential bit of self-experience is then available for "discovery" by the infant in the outer world and becomes available to be "reintegrated" as part of the developing self. Maternal reverie for the infant and analytic reverie for the patient are moments of meeting where the "fit" of this deintegrate–reintegrate process occurs.

Also relevant is the concept of mentalization as developed by Fonagy (Fonagy et al., 2002). Mentalization, also referred to as the reflective function, is a complex concept but one that centers on the capacity to consciously reflect on one's experience. Another way this is described is the capacity to think about (i.e., reflect on) one's experience. Jung (1960b, para. 246) identifies reflection as one of the five main instinctual drives, along with creativity, activity, sexuality, and hunger. Just as with Bion's model of container–contained, the capacity to mentalize begins with the infant's internalization of the mother's capacity to think about the experience of the infant and her own experience as a mother. Reverie functions in the same manner, with the patient developing or deepening their capacity for reverie through their explicit and implicit experience of the analyst's reverie. Wilkinson (2004), in reviewing research on neuroscience and subjective experience, concludes:

The developing emotional connectivity that occurs within the analytic dyad forms the essential psychic scaffolding that enables the complementary work, known traditionally as the talking cure. The vicissitudes of experience within the analytic dyad facilitate the development of self-regulatory capacity and the emergence of the reflective function.

(p. 98)

The somatic component of reverie

Because the communication of the body can only be partially mediated through language, it is a domain of analytic reverie that is easily overlooked or ignored. Christopher Bollas (1987) hypothesizes that the "unthought known"[4] of the patient is accessed as somatic knowledge and often registers in the body of the analyst if the analyst is attending at that level (p. 282). The importance of somatic influences is also registered by Jung. In "The psychology of the child archetype," Jung (1959b) writes:

> The symbols of the self arise in the depths of the body and they express its materiality every bit as much as the structure of the perceiving consciousness. The symbol is thus a living body. . . The more archaic and "deeper," that is the more *physiological*, the symbol is.

(para. 291)

Jung also makes a number of references in his writing to the "subtle body," a term he adopted from G. R. S. Mead (1919). The subtle body concept refers to "the somatic unconscious, a transcendental concept involving the relationship between mind and body" (Sharp, 1991, p. 129). The importance of discerning the activity of the somatic unconscious is emphasized by Jung (1988) in the following passage:

> The part of the unconscious which is designated as the subtle body becomes more and more identical with the functioning of the body, and therefore it grows darker and darker and ends in the utter darkness of matter; that aspect of the unconscious is exceedingly incomprehensible. . . One must include not only the shadow – the psychological unconscious – but also the physiological unconscious, that so-called somatic unconscious which is the subtle body. . . Somewhere our unconscious becomes material, because the body is the living unit, and our conscious and our unconscious are embedded in it: they contact the body. Somewhere there is a place where the two ends meet and become interlocked. And that is the place [i.e., subtle body] where one cannot say whether it is matter, or what one calls "psyche".

(p. 441)

While the somatic aspect of reverie is often subtle and easily overlooked, at times it can "speak" powerfully. With one patient, I periodically experienced a strong, irrepressible cold shiver, sometimes lasting most of the session. When this pattern initially began, I attempted to dismiss it as something other than the dynamics of the analytic setting. However, it was only with this patient that this somatic pattern infiltrated my reverie in such a unique, inescapable way, not unlike Grendel's howls before breaking into the mead hall in *Beowulf*. When I could no longer ignore "Grendel's call," I began to explore more closely my own actions, thoughts, and motives in the session. Eventually, I came to the awareness that the cold shiver consistently signaled my movement into a state of "complementary countertransference" (Racker, 1968) in which I was overly identified with and supportive of the patient's victim complex in a way that was not useful to the patient in furthering the analytic process. While this set of analytic encounters could have readily been considered solely through the concept of countertransference, I find that processing such encounters under the broad umbrella of reverie facilitates an integration of analytic experience rather than a discontinuous shifting back and forth between possible frameworks for evaluating experience.

The experience of reverie

The experience of reverie is unique to each individual and to each analytic dyad. However, I believe there are certain hallmarks of deeper reverie states. Most accounts (e.g., Frayn, 1987; Ogden, 1997; Bolognini, 2009) of reverie revolve around descriptors such as: timelessness, alterations of time (e.g., time moving faster or slower), dream-like qualities, a sense of insularity, suspension of concern with the world outside the consulting room, a sense of floating, or a sense of flow.[5] However, the entry into reverie is not like a light switch, to be turned on and off at will. It is a continuum of possible experiences, from fleeting impressions to deep states of immersion and connection. Reverie may also include states in which an absence of flow, discomfort, disconnection, or irritation dominates. Paradoxically, within reverie, such states can be viewed as a different kind of flow and as experiences that are still communicating valuable information.

Being in reverie typically includes a greater openness to metaphor. Speziale-Bagliacca (2008), Ogden (2001), and Siegelman (1990), among others, have highlighted the close relationship between metaphor and reverie. Two examples come to mind about the metaphorical qualities of reverie. In one session, I listened loosely to my patient describe an upcoming family event. She was anticipating potential problems and conflicts – wondering how she could mediate those tensions but also beginning to wonder if she should. In the background of my thoughts, I held an awareness of this patient's life-long preoccupation with responsibility; a stance adopted early on to ensure her sense of security in the face of limited external sources of security. This was an area we had examined many times in past sessions. An image emerged in my reverie of a sentry standing guard in a watchtower. I began thinking of a movie, *The Village* by M. Night Shyamalan, in which the residents of a quaint village stand watch vigilantly in towers around the edge of the village to guard against attack by monsters, which they have been falsely led to believe exist in the forest surrounding the village. I experienced a sense of deep weariness; the kind of fatigue associated with long-standing vigilance. I held the image and began to wonder what I could say to her about the image. Eventually, I felt it was possible to speak and said, "You've been standing guard in the sentry tower a long time. You survey the horizon for problems to mediate. It seems you've begun to wonder whether it's now safe enough to come down from the watchtower." The patient began sobbing and said, "I want to."

In another session, Bart, a patient with long-standing difficulties with anger and rage, was speaking of an interaction with his partner. Bart desperately wanted to be loved and accepted, yet he frequently found fault with his partner's behaviors, mannerisms, and attitudes. We had identified that Bart attacks his partner to minimize his own feelings of vulnerability, yet afterward his negative feelings about himself intensify. His partner had told him how painful it is to be criticized in this way and that he found Bart's anger intimidating. In the session being described, Bart was deliberating about going on a trip with his partner. He indicated that he was afraid he would feel controlled by his partner and that he would feel pressure to act in the "right way." I pointed to a similar pattern in his interactions with his mother. Bart agreed and indicated that it felt the same with his father. He also indicated that he was afraid of feeling overwhelmed by his feelings if he went to visit his elderly mother during the planned trip. As he was speaking, an image emerged in my reverie of a terrorist wearing a suicide vest. I began to identify imaginally with the fear and desperation of the terrorist as well as the fear of the terrorist's intended target. While the patient has not directed his anger at me, during early sessions I experienced some uneasiness as though such an explosion was possible. After listening a while longer, I said, "In the moment you are so fearful of being controlled by the expectations of others that you're willing to strap on a suicide vest and blow everyone up with your anger in order to avoid the feeling of vulnerability which that brings. Yet, the outcome is that you lose the sense of love and acceptance that you so deeply desire." The patient looked dumbstruck for a moment, but then said slowly, "You're right. . . I hadn't ever thought about it like that, but I do blow things up." Following the session, Bart went home and shared the image with his partner. While Bart still experiences anger at times, the frequency and intensity of his anger have diminished significantly, and he has become much better at modulating it.

In the case of reverie and interpretation, the analyst follows their interior flow of experience, seeing where it leads. At other times, the analyst selects a single experience from the flow and brings it into sharper focus. For example, in one session, I noticed my attention repeatedly drawn to my patient's car keys sitting on a table next to his chair. I began to wonder about my attentiveness to his keys. I wondered whether this might signal an urge for something to get "turned on" or "ignited" in the analysis. I wondered if the patient was somehow communicating to me a feeling of restlessness, or warning of his intention to leave. I wondered if there might be something within myself that was hoping the patient might make an early exit from the session that day. The willingness to let the image of the keys work within my reverie allowed engagement with processes operating outside the flow of the patient's verbalizations. Ellman (2010) provides a succinct summary of the reverie process in analytic sessions, "This state of reverie. . . allows the analyst to 'make a selection' from the material that is presented that arises not from his expectations, but organically, from out of seemingly unconnected elements in a session" (p. 534). Whether following a string of associations or focusing on a single image, I periodically reflect on several questions, "Where might this be taking me, the patient, or us?" or "What might this tell me about what is occurring with the patient, with me, or between the patient and me?"

To enter into reverie, the analyst must find a way to be present and elsewhere, whether simultaneously or alternately. This need reintroduces Sterba's (1934) concept of the analytic ego, first introduced in Chapter 5. It is a way of being with and containing the patient, but at the same time maintaining an internal space for experience and reflection independent of what the patient is communicating verbally and non-verbally. Otherwise, there is a tendency to become absorbed in the surface content of the patient's verbalizations and interactive cues; to focus too narrowly on the verbal content while neglecting the stream of reverie. To create a psychological space for fleeting impressions to coalesce during sessions, I utilize a notepad to track the analytic interaction as well as my reverie.

Some analysts are seemingly able to enter into reverie for extended periods of time, attending closely to their internal stream of experience while also remaining connected to what is transpiring in the session and with the patient.[6] Naturally, part of this is influenced by the individual tendencies of the analyst, those of the patient, and the setting or context of a particular session. While some patients are relatively adept at accessing their reverie regardless of the analytic conditions, for most patients the use of the analytic couch and increased frequency of sessions facilitates the entry into reverie.

As discussed earlier, several other important analytic qualities, such as empathy and intuition, play into an analyst's ability to utilize the reverie effectively. Certain issues can interfere with the analyst's reverie. For example, attending too closely to the patient, the felt need to track their verbalizations, or the pressure to respond to the patient's social cues can all interfere with the establishment of a reverie state. However, as Ogden (1997) points out, the biggest obstacle is often the analyst's suspicion of their own reverie process. Rather than seeing reverie as a rich source of material about the patient, themselves, and the intersubjective space, they often suspect that their emerging reverie is a result of their own preoccupations, which they assume are interfering with their ability to attend to the patient. The analyst may also interpret the presence of their reverie as evidence of their own narcissistic self-absorption, immaturity, inexperience, fatigue, inadequate training, or unresolved emotional conflicts.

Suspension and surrender in reverie

Both suspension and surrender are critical components of reverie experience. Suspension involves a setting aside of typical ego-oriented therapeutic activities:

for example, figuring out what's wrong, intentionally trying to create meaning, or attempting to categorize experience. Bion (1970) refers to this quality as the analyst's "negative capability." When not in reverie, there is a greater tendency to search for patterns in the patient's material that fit already known templates or models, whether expressed as a theory, a construct, or an archetypal amplification. While in reverie, the experience is one of impressions "occurring" or being presented for consideration, like stirring a stew pot and seeing what floats to the surface. The intentionality of searching for something is suspended.

Gordon (1985) specifically associates the capacity to set aside ego function with the ability to "surrender" to reverie. Bolognini (2009) indicates that an aptitude for suspension is a crucial characteristic for the analyst working in reverie:

> He suspends judgement, while waiting for new developments; he suspends his evaluation of the clinical work, and he may even suspend representational activity. . . in order to facilitate a more spontaneous and dynamic flow of associations after temporarily abstaining. . . Furthermore, the experienced analyst is ready to make mental room for the emergence of new configurations.
>
> (pp. 49–50)

The suspension discussed by Bolognini parallels the paradoxical Taoist concept of *wei wu wei*: "action without action" or "effortless doing."

Ghent (2001) says, "Surrender is an act of embracing the unknown" and that "surrender is not passivity; it is an active process" (pp. 31–32). Jungians primarily make reference to surrender in the context of the surrender of the ego to the Self, or more generally, surrender to the unconscious. An exception is Willeford (1975), who takes surrender fully into the relational sphere, "There must be an opening of oneself, a partial surrender of one's own subjective sphere to partial penetration by that of the other" (p. 32). Willeford's position is echoed by Khan (1983), who also associates surrender with relationship, "I feel that *relationship* implies some sort of surrender from both parties" (p. 120). Benjamin (2004) makes the distinction that surrender, in the analytic situation, is not the surrender of one person to another but rather the surrender of both patient and analyst to a mutually created thirdness. Knight (2007) indicates that surrender is often resisted by the analyst because of past conceptions of the appropriate analytic stance and because of fears around exposing their own primitive self.

Configurations of reverie

Reflecting its elusive character, reverie goes on, to some degree, all of the time in the background of our experience. However, we can loosely think of four potential configurations of reverie states: 1) when the analyst is in reverie but not the patient; 2) when the patient is in reverie but not the analyst; 3) when both the analyst and patient are in reverie together; or 4) when neither can enter reverie.

The patient's inability or difficulty entering into a reverie may be indicative of the patient's capacity to reflect or to engage with their imagination. Ogden (2003) reports that he sometimes experiences "reverie deprivation" when working with patients who are unable to dream,[7] in either a sleeping or waking state, or who actively preclude entry into reverie by being hyper-verbal yet unreflective. When both analyst and patient are able to enter reverie in the presence of each other, then conditions are available for "analytic contact" (Waska, 2007) to be made and for a "secured symbolizing field" (Goodheart, 1980) to be constellated between patient and analyst.

Capacity for reverie

In addition to being an important contributor to the interpretive process, the analyst's reverie introduces the potential for the patient to develop their own capacity to engage in reverie, which is often a fundamental shift in their relationship to their own interior processes. The patient who can be contained through reverie then has the possibility of acquiring the capacity to contain their own experience, which in turn is one of the developmental steps in acquiring a symbolic relationship with one's interior life and imagination.

Reverie is a capacity that can be developed, like mentalization or the acquisition of a symbolic attitude. Ferro (2006) places the development of the patient's capacity for reverie at the very center of the analytic process:

> The purpose of analysis is first and foremost to develop this capacity to weave images (which are not directly knowable). . . . This baseline activity of reverie is the engine of our mental life, and psychic health, illness, or suffering depend on its functionality or dysfunctionality.
>
> (p. 1053)

There is much experience that is not represented in the psyche (Botella & Botella, 2005) and therefore can only become a presence in the analytic encounter through reverie. Reverie sometimes allows these experiences to become represented in the psyche, not as an image, thought, or word, but as an "inchoate awareness of something having occurred" (Botella & Botella, 2005, p. xix).

The analyst's capacity for reverie and development of that capacity is also an important consideration. Ogden (1994) emphasizes the importance of "the analyst's capacity to recognize and make use of a form of intersubjective clinical fact manifested largely through bodily sensation/fantasy" (p. 84). Pelled (2007), drawing from the work of Bion and Buddhist philosophy, suggests that reverie is closely akin to meditation. She associates both meditation and reverie with the capacity to learn from experience.

The more the analyst is able to move to a place of reverie, the greater the possibility that the patient can join the analyst in a similar state. As one, or both, of the analytic participants increase their capacity for reverie, the potential for the emergence of transformative interpretive exchanges also increases. This involves an experience of "faith" in the sense that Bion uses the term, that is, not faith in a religious system but faith in an experience or process. In many instances, the patient first borrows the faith of the analyst before coming to have faith in their own unconscious processes. Often, this occurs first on an implicit level and only later becomes an explicit awareness leading to internalization of faith. For Bion (1970), the term denotes the mindset, or stance, of the analyst that allows an approach to the ineffable unknown mystery which he referred to as "O." According to Eigen (1981), "In Bion faith is linked with openness to O or the (unknowable) ultimate reality of a session and is the operative principle of the psychoanalytic attitude" (p. 432). Weir (1996) indicates:

> The hard part is having faith in the validity of thoughts and feelings that percolate up as if from nowhere. It is important to find ways of usefully using our subjective feelings, images, sensations, and states of mind for our work.
>
> (p. 331)

Weir's statement underscores the intimate link between reverie and interpretation. It is interpretation that allows the analyst's subjective and intersubjective experiences of reverie to be put to use in the service of the analysis.

Some patients are unable to engage in symbolization (Bovensiepen, 2002), utilize their imagination or fantasy (Plaut, 1966), or even dream (Ogden, 2003). Often, this is a result of past trauma, defenses against imagination or connection, deficits in the emotional responsiveness of their environment, or inhibition as a result of cultural conditioning. Plaut (1966) associates a disruption in trust with difficulties in being able to imagine, although a contemporary understanding of this issue suggests such a disruption is probably better understood as a difficulty in terms of attachment style (Osofsky, 1988). These limitations interfere with the capacity for reverie because reverie involves the use of the functions that have been disrupted. For these patients, the need for the analyst to be able to engage their own reverie in the absence of the patient's reverie becomes even more significant. As Giustino (2009) points out, the importance of reverie, as a process engaged in by the analyst, is crucial even with those patients who are able to dream:

> By contrast, the patients. . . who are far less severely traumatized, do dream – and often at a very early stage in their analysis but do not understand what they have dreamed. It is then the task of the analyst, who is capable of reverie, to try to restore their function of emotional comprehension, the lack of which prevents them from getting in touch with their internal world and understanding their dreams.
>
> (p. 1066)

Jung (1954b) speaks of a similar process when referring to the need of the patient to project the Self onto the analyst. Jung felt that the willingness of the analyst to carry the projection of the Self for a period of time was often essential, especially during the early phases of analysis.

Utilizing reverie

Naturally, the question eventually arises about what to do with the material emerging from the reverie. Reverie is a continuum of experience – a state we can attempt to enter into but which we may be unable to access depending upon our own psychological state and the state of the patient. Bolognini (2009) speaks clearly on this point: "The unconscious cannot be tamed on demand, and the preconscious is intolerant of too purposeful an attitude on the analyst's part" (p. 37).

Ogden (1997) provides some useful guidance about the use of material arising from reverie, which also has relevance to ideas around the issue of self-revelation in analysis:

> As is the case with other highly personal emotional experiences of the analyst, he does not often speak with the analysand directly about his experiences, but attempts to speak to the analysand from what he is thinking and feeling. That is, he attempts to inform what he says by his awareness of and groundedness in his emotional experience with the patient.
>
> (p. 158)

Civitarese (2015) adopts a similar position: "It is not a question of the analyst explaining the content of the reverie to the patient (except in exceptional cases) but of talking (or remaining silent) about the emotional experience it registers and relaunches at the same time" (p. 197). A clinical situation illustrating the perspective offered by Ogden and Civitarese began with a desert scene emerging in my mind. The scene seemed strongly connected with what the patient was speaking about. I could have simply shared the image and said, "As you're talking, I'm having a strong image come to mind of a desert." However, I felt this was not sufficiently metabolized. The image was still too closely connected to me, that is, the image as it entered my reverie. I needed to translate my image into words more closely associated with the patient's experience. Upon further reflection, I interpreted, "In what you're describing, I have a strong sense that everything feels rather dry to you, as though you're out in a desert with nothing to drink, and have no hope of quenching your thirst with anything around you."

Both Cooper (2008) and Ogden (1997) emphasize that many reverie experiences are not immediately translatable in a one-to-one fashion about what is happening in an analytic relationship. As with many aspects of analytic work, there are often many ways to do or think about any given situation. For example, Cwik (2011) has a somewhat different perspective regarding the use of reverie than Ogden. Ogden's position, outlined above, is primarily to use his reverie content to inform what he communicates interpretively to the patient – that is, speaking from the analyst's reverie. Cwik indicates that the assessment of whether to speak "from" or "about" reverie contents should be based predominantly on the developmental capabilities of the patient. Patients, particularly those who have impingement in their capacity to engage in reverie and to "dream,"[8] often find it emotionally overwhelming to hear directly what is going on within the analyst. Similar positions are articulated by Riesenberg-Malcolm (1995), who considers the patient's developmental state (i.e., paranoid-schizoid versus depressive position[9]) as it relates to the interpretive process; and Cooper (2008), who makes a distinction between "analyst disclosure" (p. 1052) in the service of the analysis and self-disclosure. For Cooper, analyst disclosure involves some sharing of the analyst's emotional response in reference to the countertransference but "not to provide gratuitous, exhibitionistic, or diversionary statements of personal feeling" (p. 1052), which he associates with self-disclosure. Cooper also introduces a post-reverie phase of reflection which he calls "ethical imagination" (p. 1050). In this phase, the analyst engages in an imagining of the potential usefulness or impact of a particular interpretation being considered following reverie. Like Cwik, Cooper, and Riesenberg-Malcolm, how I incorporate the content of my reverie depends on the psychological state of the patient, my own internal state, and the overall status of the analysis.

Summary

The concept of reverie serves as a useful container for a number of analytic processes previously considered in relative isolation. To summarize, reverie serves as a process for experiencing connection, gathering information, metabolizing of intolerable or unrepresented bits of experience, deepening interpretation, facilitating individuation, and increasing the capacity for reflection. While this list of functions is not exhaustive, it serves to underscore the significance of reverie as an analytic activity, particularly during the interpretive process.

Reverie states encountered in the analytic setting are clearly an example of participation mystique, but one in which the infection or contagion spoken of by Jung (1954b, para. 364–365) serves to deepen analytic experience, connection, understanding, and insight. Possessing elements of imagination, reflection, mutual influence, and receptivity to unconscious influences, reverie fits well within Analytical Psychology, even though the concept originated apart from Jung's conceptual framework. Looked at broadly, most of Jung's central concepts were acquired from a wide variety of sources: theology, anthropology, philosophy, religion, mythology, alchemy, physics, and biology. As Casement (2007) points out, Jung was a *bricoleur*, that is, one who assembles something useful from whatever materials are available: "borrowing a metaphorical screw from here, a figurative nut from there and, from elsewhere, an imaginative bolt. This 'bricolage' reflects Jung's view of the diversity and complexity of the psyche" (p. 97). Jung's example suggests that a willingness to incorporate ideas, concepts, and practices that fit within the overall ethos or attitude of the Jungian analytic project is essential.

To adopt reverie fully into the practice of Analytical Psychology is not solely an act of incorporation because Analytical Psychology also has something to add to the concept of reverie. Analytical Psychology, with its concept of the collective unconscious (whether considered from an *a priori* or emergent perspective), introduces a deeper, more complex understanding of the analytic third. Within Analytical Psychology, the analytic third is not just a mutual construction; it also includes something that transcends the personalistic contribution of the analytic dyad.

Reverie has become central to my interpretive technique and the analytic process as a whole. While not always able to "drop into" a reverie state during sessions, I am always attempting to move toward that state or trying to sense what is obstructing that movement. The presence, absence, or deepening of a capacity for reverie in my patients is also a central focus. Reverie is a move from *doing* to an experience of *engagement* and *being with*. Reverie has the potential to transform the session into a sanctuary of attentional flow, engagement, and embodiment.

Exercises for the reader

1) Begin by practicing reverie outside of sessions. At the end of your day, take a few moments before leaving the office. Lie down or sit comfortably with your eyes closed and permit sensations, thoughts, and feelings to float up about the sessions of the day.
2) During sessions, begin to "listen loosely," attending to the flow of the patient's narrative and paraverbal communication, while also attending to the flow of your internal experience with as little evaluation as possible.
3) During sessions, use a notepad to write down words or short phrases that capture the essence of experience arising from your reverie. Permit yourself to wonder how those experiences might be related to what is transpiring for the patient, or between you and the patient.
4) Begin to formulate interpretations informed by your internal reverie.

Notes

1 Portions of this chapter were also included in Winborn (2014), Chapter 3.
2 Bion's concept of the alpha function has strong similarities with Jung's concept of the transcendent function.
3 See Winborn (2014, Chapter 3) for a fuller discussion of reverie as an experience of participation mystique.
4 The "unthought known" is the term Bollas coined for the experiences of infants that are processed through actions rather than thoughts.
5 "Flow" is a term coined by psychologist Mihály Csíkszentmihályi to describe the experience of becoming fully immersed in an activity.
6 For extended examples of the use of reverie, see Ogden (1997, pp. 143–151 and 164–197).

7 Ogden has developed a broad definition of dreaming to include waking experiences as well as experiences while asleep. In Ogden's model, the analytic interaction is a form of dreaming in which dreams can be dreamt which the patient is unable to dream while asleep. He proposes that each analytic session should be viewed as a dream in which significant primary-process thinking is occurring. For a fuller exploration, see Ogden (2003, 2005, 2009).

8 Referring here to Ogden's concept of dreaming, which is the capacity to do psychological work with unconscious material – whether in a waking or sleeping state.

9 In Melanie Klein's model of psychic development, the paranoid-schizoid position refers to a less developed state in which part-object relationships dominate the patient's internal world and the intersubjective field. The depressive position refers to a state of increased development in which whole-object relationships are typical.

Chapter 9

Confrontation and interpretation[1]

Confrontation, both in attitude and action, is a central aspect of the interpretive process. While confrontation could have been included in Chapter 4 as one of the component attributes of the analytic attitude, or in Chapter 6 as a category of interpretation, it is of sufficient significance to be addressed separately. Confrontation typically involves engagement with the patient's defense processes deployed to protect the patient's ego or to maintain a particular configuration of activated complexes. Ferro and Civitarese (2015) highlight the central role of confrontation in the analytic process:

> Confrontation in general is directed to matters that are evident to both parties, such as ego dysfunctions, resistances, enactments, or breaches of the setting. If used correctly, it can facilitate integration in the patient, help him to control his impulses, overcome an impasse, tackle the onset of acute symptoms, and preserve the therapeutic alliance. In addition, by way of interpretation it prepares the patient to engage with deeper levels of unconscious life.
>
> (p. 97)

Confrontation also involves engagement of the patient's resistance to change and challenges the patient to experience herself in a new way. For some patients, this involves confrontation of the patient's difficulty in assimilating positive aspects of their emerging self.

Smith (2016) describes the role of confrontation in the analytic process even more broadly, "Contemporary analytic process can be seen as a series of confrontations between two people by virtue of the intrinsic differences between them" (p. 323). Smith's description can be considered the interpersonal equivalent of the intrapsychic confrontation described by Jung (1963), "*The experience of the self is always a defeat for the ego. . .* The ego enters into the picture only so far as it can offer resistance, defend itself, and in the event of defeat still affirm its existence" (para. 778, italics in original). Elsewhere, Jung (1967) indicates that confrontation is at the heart of overcoming dissociation within the psyche:

As I have said the confrontation with the unconscious usually begins in the realm of the personal unconscious, that is, of personally acquired contents which constitute the shadow, and from there leads to archetypal symbols which represent the collective unconscious. The aim of the confrontation is to abolish the dissociation.

(para. 481)

By confrontation, I refer to the need, at times, for the analyst to be persistent or even pressuring in the face of defenses, resistance, patterns of being, and attitudes that limit the patient's functioning and meaning in life. While confrontation often facilitates the development of psychological freedom, it also involves diminishing something the patient has relied on to cope with life or that has promoted survival. Auld and Hyman (1991) indicate that confrontation is the process of calling the patient's attention to a pattern that is not yet conscious. They point out that the act of focusing attention on these patterns can be experienced as threatening to the patient. Adler and Myerson (1991) indicate that confrontation refers to a forceful way to intervene as a means of uncovering hidden affects, denial, resistance, wishes, and fantasies. With experience comes the awareness that the analyst's development frequently includes ever greater capacity for navigating the patient's darker emotions and suffering. Over the years, I have developed a greater appreciation of the patient's defensive operations used to maintain psychic equilibrium, for the pervasiveness and complexity of defensive operations, and for the power of these defensive operations to interfere with efforts to stimulate growth and transformation.

The analyst's capacity for confrontation in the analytic process is analogous to the attitude medical professionals in hospital burn units must adopt during the process of debridement; the painful process of removing of the patient's dead, damaged, or infected tissue to facilitate the healing potential of the surrounding healthy tissue. Significant danger arises during the debridement process if the medical professional acts too conservatively, out of concern for creating too much pain for the patient, and fails to excise all of the dead tissue, resulting in a necrotic wound – that is, the death of living cells and healthy tissue.

Often, the confrontational activities of the analyst are experienced as a threat to the patient's ego or persona. Yet, as Redfearn (1982) points out, "caring by no means precludes ruthlessness, but rather demands it" (p. 234). The confrontational capacity of the analyst is cultivated out of compassion for the patient's suffering and their imprisonment by their current psychic reality, not out of the will to power or a desire to wound. This perspective has similarities with Bollas' (1992) observation that the patient's response to trauma often becomes aligned with the death instinct and that the activity of the analysis must be rooted in the life instinct. In such a context, confrontation is not intended to shame, embarrass, or belittle, even though a confrontational interpretation may sometimes evoke such reactions from the patient. It is an attitudinal perspective that goes beyond the concerns of the patient's ego perspective to the needs of the whole individual which, when utilized appropriately, is an attempt to work synergistically with the teleological thrust of the Self and in primary service to the analytic process. This chapter focuses on confrontation as a consciously held facet of the analytic attitude, used in the service of the analytic process, and carried out through interpretation.

Conceptual parallels of confrontation

Confrontation in analysis has parallels with discussions from other theoretical constructs, such as the conceptual overlap that exists between confrontation and "hate in the countertransference" as discussed by Winnicott (1949), Epstein (1977), Micati (1990), and Frederickson (1990). These analysts highlight the necessity of the analyst becoming aware of, metabolizing, and utilizing their experience of "hating" the patient in the service of the analysand's development and in facilitating the mutual capacity for empathy in both the analyst and analysand. They also emphasize the potential dangers that emerge when the analyst defends against or fails to acknowledge this hatred. Addressing another aspect of the analytic interaction, Wolf (1988) points out that certain patients need an "adversarial selfobject transference," which he describes as "the need to experience a supportive yet oppositional selfobject relationship, an ally-antagonist selfobject experience" (p. 126).

More directly related to the issue of confrontation, Hart (1999) speaks of the need to "reclaim the analyst's disruptive role in analysis," while Ogden (1997) highlights the necessarily disruptive impact of the analyst's use of language on the patient's conscious beliefs and narratives. Similarly, Kradin (2005) uses the term "analytic aggression" to describe the necessary activities of the analyst, often involving the interpretation of defenses and resistances, which have a propensity to evoke negative feelings in the patient.

Hate, disruption, and aggression all bear on the issue at hand. Hate speaks to the analyst's emotional reaction to the patient, aggression speaks to a quality of the analyst's actions toward the patient, and disruption speaks to the patient's reaction to the analyst's actions. Incorporating confrontation as a quality of the analytic attitude facilitates a willingness to acknowledge hate in the countertransference, to act in a therapeutically aggressive manner towards the patient, and to tolerate the patient's experience of disruption in the face of the analyst's interventions. Confrontation highlights an important aspect of the analytic attitude and is directly connected to the overarching work of the analytic endeavor.

Jung (1954b) addresses the importance of confrontation in the cultivation of consciousness, stating that analysis is, "a process that requires the patient to face his problems and that taxes his powers of conscious judgment and decision. It is nothing less than a direct challenge to his ethical sense, a call to arms that must be answered by the whole personality" (para. 315). Elsewhere, speaking of the experience of God, Jung (1958b) adopts a similar position: "It is far better to admit to the affect and submit to its violence than to try to escape it by all sorts of intellectual tricks or by emotional value-judgments" (para. 562). Clearly, Jung (1965) understood the importance of confrontation to the analytic process, having referred to his own descent experience during the years from 1913 through 1917 as his "confrontation with the unconscious" (pp. 170–199). Elsewhere, Jung (1983) quotes Jakob

Boehme: "Without opposition no thing can become apparent to itself; for if there is nothing in it which resists it, it goes forever outward and does not enter again into itself" (para. 202).

Archetypal aspects of confrontation

In Analytical Psychology, archetypal material is often interpreted from an intra-psychic perspective, for example, reflecting the dynamic relationship between the ego and the Self. However, as Jung (1954b) demonstrates in his analysis of the *Rosarium philosophorum*, archetypal themes can also be utilized to understand patterns in the analytic process, including certain attitudes necessary for engaging developments in the intersubjective field. Thus, the psyche interacts via a process of mythopoesis and the transformative aspect of confrontation is revealed in many archetypal narratives.

The Bible is replete with examples of confrontation in the service of transformation. Yahweh's engagement with Adam and Eve is inherently confrontational as he casts them out of the Garden of Eden for eating from the tree of the knowledge of good and evil (Holy Bible, Genesis, Chapter 3). Through the painful experience of being cast out of Eden, Adam and Eve are able to differentiate from the Godhead and initiate movement towards consciousness. Similarly, there is a ruthless confrontation between Jacob and an angel, wrestling throughout the night, and resulting in injury to Jacob's hip (Holy Bible, Genesis, Chapter 32). Jacob not only survives this struggle but is transformed by it – symbolized by the angel bestowing a new name upon Jacob, *Israel*, which means "the one who wrestles with God." In the conflict between Jacob and the angel, there is no victor – the emphasis is on the experience of the confrontation. Confrontation is also depicted in the willing sacrificial crucifixion of Yahweh's son, Jesus: a confrontation seen as the central transformative moment in the metamorphosis of Jesus into the figure of Christ (Holy Bible, Luke, Chapter 23).

In another example, the theme of confrontation invoked in the service of transformation is portrayed in the fairytale of *The Bewitched Princess* (von Franz, 1970). In this tale, a young man named Peter falls in love with a princess who has been bewitched by a mountain spirit. Peter's advisor is a ghost who provides Peter with an iron rod and instructs Peter to pummel the princess with the rod, causing her to flee to the arms of the mountain spirit. Peter follows her to the home of the mountain spirit and is provided with a sword. He utilizes the sword to cut off the head of the mountain spirit and throws it at the feet of the princess, releasing the princess from her enchantment. This tale provides a metaphorical template for the confrontation of defenses in analysis. Like the tale of *The Bewitched Princess*, the goal of interpreting the patient's defenses is not simply the confrontation of the defense but the revelation of the motivating factor that lies beneath the defense, that is, following the defense back to its source, just as Peter had to locate the home of the mountain spirit who had bewitched the princess. Many other examples exist in which the archetypal narrative calls for confrontation in the service of progression, adaptation, and transformation.

Ambivalence about confrontation

Confrontation is an aspect of analysis about which many therapists and analysts are uneasy. Perhaps this reflects a lack of knowledge and tools to draw upon when confronting patients. Perhaps there is not a sufficient psychological buffer separating the analytic use of confrontation from unrecognized sadistic impulses; a situation wherein the goal of confrontation becomes contaminated with the urge to inflict psychological pain. It is a difficult tension for the analyst to hold; feeling uncertain in the moment whether one's confrontational intervention is an abuse of the patient or an attitude adopted in the service of the analysis.

The struggles experienced around confrontation likely reflect the type of individuals often drawn to analytic work. McWilliams (2004) observes, "Most people who are attracted to being psychotherapists like closeness, dislike separation, fear rejection, and suffer guilt readily. They tend to put other people's needs before their own" (p. 105). Similarly, Maroda (2010) reflects:

> From my experience working with therapists, many suffer from being too passive, masochistic, and conflict avoidant. . . . therapists gravitate toward soothing and peacemaking behaviors . . . a wide variety of other attitudes and interventions are therapeutic yet may not be part of the repertoire that many therapists established in their childhood training as caretakers.
>
> (pp. 179–180)

Maroda goes on to say that therapists often fail to develop their capacity to engage with negative affects because their own analyses were frequently conducted by an analyst who also was not comfortable with conflict or confrontation. Levy (1990) and Kradin (2005) both observe that many therapists have conflicts around their own sadistic urges, fear of hurting patients with their words, and guilt around seeing and knowing too much about their patient which the patient considers taboo. Levy goes on to say that therapists often fall into patterns of pseudo-uncertainty; becoming overly speculative and/or tentative in their interpretations when these internal conflicts are prominent.

In addition to these characterological factors of self-selection, the fields of Analytical Psychology and psychoanalysis have been significantly influenced by a large shift in the gender composition of the analytic profession, the relational shift in contemporary psychoanalysis, post-modern philosophy, intersubjectivity, feminist theory, and infant observation research. All of these influences have resulted in a needed compensatory move away from the traditional view of the analyst as an objective, detached, cold, and authoritarian presence who rarely speaks. What has emerged is a field in which there is a greater appreciation of the mutuality of influence in analysis, a greater focus on the interactions of the mother–infant dyad for understanding analytic interactions, and a general questioning of the position of authority of the analyst in the analytic dyad.

However, the integration of these compensatory influences seems to have resulted in throwing the baby out with the bathwater. Hart (1999), Kradin (2005), Kernberg

(1996), Imber (2000), and Tuch (2001) all point to new imbalances that have emerged as the analytic community has sought to correct old patterns of one-sidedness. Hart (1999) warns, "The analyst who defensively identifies with the maternal role may turn the analytic relationship into a single-parent family where 'the father' (representing the capacity for analytic disruption) has been banished because he threatens the safety of the two" (p. 198). Bollas (1996) cautions that, unless the analyst finds a way to move between the maternal and paternal, our analytic theorizing and practice will be carried out in a matricidal or patricidal manner, resulting in an analysis that is conducted from the perspective of a single-parent family. The opposing parental principle is then dismembered by the principle being embraced in a one-sided manner. By striving to embody the mother, we slay the father; and in an attempt to embody the father, we slay the mother. Finding a combination of analytic values that derive from both the maternal and paternal positions allows the formation of an analytic syzygy (Jung, 1959a).

Confrontation and the tension of opposites

The preceding passage illustrates how intimately the issue of confrontation is connected to the Jungian concept of the tension of opposites. As Jung (1953a) states, "all energy can proceed only from the tension of opposites" (para. 34), and elsewhere he observes (1960b), "The confrontation of the two positions generates. . . a living, third thing. . . a movement out of the suspension between opposites . . . The transcendent function manifests itself as a quality of conjoined opposites" (para. 189). The analyst working with the tension of opposites considers what is missing, what is out of balance, or what has yet to be developed. From a Jungian perspective, there is an emergent tension of opposites discovered in the patient's material as well as a tension of opposites embodied in the analytic activities and attitudes of the therapist.

At times, analytic activity can become stuck in a one-sided approach to analytic interactions – that of passivity, receptivity, holding, and containing; activities associated with Eros or the maternal function of the analyst. Fordham (1979) warns against the tendency to fall into such one-sided analytic functioning: "If an analyst believes that being loving, tolerant, kind, understanding, and long-suffering is enough for the relationship he is mistaken" (p. 637). Melanie Klein (1950) adopts a similar position:

> Idealization is used as a defense against persecutory anxiety and is its corollary. If the analyst allows excessive idealization to persist – that is to say, if he relies mostly on the positive transference – he may, it is sure, bring about some improvement . . . . It is only by analyzing the negative as well as the positive transference that anxiety is reduced at the root.
>
> (p. 80)

Well-intentioned and necessary efforts to be kind, understanding, empathic, warm, and supportive sometimes hinder actions that sustain the tension of opposites inherent in analytic process, that is, the balance between passivity, receptivity, holding and containing, and the equally needed activities of conscious discrimination, differentiation, action, and penetration (activities largely mediated through the interpretive process). In this vein, we could also include the balance between hardness and softness, knowing and not knowing, questioning and interpreting, and masculine and feminine.

Seinfeld (1993) describes the reciprocal processes of interpretation and holding as the paternal and maternal functions of the psychotherapist. Seinfeld sees the paternal functions as originating with Freud's model of analytic activity and associates the maternal mode of engagement as emerging from Winnicott's modifications to the psychoanalytic model. In like fashion, Josephs (1995) speaks of balancing empathy and interpretation, wherein the analyst pursues parallel analytic paths of understanding from both objective and subjective positions.

Kradin (2005) points out that "empathy is a cardinal feature of Eros. But it should be recognized that empathy is invariably ego-syntonic, so that critical unconscious factors operating beyond consciousness cannot be directly accessed via this approach" (p. 431). Kradin goes on to say:

> Although consciously repelled, the hard-minded and tender-minded approaches are unconsciously attracted and depend upon each other. The Greeks resolved this problem by imagining the offspring of Love and War as Harmony . . . Empathy and interpretation, love and aggression, all contribute to the fullness of experience. Only by carefully and appropriately balancing empathy with analytic aggression, without overtly or subtly valuing one over the other, can the tension engendered by their aims be appreciated as complementary in the service of promoting psychological freedom.
>
> (p. 447)

Confrontation and analytic roles

In the analytic relationship, there is an implicit contract to assist our patients in cultivating the fullest relationship with their psyches despite the pain, discomfort, and dis-ease that may be created in the process. The analyst's capacity to confront is a part of this implicit contract. When the analytic moment requires confrontation and there is a failure to confront, the analyst has neglected an inherent responsibility of the analyst's role. The patient needs to be able to trust that the analyst is able to interact with them in whatever manner serves their transformation, even if it is painful or uncomfortable for both analyst and patient. Fordham (1974b) speaks of this necessity when he writes:

> Nor is it desirable to become excessively passive or guilty at the amount of pain, terror and dread that the patient asserts the analyst causes . . . It is important also to recognize a feature of the pain: it is a sign that the patient is struggling and of his will to live. It is even secretly valued by the patient as such, so it is mistaken to try and take it away from him.
>
> (pp. 195–197)

Or, as Jung (1954a) succinctly states, "There is no birth of consciousness without pain" (para. 331).

The capacity to utilize confrontation generatively involves a degree of trust or therapeutic alliance which permits both the patient and the analyst to move into new configurations of their role relationships (Hart, 1999; Kradin, 2005). Optimally, these new configurations will result in a realignment (i.e., an experience of emergence or transcendence) of previous habitual relationship patterns (Stern et al., 1998) and the development of patterns better suited to progressive movement in the analysis; however, the patient's comfort will often be challenged in this process.

As pointed out earlier, the analytic profession has undergone a significant paradigm shift in regard to the analytic dyad, particularly in attitudes about objectivity, authority, power, influence, and knowledge. These developments have caused those in the analytic community to re-examine their perspectives on analytic authority and the potential difficulties associated with authority: a re-examination that is needed on an ongoing basis.

To begin, there is the issue as to what analytic authority is, how we hold it, and whether it can be abused. Kernberg (1996) draws a distinction between authority and authoritarianism. He indicates that authority refers to the functional exercise of power in a social setting to carry out necessary tasks. Kernberg terms this functional authority. In contrast, he describes authoritarianism as the illegitimate use of power beyond what is required for the sanctioned task. Friedman (1996) distinguishes between authority as rightness and authority as influence. He goes on to state that authority as influence is an inevitable and unavoidable part of any analytic relationship. This is similar to the position taken by Imber (2000), who says, "No matter how much mutuality and democracy have replaced authoritarianism in the consulting room, the analyst is still the professional and the patient is still the one who comes seeking help" (p. 623); a position also advanced by Fordham (1979). Imber (2000) points out that every analyst, even those attempting to relinquish their position of authority and create a feeling of mutuality, are still making an authoritative decision about what they believe is best for the patient. Sandler and Dreher (1996) make the case that every analyst acquires, through their training and experiences, a set of implicit and explicit ideas about the nature of therapeutic change. They go on to argue that no analyst, regardless of the analyst's desire or intent, is capable of "turning off" that knowledge base which forms the foundation of their functional authority in the analytic dyad.

The idea of analytic authority can bring to mind images of the stereotypical psychoanalyst of the past; the psychoanalyst who remains cold and unrevealing of his inner emotions, responding only through experience-distant, meta-psychological interpretations delivered from a hierarchical position of objective knowledge gleaned from theory. Confrontation in analysis certainly has the shadowy potential to reinforce the hierarchical relationship inherent in the analytic setting (Guggenbuel-Craig, 1971). However, another danger, as Tuch (2001) points out, is that, "discounting the analyst's authoritative knowledge about the patient threatens to rob the analyst of the leverage needed to facilitate change" (p. 495).

During supervision sessions, I have frequently observed a tendency for supervisees to become caught up asking their patients a long series of questions which do not appear to facilitate the emergence of meaning or deepen experience. When these instances occur, I often interrupt the supervisee to ask them what they know about the patient, or the interaction, at that specific moment of the session. The supervisee often articulates something particularly insightful or useful. When I ask why they did not share their observation with the patient through an interpretation, the supervisee will often respond, "I didn't know I knew that until you asked me," or "I've been told not to say things directly like that – that it is always better to ask a question." Such responses reflect the difficulty involved with the incorporation and utilization of functional authority as part of one's analytic attitude. The comments of my supervisees also underscore how the assimilation of functional authority and interpretive competency can be inadvertently discouraged in the analytic training process. There are many times throughout an analysis in which it is important to remain in a position of unknowing, to leave space for the teleological actions of the Self, and to remain in a receptive position to what is emerging in the analysis. However, there are also frequent occasions when the therapist has an intuition or hypothesis about what is happening with the patient but fails to make an interpretation because of a lack of well-integrated analytic authority.

Those who are critical of analytic authority often point to the use of interpretation as a process for the analyst to impose their views on the patient. Certainly, there are analysts who experience a narcissistic need to have their interpretations validated by the patient, resulting in authoritarian maneuvers to ensure that the analyst's views are accepted and the analyst's ego ideal is protected. However, critics of interpretation often presume that the analyst is delivering the interpretation in an overbearing manner in an attempt to force the patient to accept the analyst's "objective truth," or that objectivity is the only basis by which an interpretation can be formulated.

More often, in our current state of analytic understanding, interpretations are framed from within the patient's subjectivity (Atwood & Stolorow, 1993), not from the stance of a detached, objective observer. Or, as Giordanelli (1990) suggests, interpretation provides a structuring function, emerging from and operating within a shared relational field:

> the analyst does not present the patient with appropriate interpretation at the appropriate moment; rather, interpretation is jointly conceived and perceived as the meaning of salient material. The skill of the analyst lies essentially in his ability, which is greater than the patient's, to gather the import of both parties unconscious.
>
> (p. 6)

The inherent tension between subjectivity versus objectivity is what Spence (1982) refers to as "narrative truth" versus "historical truth," with an understanding that any interpretation is offered as a hypothesis about the patient's narrative truth and how that truth appears to influence the patient's sense of self and functioning in life. As Kernberg (1996) points out, the "psychoanalysts' legitimate authority does not imply that they understand all the time what is going on, or that in their understanding and interventions, they are always doing 'the right thing'" (p. 150).

When used appropriately, an interpretation is a means of accessing and engaging an area of psychic experience that might otherwise remain split off and unavailable for transformation. Owning our analytic authority enables us to know what we can know in the moment; not holding it as absolute truth, but rather holding it as an ever-evolving experiential truth. Analytic authority involves saying what needs to be said based on the moment we are embedded within.

As a field, analytic therapy is in danger of diminishing a useful and necessary aspect of the analytic process because of well-intentioned efforts to increase the symmetry or equality of the analytic relationship. This shift has resulted in a gradual erosion of analytic authority, making that quality less available for use by the analysand. Rather than creating artificial bulwarks intended to eliminate authoritarianism, analysts benefit from recognizing the functional authority of their role so that it can be utilized for the benefit of the analysis. It requires courage on the part of the analyst to integrate analytic authority in a way that includes a willingness to risk temporary wounding of the patient as part of the process of healing. To paraphrase the inscription over the entry to Jung's home, "Invited or uninvited, authority will be present."[2] The issue of analytic authority will be present whether we have identified with it, whether it emerges out of the asymmetrical intersubjective matrix, whether it is projected onto us by the unmet needs and wishes of our patients, or whether it is conferred upon us by our training institutions and culture.

The language of confrontation

Confrontation is widely undervalued within the analytic community, often not perceived as an attribute requiring cultivation in the same way other analytic attributes are cultivated – such as the symbolic attitude. We need only examine the conceptual language of analytic theory to observe the positive connotations associated with certain aspects of the therapeutic relationship: containment, holding, receptivity, maternal presence, Eros, *coniunctio*, therapeutic alliance, transference love, rapport, and good-enough mothering.

In contrast to the richness of the language around more comfortable aspects of the analytic relationship, there is a limited vocabulary around more confrontational aspects of the analytic relationship. The language of confrontation is sometimes used in describing the patient's orientation towards the analyst, particularly in the case of patients diagnosed with borderline personality disorder and other patients who are significantly regressed. But there is a poverty of language to describe confrontational aspects of the analyst's attitudes and actions with the patient. Ogden (1997) points out the importance of the disruptive aspects of the analyst's language to the analytic process:

The analyst relies on language to upset (unsettle, decenter, disturb, perturb) the given – the given of the patient's conscious beliefs and narratives by which he creates illusions of permanence, certainty, and fixity of the experience of self and of the people who occupy his internal and external worlds. A central part of "the given" that is disturbed by language is the given of the patient's and the analyst's understanding of what is "going on" in the analytic relationship . . . Language is at its most powerful when it disturbs, not by arriving at insights/understandings, but by creating possibilities.

(pp. 218–219)

Hart (1999) indicates that the very act of languaging experience in analysis is necessarily violating:

In a sense, putting the unformulated into words through interpretation amounts to a violation. . . As the analyst introduces language for experiences, the analyst intrudes on the analysand's private safety. Now experience that had been left disconnected is potentially connectable. Dreaded experience is no longer nameless, no longer isolated, no longer easily forgotten. . . The analyst violates with inquiring.

(p. 192)

Confrontation of defenses and resistance

As Lambert (1981), Van Eenwyk (1991), and Kalsched (2010), among others, have pointed out, there is a significant lack of emphasis on the analysis of defense and resistance in Analytical Psychology. The essential presence of a safe, containing *temenos* is certainly an essential condition for the analytic process, but it is rarely sufficient to allow the emergence of experiences that are actively defended against. It is primarily in the confrontation of the patient's defenses and their resistance to analysis where confrontation is of the greatest necessity. However, the analyst's concern about the patient's ego response often interferes with the analyst's use of confrontation.

Frequently, the patient's defensive processes must be actively engaged. For example, Kalsched (1996) and Waska (2006) indicate that certain patients unconsciously experience the possibility of change as a new trauma and organize their defenses around blocking out the experience of the analyst as a good object – hence the analyst's efforts to be warm and receptive are experienced as a threat to the patient's psychic situation. Fordham (1974b) refers to this pattern as a "defence of the self." In a similar vein, Bunster (1993) highlights the need for flexibility in treating "the difficult to reach patient" and speaks to the necessity of moving between a holding/containing position and consistent interpretation.

Often, the interpretive confrontation of defenses or resistance occurs over longer periods of time than with other forms of interpretation. The interpretive illustrations provided thus far have largely focused on interpretations offered during single sessions. With patients who are strongly defended, it is often necessary to patiently sustain interpretive threads over long periods of time. The need for interpretive sequences maintained over time is in keeping with Jung's (1960a) statements about the "chronic effect of complexes" which can have a "continuously active feeling tone" over a number of years or even a lifetime (para. 88–91).

With one patient, Jamie, it has been necessary to consistently confront magical thinking around her connection to her ex-husband, from whom she had been divorced for more than a decade. The confrontational process began even before her divorce, confronting her fantasy that her husband desired a relationship with her despite all of the indications to the contrary. The process has continued over a decade; for example, regularly confronting her fantasy that her husband is coming back or that they would be reunited even after he had already remarried. This fantasy has remained subtly fixed in her psyche in a variety of ways that has limited her capacity to advocate for her needs during the divorce, create a new center of identity, or respond adaptively to her post-divorce life.

Part of her resistance to change involving the internal image of her husband is an avoidance of her grief over the loss of the marriage and her sense of identity as his wife. The fantasy interferes with other psychological changes; working to keep her from investing in her present life or forming an identity that can function independently of her attachment to her ex-husband. Often, my confrontation is rather simple, such as saying, "But he isn't here to participate in the scene you are describing." At other times, there is a fuller interpretive process linking her avoidance of grief with her unconscious fear of embracing an identity that is not connected to being the wife of her husband. The ongoing interpretive confrontation of the fantasy has resulted in a weakening of the dream lover attachment she created around the internal imago of her ex-husband. As a result, Jamie has begun a hard-won but tangible investment in an independent identity and life during the last few years. Additionally, her capacity to grieve her loss in a more embodied manner has begun to emerge.

A second illustration can be conceptualized as a confrontation of the patient's resistance to the transference. This case involves another patient with a significant history of childhood trauma. The patient, Nina, experienced a positive transference with me, but also continuously defended against her experience of a positive transference. She also defended against any deepening of the analysis, any sense of emotional closeness, or any emotional experience which caused her to feel weak and vulnerable. She would respond to any emerging feelings of dependence (and a corresponding fear of rejection) by telling me, "You can stop seeing me if you want to. I'll be okay," or "We don't need to meet next week if you don't want to." She was caught between her desire to form connection, thus breaking her sense of isolation, and her fear that making her need known to herself and to me would expose her to unmanageable feelings of vulnerability and dependence. Waska (2006) evocatively describes this emotional bind as "I hear you knocking but you can't come in" (p. 3). These defensive processes were so prevalent and persistent for Nina that the analytic process would have been severely attenuated if I had not consistently confronted her defenses. In crafting the interpretations offered to Nina, I attempted to capture both sides of her emotional dilemma, as well as articulating the likely outcome if she remained caught in that dilemma, for example, "You've come to feel that the only way to experience a sense of safety in relationships is to maintain a buffer of emotional distance. You also seem to believe that hiding all of your good feelings about me and our work together is necessary to avoid feeling vulnerable in our relationship. However, that effort to remain safe also keeps you feeling alone in the world and having to rely completely on your own fragile self-sufficiency." While my interpretation of her defense processes often made her uncomfortable, she was eventually able to recognize and tolerate my presence as a "good object." Over time, Nina came to hear my repeated interpretation of her defenses as, "I'm knocking at your door. In order to change, you'll have to let me through the door and break the isolation that you've imposed in order to stay safe." She also came to recognize that keeping me at a distance did not allow her to address the deeper, painful emotions that have maintained her self-rejection and created obstacles to relational connection.

Confrontation and curative factors

Much of the curative factor associated with confrontation can be attributed to the uncovering and engagement of various split-off, hidden, dissociated, or repressed psychic contents; allowing them to become more available for conscious reflection and assimilation. However, this influence can be identified as a curative or transformative aspect of many analytic actions. Two factors associated more exclusively with confrontation are the centrality of rupture in the healing process and the application of the *law of similars*.

Rupture and healing

Analytic literature and training often focus on the importance of creating and maintaining a positive therapeutic alliance, but there is comparatively little discussion of the progressive aspects of disruption and rupture in analysis. Self psychology recognizes the potential therapeutic benefit of analytic rupture in the concepts of optimal frustration[3] and optimal failure.[4] Optimal frustration and optimal failure are experienced by the patient as disruptions in the therapeutic relationship (Kohut, 1984). Self psychologists propose that progressive intrapsychic structuralization is occurring through experiences of rupture and subsequent reparative interaction (Lee & Martin, 1991). In fact, Kohut (1971) indicates that the greatest potential for intrapsychic structuralization occurs in these moments of rupture and restoration, which he termed "transmuting internalization."

More recently, the Boston Change Process Study Group (Stern et al., 1998) has proposed that "disjoining" experiences and "missed now moments" form a cyclical process in any functional transformative relationship. When these disruptive moments are recognized, acknowledged, and repaired through the interactions of the analytic dyad, they ultimately contribute to the development of new capacities, intrapsychic structures, and interpersonal patterns. Similarly, infant observation researchers have also documented the developmental progression when ruptures are successfully navigated and repaired in caregiver–infant dyads (Tronick, 1998). Summarizing the creative aspects of rupture in the analytic container, Hart (1999) proposes, "The analyst must attempt to hold . . . the sense that *analytic disruption is the basis for analytic creation*. . . . Disruption is present in all instances of analytic work that feel alive, emergent, in motion" (pp. 205–206, italics in original).

The following case provides an example of this sequence of rupture, repair, and structuralization mediated through interpretation. Jessica, who was being seen twice weekly, was discussing the various things she does to maintain a sense of security. As we spoke, she began to feel I did not understand how difficult it is for her to change these patterns and to experience a sense of pressure from me to change the patterns she utilizes for security: an empathic break had occurred. Jessica expressed her anger towards me for not understanding how difficult it was for her. Then she began to feel frightened and indicated this to me. I interpreted, "It seems like you feel I'll become angry at you for being angry at me and that I'll attempt to punish you for being angry with me for not understanding you." She agreed and near the end of the session she requested my reassurance that I was not angry with her. I inquired whether she had a sense that I was angry at her. She said, "No, but I'm afraid you still might be." I replied, "It seems difficult to trust your own perceptions about whether I'm angry or not. Perhaps it would be better if you remain aware of this fear and wait to see what happens on Friday so that you can discover whether your perception of me is accurate or not." On Friday, she returned and indicated she stayed frightened for a day or two but that the feeling passed. Later in the session, she began to talk about a feeling that people were looking at her and talking about her, but she also expressed the feeling that I seemed to understand her again. I replied, "It was important for you that I seemed to understand you today. It was frightening for you on Tuesday when you felt that I didn't understand. Often, it feels as though I'm the only one who understands you, and when you feel I don't understand it feels like something necessary for your sense of security has been lost." After this exchange, she began to tell me about altering one of the security rituals she engaged in. Her willingness and capacity to alter one of her security rituals and to share that information with me was an indication that empathic connection had been restored. This shift also suggested that a transmuting internalization had occurred, permitting her to take greater emotional risks and maintain fewer restrictive internal controls.

In another example, Samantha actively disagreed with many of my interpretations. When she entered analysis, Samantha was monetarily supported by her father, for whom she carried significant fears of disappointing or engendering his disapproval. Because of the consistency of Samantha's objections to my interpretations during the early phases of the analysis, I questioned my understanding of Samantha and her inner world. Over time, I developed the sense that her disagreement with my interpretations was part of her process of differentiation, that is, beginning to develop an experience of herself through opposition. Through her disagreement with my interpretations, she began to develop an experience of herself; an experience she could sense through her acts of opposition. My willingness to tolerate her disagreement with my interpretations and remain engaged facilitated an "optimal failure" situation for Samantha. Through the transference, I became the father that she could disagree with without fear of retaliation, thus allowing her ego to develop and create a sense of efficacy.

The law of similars

In addition to the centrality of rupture for growth, the healing potential associated with the adoption of confrontation is also reflected in the *law of similars,*[5] which states "let like be cured by like" (*similia similibus curentur*). Jung (1960b, para. 488) proposes that the law of similars is often reflected in dream processes, while Schwartz-Salant (1991b) has advocated "leaning into the pathology" – an activity of the analyst that can be seen as a behavioral application of the law of similars. An analogous idea is also observed in the alchemical Axiom of Ostanes: "A nature is delighted by another nature, a nature conquers another nature, a nature dominates another nature." As Kalsched (1996, 2010) points out, the inner world of the patient can be ruthless in response to the analyst's efforts to connect and facilitate healing in the patient. Clinical experience and the archetypal patterns of the objective psyche provide support for the idea that there are times when confrontation is necessary in order to navigate the barriers erected to protect the inner world of the patient and to maintain psychic homeostasis.

Summary

In the effort to embrace the essential, and previously under-appreciated, maternal functions of the analytic relationship, an *enantiodromia* has emerged; one in which the analytic culture has swung too far toward the other extreme. Poland (2008) asserts, "In agreeing to work psychoanalytically with someone, the analyst commits himself or herself to stay with that work with whatever ruthless honesty he or she can command" (p. 557). By making room for confrontation in our repertoire of analytic behaviors, we initiate a movement towards a new position in which both sides of the maternal–paternal continuum can be embraced, appreciated, and utilized; a center from which acting in the service of the analysis is the greater goal. Ghent (1989) captures this position in a simple metaphorical image, "My own view is that there is more than one way to help a flower grow. Sometimes selectively nourishing or watering it is what is required; sometimes clearing some weeds will be helpful" (p. 196). Finding a balance between the maternal and paternal aspects of analytic activity is a characteristic that differentiates a process that is analytic from one that is merely therapeutic. In order to embrace confrontation as part of the analytic attitude, there is an ongoing need to challenge comfortable roles, patterns, and ideas. Each confrontation with a patient is also a confrontation of our own anxiety; our own fear of becoming a source of our patient's wounding. In this regard, it is essential to hold in mind that we are, first and foremost, servants of the analytic process.

Exercises for the reader

1) Inventory your personal history and relationship with confrontation. Try to identify the reservations you carry regarding confrontation.
2) Think back through your previous patients. Try to identify patients whose analytic process would have benefited from a greater degree of confrontation.
3) Identify the reason(s) why confrontation was avoided with those patients. Consider what it was about the patient, the therapist, or the analytic couple that inhibited confrontation.
4) Mentally review the sessions of the past week with your current patients. Attempt to identify specific moments that would have been well served by confrontation. Select at least one of the moments and write out an imagined analytic dialogue in which an interpretive confrontation is made. Include the feeling response you imagine from your patient as well as your own feelings.

Notes

1 This chapter is based on a paper, "The fate of ruthlessness in analysis," presented March 14, 2011, at the Spring Meeting of the Inter-Regional Society of Jungian Analysts in Boulder, Colorado.
2 The actual inscription (*Vocatus atque non vocatus, Deus aderit*) translates "Invited or uninvited, God will be present."
3 Optimal frustration refers to the analyst's inability to meet all of the patient's needs and expectations while meeting the patient's frustrated response with acceptance and understanding. When the level of frustration is tolerable to the patient and the analyst's efforts to address the patient's frustration are adequate, increased cohesion and structuralization of the patient's psyche occurs through internalization and introjection.
4 Optimal failure refers to the unavoidable but temporary instances when the analyst fails to understand, empathize with, or interpret the patient's current psychological situation. Kohut often referred to these failures as "empathic breaks." When the analyst's failures are tolerable to the patient and the analyst's efforts to respond to the failure are adequate, increased structuralization and cohesion of the patient's psyche occurs through internalization and introjection.
5 Proposed by Samuel Hahnemann, the founder of homeopathy.

Chapter 10

Fluidity and consolidation

This last chapter addresses two themes: fluidity and consolidation. Fluidity refers to the capacity to move in and out of the interpretive process with dexterity, finesse, and spontaneity. Consolidation addresses the various skills and focal areas of the interpretive process as yet unaddressed in this volume.

Fluidity

Developing fluidity with interpretation requires the analyst to sufficiently internalize the process so that interpretations can be offered in the flow of the analytic moment without sounding contrived, distant, mechanical, or overly intellectualized. In addition to the technical skills of interpretation, fluidity also involves the capacity to recognize and link together elements of the analytic experience while also participating in the moment. Therefore, fluidity involves the capacity to recognize meaningful patterns in the patient's affective, somatic, verbal, and behavioral presence as well as in their life narrative and in the transference–countertransference matrix. Noticing these patterns often involves recognizing the action of metaphor and symbol.

Much like the practice habits of the poets, painters, and jazz musicians alluded to in the Introduction, the integration of the interpretive model outlined in this volume will be facilitated by time spent working with interpretation outside the analytic session. Dancers, musicians, and actors all recognize the need for hours of practice prior to performing. They spend years mastering the fundamentals of their art forms in order to be able to present their art at a consistently high level on the day of the performance. In order for their performance to be fluid and natural, rather than stiff and awkward, those fundamentals must be so fully integrated that they operate outside of conscious awareness, enabling the artist to concentrate on the artistic elements of the performance rather than the mechanical or technical aspects of the art form. For the jazz musician, this involves learning music theory, such as scales, chords, and modes, as well as developing physical proficiency with their instrument and the repertoire of "jazz standards." Proficiency in these areas is necessary before the jazz musician can improvise fluidly; creating spontaneous, original musical interactions with other musicians in the midst of a musical performance. As the great jazz saxophonist Charlie Parker said, "Master your instrument, master the music, and then forget all that [stuff] and just play."

The role of the analytic therapist is much like the role of the improvising jazz musician. As with the jazz musician, the analyst does not "perform" alone; there is always an interactive-improvisational partner, the patient. The various technical elements of interpretation are outlined in this volume, but to develop proficiency those elements must be cultivated, both in session and out of session. Art Tatum, a giant of jazz piano, emphasized that even improvisation must be practiced, "You have to practice improvisation, let no one kid you about it!"

Advice for learning to interpret fluidly

- Practice for the interpreting analyst involves working with verbatim transcripts of sessions. I suggest working with audio recordings of sessions[1] or detailed process notes taken during the session and fleshed out immediately after the session. Record and transcribe, word for word, as many sessions as possible with your patients. Naturally, the patient's permission must be obtained prior to recording. During the transcription process, include notes regarding your countertransference reactions and reverie. It is time-consuming and humbling work to transcribe yourself engaging in analytic therapy, but the reward is rich. There are many nuances of the analytic interaction picked up in recordings that are easily overlooked or forgotten when attempting to reconstruct a session from memory or when writing a case summary.

- After transcribing a session, identify patterns that were overlooked, the places where opportunities to interpret were missed, and where interpretations were offered but fell flat, missed the mark, or were awkwardly phrased. Spend time writing out possible interpretations for those openings missed and alternative interpretations for the awkward interventions. Over time, it becomes easier to see these openings as they arise in the session.

- Make a practice of supervision, peer supervision, and self-supervision with transcripts of recorded sessions. Locate supervisors who are experienced in working with verbatim transcripts. Supervisors who are more comfortable supervising from summarized material are often uncomfortable with the close attention to the nuance and detail of the analytic interaction that verbatim transcripts permit. Recruit peer colleagues who are also interested in working with verbatim patient material. Hearing how colleagues construct interpretations and other interventions also provides new insight into working interpretively.

- As author Henry Miller points out in *The Books in My Life* (1969), every good writer is first an accomplished reader: reading great writers encourages greater depth of writing. Therefore, in addition to transcripts from your sessions or the sessions of colleagues, there are also excellent resources for verbatim material in the analytic literature, although there are few verbatim transcriptions available in the Jungian literature in comparison to the psychoanalytic literature. Read as many verbatim transcripts of actual sessions as you can, from any school of psychoanalytic thought. When reading published transcripts, experiment with covering over the analyst's interventions and formulate your own interpretation before reading the analyst's intervention. In the psychoanalytic literature, most articles with the phrase "case study" or "case presentation" in the title will include verbatim material. The *International Journal of Psycho-Analysis* regularly publishes verbatim case material in the recurring series *The Analyst at Work*. The series also includes commentary on the presenting analyst's case by several other analysts. It is quite enlightening to see how analysts from different theoretical perspectives approach the same material. *Psychoanalytic Inquiry* is another journal that regularly features verbatim analytic dialogue. In addition to the transcripts available in analytic journals, a number of books feature extensive verbatim transcriptions: for example, Bollas (2009), Gill and Hoffman (1982), Grotstein (2009, Vol. 2), Labije and Neborsky (2012), Langs and Searles (1980), Thoma and Kächele (1988, Vol. 2), and Winnicott (1994).

- In addition to this volume, I also highly recommend Levy's *Principles of Interpretation* (1990). It is one of the first books I read on interpretation and one that I have returned to many times. All analytically oriented therapists will gain new insights into the interpretive process from Levy's book.
- Finally, attempt to make one clear interpretation in every session. A single well-crafted, empathically connected interpretation in each session often provides sufficient reflective stimulus to keep the analytic process engaged and moving prospectively.

Consolidation

This section gathers the various bits of practical advice, guiding principles, and suggestions for interpretation that have not yet found a place in this volume.

Frequency of interpretation

The analytic process does not require the analyst to interpret constantly. In fact, it would be detrimental to the process to interpret too frequently. Interpretation undertaken too frequently often leads to an over-"saturation" (Bion, 1965) of the analytic field in which reflection is disrupted rather than facilitated. Extended periods of silence on the part of the analyst (and sometimes the patient) are not uncommon in analytic therapy. Often, just a few interpretations per session is sufficient to keep the analytic process engaged and progressing. In fact, in some sessions, the analyst will decide not to offer any interpretations. Yet, it remains important for the analyst to be aware of opportunities to make interpretations even if those opportunities are not ultimately acted upon. However, when no interpretations occur to the analyst over several sessions, that may also reflect a particular constellation of the intersubjective field. The absence of interpretive impulse may reveal the presence of strongly constellated defenses, or it may reveal a deadness or emptiness within the analytic field. It is often better to risk an interpretation and be off the mark than it is to be overly conservative, by not interpreting, and never stimulate the possibility of transformation. If the patient is put off by the interpretation, a therapeutic rupture may have occurred that must be acknowledged and repaired. As Kohut (1971, 1984) points out, the analyst's recognition and interpretive acknowledgment of therapeutic ruptures is also transformative as long as rupture does not become the norm of the interaction.

The frequency of interpretation is also affected by the frequency of sessions. When sessions are occurring less frequently, such as in weekly therapy, there is a need for the analyst to become more active interpretively. Patients being seen on a weekly basis often return to each session having re-established unconscious defense processes between sessions. Offering fewer interpretations per session is possible when the patient is being seen two or more times a week. In this setting, the patient's defenses have less time to become re-established and the patient has more opportunity to internalize the analyst in other ways. We can refer to this as the patient's analytic availability, or as their capacity to make analytic contact (Waska, 2007). In my experience, the greatest leap in analytic availability comes in the change from once a week to twice a week sessions. In general, when the analytic sessions are less frequent, then the analyst has to be more active interpretively.

There is also often a significant difference in the field created with the patient being seen on the couch versus sitting in the chair. When the patient is on the couch, there is often a qualitative shift in the depth of affective engagement and associative material generated. My own capacity for reverie and containment also increases when the patient is on the couch. It becomes easier to hold my internal space while also holding the patient in my psyche. In combination, the session frequency and the physical position of the patient are significant influences on the interpretive process and analytic experience.

Focus on experience

The theme of experience is addressed in Chapter 4 as an attribute of the analytic attitude; however, it bears reiteration here because analytic therapy is fundamentally a process based upon engaging, digesting, and assimilating experience. The principal focus of interpretation is experience. Experience is mediated through a variety of domains, including language, cognition, image, somatic, kinesthetic, and affect. As Freud (1915) indicates, "To have heard something and experienced something are in their psychological nature two quite different things, even though the content of both is the same" (p. 176). Experience is our ultimate ground; the medium through which meaning and being are transmitted.

In terms of analysis, Ogden (2009) suggests: "People can only do psychological work with a bit of their lived experience" (p. 79). Elsewhere, Ogden (1997) frames the analytic focus on experience in terms of a feeling of aliveness or deadness: "I have become increasingly aware. . . that the sense of aliveness and deadness of the transference–countertransference is, for me, perhaps the single most important measure of the moment-to-moment status of the analytic process" (p. 23). According to Jung (1965), the experiential nature of the analytic process necessarily includes both patient and analyst, "In any thoroughgoing analysis the whole personality of both patient and doctor is called into play" (p. 132).

In this vein, Aldous Huxley's (1933) statement, "Experience is not what happens to a man; it is what a man does with what happens to him" (p. 5), enters my reverie often in any given week. Huxley's statement speaks to experience as the foundation stone of analytic therapy. In conjunction with Huxley's statement, I frequently think in terms of the limitations on experience emanating from within the patient. In other words, I consider the internal constrictions, in the form of defense processes that restrict the patient's range and possibilities of experience, especially self-experience. In such moments, my reverie often turns to the sculpture *Freedom* by Zenos Frudakis which vividly depicts the human struggle to gain freedom from internal constrictions.

Utilize action language

Schafer (1976) advocates for the use of action language in the interpretive process. For Schafer, the analysand "both in analytic session and throughout psychological existence, is to be understood as being active, goal-directed, choice-making, meaning-creating, fantasying, and responsible" (pp. 145–146). He also states, "the person as agent has always stood at the center of psychoanalytic understanding" (p. 361). Based upon these premises, Schafer advocates for the use of action language when making interpretations, and also when thinking, writing, or speaking about patients. The use of action language guards against reification and orients the patient as the center of experience. Also, action language is experiential language; keeping life in the material being interpreted. The inclusion of action language has become central in my orientation to interpretation, helping me organize my thoughts about how to frame interpretations from an active, dynamic perspective, rather than from a static or passive perspective.

As Carsky and Chardavoyne (2017) put it, "Action language underscores the agency of the individual" (p. 399). Incorporating action language involves framing interpretations in terms of actions (real or imagined), both private (i.e., thoughts, feelings, sensations, and images) and public (i.e., speaking and moving). Actions are best designated by verbs (action words) and adverbs (qualifiers to verbs) rather than nouns (terms that name) or adjectives (modifiers to nouns). An emphasis on nouns (e.g., id, ego, superego, anima, or shadow) and adjectives (e.g., dependent, introverted, grandiose, or obsessive) encourages reification and a focus on static traits. Actions of the patient include feeling, sensing, thinking, and choosing. Additionally, when forming interpretations, use words like *act* or *behave* (e.g., "you act as if. . .") instead of *is* or *are* (e.g., "you are. . . ."). *Is* and *are* imply static, unchangeable aspects of the psyche, whereas *act* and *behave* imply non-static, changeable aspects of the psyche. For example, "You seem to *feel* more depressed when you *hear* the negative voice of your father" is framed from an active position, whereas "Your depression builds when your father complex is active" is framed from a passive perspective that reifies the experience of the father complex. As established in Chapter 2, words do matter.

An example of action language

P: My job search is stressing me but I'm still not on any medication. I've been dreaming about my mother. I'm grateful to see her. I can't. . . . it's still so hard not to reach for the phone several times a day. I feel lost without mom. I didn't expect this reaction now. I have the urge to make it stop.

A: The feeling of love and loss is uncomfortable.

P: Yes. I now have doubt about whether I can get through this.

A: And you don't like being unable to anticipate the movement of your psyche.

P: Yes, it seems strange it hit that hard. It's hard to breathe and I want to get away.

A: The funny thing is that the more we talk about this feeling, the further it seems we get away from the feelings about your mother.

P: I had to shut it off. It hurt too much.

A: What do you do when you notice yourself wanting to call?

P: Nothing. I guess I feel mildly frustrated or annoyed and then put it out of my mind. It's the permanence of it that. . . . even with a break-up, there is a slight hope no matter how bad it was. But there is no chance to get her back.

A: It can be a terrible thing to feel so alone in the world.

P: It's the worst feeling and I'm tired of it.

A: But it seems somehow that these feelings you toss away are like those bodies from the hurricane that float back to the surface after a few days.

P: Yes, that one always comes back. . . I think. . . I know being home most of the day isn't helping.

In this exchange, the point of emphasis is on the patient's psychological action of closing down her thoughts and feelings about her mother's death. My interpretation utilizes action language, *toss away*, to call the patient's attention to her defense against the grief following her mother's death. The interpretation metaphorically incorporates images from the aftermath of Hurricane Katrina which had just occurred a few weeks before this session. In a previous session, the patient had mentioned being haunted by the images of the submerged bodies floating to the surface after a few days.

Another patient consistently came to sessions reporting what was occurring in his outer life and would then wait for me to ask him questions about his report, although these encounters rarely seemed to result in affective engagement. I reflected to him that he might consider whether our sessions could be a place where it was safe enough to experiment with doing something other than waiting for my reaction or questions. It was important that the patient hear this observation as an invitation to discover something different about himself rather than as an injunction to behave in a different way as a means of being compliant. Initially, he responded by saying, "Maybe between sessions I'll make a list of topics to talk about." I responded, "What I'm referring to is discovering those elements of yourself you might want to share but which it feels safer to leave alone unless someone else discovers them for you." Here the emphasis in the interpretation is on verbs, that is, action words: *discover*, *share*, and *leave*. The action language of the interpretation is also closely tied to an affective state – *safer*.

Clarity and provisionality

Clarity and provisionality form a creative tension of opposites in the field of interpretation. On the one hand, clarity is an important characteristic of analytic interpretation, and it is beneficial to be as clear and specific as possible when interpreting. Clear interpretations can be likened to the experience of the maternal body, wherein the directness, accuracy, and depth of an interpretation correspond to the infant's sense of the boundaried firmness of the mother's body. An analytic interpretation, as Fordham (1991a) points out, is most effective when clearly structured:

> An interpretation is composed of that part of the patient's unconscious digested and thought about by the analyst. The result is then communicated to the patient in such a way as to give meaning to the patient's material. To do this it must have a clear structure and contain a verb.
>
> (p. 209)

As much as possible, avoid words and phrases like: *Something seems to be happening; something in you ____; a place in you ____; or a part of you ____.* Phrases such as these introduce uncertainty for the patient about which aspect of experience the analyst is referring to. Often this occurs because the interpretive statement is constructed using indefinite pronouns and nouns. If the analyst is unable to be more specific about the feeling or aspect of the psyche being interpreted, perhaps it would be more useful to wait until a more refined focus for the interpretation has developed or sufficient information for the interpretation has been gathered. The triangle of conflict, introduced in Chapter 5, encourages clarity of interpretation by delineating the content of the insight-oriented interpretations: 1) a feeling or impulse that is hidden or repressed, 2) a defense used to prevent the expression of the hidden feeling, 3) and the anxiety associated with the possibility that the hidden impulse or feeling will be exposed despite the presence of the activated defense mechanism.

However, it is also possible to become overly specific in delineating an interpretation so that all of the unknown, the mystery of the psyche, is removed. Under such conditions, elements on the periphery of consciousness can be pushed out by too much specificity or premature clarity. While highly saturated interpretations often leave little room for the patient's response to the intervention, provisionally stated interpretations often leave more room for the patient to join in with the analyst's interpretive process. Some interpretations are better delivered obliquely to allow space for the patient's recognition to materialize. The provisional or oblique interpretation functions somewhat like a Zen koan or biblical parable, stirring a question to form in the mind of the patient, followed closely by insight. Initiating interpretations with semi-speculative phrases suggests the provisional nature of such interpretations: "Perhaps we could think of this as ____"; "Do you think it is possible to consider ____"; "It may not readily occur to you, but it seems likely that ____"; or "I wonder if we might think of this as ____." Provisionality invites the unknown into the analytic moment.

Avoid the use of jargon

As discussed in Chapters 4 and 7, the utilization of psychological jargon during analytic sessions increases the risk of reification. Analytic therapy does not require the patient to become familiar with analytic concepts. As a patient once said to me, "I can't see the method in our sessions. It seems like we just come in here and talk. But I know when I go home afterward that something has happened." Jargon, technical terms, labels, and abstractions tend to diminish the experiential nature of interpretations and reduce the patient's capacity to develop a sense of agency. For example, for a patient with a domineering negative father complex, it is more experientially engaging for the analyst to say, "Your silence today suggests you experience me as intimidating." Calling attention to a behavioral pattern, and linking it to the affective tone in the here-and-now of the analytic session, lays the experiential groundwork to move more deeply into the origins of this feeling and behavioral response, than if the analyst bluntly stated, "You're projecting your domineering father onto me today." Therefore, it is important to frame interpretations in *experience-near* terms rather than couching interpretations in concepts and analytic jargon (Kohut, 1971; Stolorow, 1992).

It is entirely possible to progress through an entire analysis without educating the patient about Jungian terms, such as shadow, anima, complex, persona, or Self. It is not that these terms are not meaningful and useful for the analyst's reflections; however, in terms of interacting with the patient, it is typically more useful to use operational descriptions of concepts rather than Jungian conceptual terms. Examples of such operational descriptions are provided in Chapter 7. When attempting to delineate an intrapsychic process, structure, or dynamic to a patient, it is also useful to utilize images and metaphors drawn from the patient's dreams and statements – such as my patient who dreamed of a "man in a gray suit." The image of the man in the suit became our shared metaphorical reference when engaging her father complex. An exception to this rule of thumb about avoiding jargon is when the patient introduces the terminology themselves. In those instances, I will often meet the patient where they are and use the language they utilize. However, I also remain aware that the patient could be using psychological terminology as an intellectual defense against deeper affective engagement.

Relationality and interpretation

As alluded to in earlier chapters, Jungian therapy requires a balance between theory, technique, relationship, and knowledge of archetypal and cultural amplifications.

The inherent relationship between interpretation and the analytic relationship can be expressed through the metaphor of the violinist. The left hand of the violinist fingers the notes but it is the right hand, drawing the bow across the strings, that gives voice to the notes, bringing them to life and investing them with feeling. Notes without feeling and feeling without notes are not music, they are just sound. The same holds true in the relationship between interpretation and the relational aspects of analysis. The analytic relationship and the person of the analyst are absolutely essential to a transformative experience in analysis. However, unless the analyst's relational capacity is well integrated with theory and technique, their effectiveness will be limited. The analyst's capacity to make relational connection, enter into affective-imaginal domains, hold theories in their mind, and to effectively translate experiences into interpretations are all essential to the analytic process.

Tips and reminders for consolidation

- Be aware when you have gathered enough information to make an interpretation rather than asking another question.
- Form interpretations around material that is most emotionally available and present in the session, for example, when a complex is activated.
- Beyond the content of the patient's communication, always listen and watch for the emotional node/center of the patient's communication (verbal, non-verbal, somatic, or behavioral). Incorporate that emotional center as the focus of the interpretation.
- One of the essential tasks of the analytic therapist is that of "pattern recognition" – that is, recognizing and articulating links between the somatic, behavioral, affective, and cognitive experiences of the patient. Or between the past, present, and future; inner and outer; conscious and unconscious; represented and unrepresented; or archetypal and personal.
- When possible, incorporate the patient's images and phrases into interpretations.
- No interpretation can be fully evaluated in isolation, apart from the context in which it takes place, that is, in a specific moment, with a specific patient–analyst dyad. This includes the gender and sexual orientation of the patient and analyst, as well as other factors such as cultural influences, spiritual orientation, and socio-economic status.
- Be aware of the *level* or *levels* of experience being addressed by each interpretation. By levels, I am referring to: archetypal experience, cultural experience, proto-experience (i.e., experience not yet represented in the mind), repressed experience (i.e., experience held out of awareness by defenses), implicit experience (i.e., experience occurring out of awareness but not repressed), pre-symbolic experience (i.e., experience being processed by the patient in a concrete or literal way), symbolic experience (i.e., experience that has meaning beyond the concrete or literal), and individuation experience (i.e., experience that is associated with the patient's movement towards individuation or coming into being). Naturally, an interpretation may address, or touch upon,

more than one level, and the boundaries between these domains of experience are not always clearly delineated.

- Interpretations rooted in metaphor are almost always more effective at involving the patient at affective and somatic levels.
- Interpretively, work from surface to depth, for example, interpreting the presence of a defense before interpreting that which is being defended against. Similarly, identify the particular feeling or experience that is being defended against before interpreting the meaning behind that experience or feeling.
- In general, seek to offer interpretations framed a half-step ahead of where the patient is at psychologically. Interpretations can be, and often are, built up over several exchanges.
- The movement from confrontational observation, to clarifying inference, to interpretation is one way of conceptualizing such a step-wise approach in which the full scope of an interpretation, or series of interpretations, is gradually built up and revealed.
- There are always several possible interpretations available at any moment in analysis, many of which may be valid on some level. However, some interpretations are more effective and digestible to the patient than others. Frequently, the analyst must sacrifice interpretations that the analyst might find more satisfaction in offering to the patient.
- Mild anxiety and a feeling of risk in the analyst are associated with effective interpretations. Bion (1990) indicates that such feelings allow us to know when we are close to something worth engaging:

> When approaching the unconscious – that is, what we do *not* know, not what we *do* know – we, patient and analyst alike, are certain to be disturbed. Anyone who is going to see a patient tomorrow should, at some point, experience fear. In every consulting room there ought to be two rather frightened people: the patient and the psycho-analyst. If they are not, one wonders why they are bothering to find out what everyone knows.
>
> (pp. 4–5, italics in original)

- The best interpretations come as a surprise, first to the analyst and then to the patient.
- Listen poetically and speak with a poet's heart whenever possible.

Note

1 While there has traditionally been a bias against audio-recording in the Jungian community, my personal experiences with audio-recording, and the actual research on the impact of recording, do not support this bias (see Haggard, Hiken, & Isaacs, 1965; Gill, Simon, Endicott, & Paul, 1968; Simon, Fink, Endicott, Paul, & Gill, 1970). Additionally, several authors (see Karp, Hyler, Wald, Whitman, Herschkowitz, & Goldberger, 1993; Firestein, 2001) argue that the use of audio-recordings positively impacts the analytic learning process, particularly in the development or progression of the techniques of analytic therapy.

Conclusion

Interpretation is an essential tool of transformation in analytic therapy. Relational elements, moments of meeting, the discovery of meaning, symbolic processes, and interpretation all contribute significantly to transformation and individuation. However, the transformational possibilities of interpretation have often been under-appreciated by the Jungian community. As Charlton (1986) points out:

> Despite attempts at clarification, technique within Jungian analysis remains confused and confusing. There exists a wide range of acceptable techniques often without much understanding of the rationale for their use. There has been little discussion in the Jungian literature of the overriding parameters of analytic method in particular situations.
>
> (p. 153)

In this volume, I have made the case for interpretation as an essential element of all analytic therapies, offered a reappraisal of interpretation for the Jungian world, and created a bridge between Jungian and psychoanalytic approaches to interpretation.

Naturally, simply reading this book will not make the reader fluent in the interpretive process. As with the acquisition of any language, fluency requires intensive study and immersion. This volume outlines the role of and rationale for interpretation in the analytic process. It also provides the basic tools, templates, and resources to begin cultivating interpretation as an analytic skill. The Jungian practitioner who integrates interpretation with other analytic skills creates a compelling *mixtum compositum*; combining the well-developed psychoanalytic emphasis on the technique of psychoanalysis with the richly cultivated emphasis on symbol and metaphor of Analytical Psychology. As Kadinsky (1970) points out, technique is not simply a set of mechanical processes to be carried out by the analyst with a cookie-cutter mentality. Rather, Kadinsky emphasizes that the very process of technique is a means of communicating symbolic material; communicating meaning through analytic action just as the analytic frame conveys the symbolism of the alchemical vase.

Developing the skills associated with interpretation is initially difficult because it involves a specific way of structuring verbalizations that can feel awkward, mechanical, or risky. Making declarative interpretive statements can also feel arrogant to the ear of the analytic therapist struggling to find an interpretive voice that moves beyond mimicking the voices of mentors. However, as Gabbard and Ogden (2009) point out, "With each patient, we have the responsibility to become an analyst whom we have never been before" (p. 322).

This volume presents ways of looking at, thinking about, and engaging experience while with patients, as well as ways of translating those experiences and insights into interpretations. There are always several useful ways of interpreting any analytic moment, as well many unproductive ways to intervene that may actually hinder the progress of the analysis. In reading through this volume, the goal is not to sound like me or offer interpretations exactly as I have. The examples provided reflect my style and voice. I began by trying to emulate a supervisor, Mel Marshak. Over time, I realized I could not create interpretations that sounded like Marshak's interpretations, but I began to discern the elements of experience she was engaging with her interpretations and why she was framing her interpretations as she did. Hopefully, the reader will use my clinical excerpts as examples of how an interpretation might be formed and develop a style of their own. The beauty of poetry is found in the individual visions and voices of the poets. Imagine the loss and sadness we might feel if suddenly Rumi, Virginia Woolf, Antonio Machado, Rainer Maria Rilke, Anne Sexton, and T. S. Eliot all sounded the same. As Bion (1994) put it, "The way that I do analysis is of no importance to anybody excepting myself, but it may give you some idea of how you do analysis, and that is important" (p. 224). According to Bion (1994), "The analyst you become is you and you alone; you have to respect the uniqueness of your own personality – that is what you use" (p. 15). With practice, you will create, through trial and error, your own approach to interpretation, learning to speak with "words that touch".

Analysis is the utilization of imagination, language, and relationship to explore the unknown, without eradicating the unknown; to learn to tolerate the truth of one's being; and to promote the growth of the personality while removing obstacles to growth. Over time, the analyst assists the patient in seeing how their inner world shapes their perceptions and experience of the outer world. In coming to this awareness, the patient can participate in the transformation of those perceptual patterns and the reduction of internal obstacles to individuation. Contemporary analytic therapy no longer views the analytic process as solely addressing the horizontal split between consciousness and the unconscious. The primary function of interpretation is to form linkages across various levels of experience, including experience that has been dissociated, repressed, or not yet represented in the psyche. Overall, interpretation facilitates a movement towards greater integration.

Yet, the process of integration is ongoing. Over time, my appreciation for the complexity of the psyche has grown. As that appreciation has deepened, so too has my awareness of the ways in which the various schools of analytic theory overlap and complement one another. Jung (1960b) offers this perspective on the complexity of the psyche:

> The psyche, as a reflection of the world and man, is a thing of such infinite complexity that it can be observed and studied from a great many sides. . . the psyche is the only phenomenon that is given to us immediately and, therefore, is the *sine qua non* of all experience.
>
> (para. 283)

A perspective that is mirrored by Bion (1970):

> The domain of personality is so extensive that it cannot be investigated with thoroughness. The power of psycho-analysis demonstrates to any practicing psycho-analyst that adjectives like "complete" or "full" have no place in qualifying "analysis." The more nearly thorough the investigation, the clearer it becomes that however prolonged a psycho-analysis may be it represents only the start of an investigation. It stimulates growth of the domain it investigates.
>
> (p. 69)

The tool of analytic interpretation is essential to engaging the complexity of the psyche.

Working to craft useful, transformative interpretations in the ever-fluid flow of the analytic process is always an elusive endeavor; always involving a struggle for the interpreting analyst. The interpretive path of analysis can be steep, demanding a great deal of the analyst. Once the art and craft of interpretation are taken up, there is little opportunity to "coast" in an analysis. However, it is an endeavor that keeps the analyst mindful of and actively engaged with the emergent process unfolding in the room. Interpretation can be a rich source of creative, intellectual, and emotional nourishment for the analyst and a powerful tool of transformation for the patient. For myself, my analytic journey would be much less fulfilling and alive without an interpretive focus. I hope this volume provides the impetus for others to discover similar fulfillment through the art and technique of interpretation in analytic practice: embracing the *operatio* that paves the path to the philosopher's stone.

Appendix

Research on interpretation in analytic therapy

There has always existed an uneasy tension regarding research into analytic therapies (Fonagy, 2013; Winborn, 2016). Many analysts are of the opinion that psychoanalysis and psychoanalytic psychotherapy are too nuanced and complex to adequately be examined within traditional research designs. Some see research into psychoanalysis as a disruptive intrusion into a sacred space that should be protected from intrusion at all costs. There are others who feel a lack of systematic research has contributed to a decline in the position of analytic therapy in the face of competition from newer forms of therapy such as cognitive behavioral therapy (CBT), eye movement desensitization response therapy (EMDR), dialectical behavioral therapy (DBT), and acceptance and commitment therapy (ACT). The relatively limited research on the effectiveness and function of analytic therapies also makes it more difficult to advocate effectively for analytic therapies with universities, insurance companies, and governmental agencies. Much of the research that has been done on analytic therapies has centered on the effectiveness of analytic therapies in general or on the effectiveness of analytic therapies in comparison to other forms of therapy or psychotropic medications (e.g., Shedler, 2010). The tension around research is particularly pronounced in the Jungian world. As Roesler (2013) points out, there has been only a few systematic research studies examining the effectiveness of Jungian analysis or psychotherapy.

Most of the other forms of therapy listed above can be conducted relatively effectively by less experienced therapists, and research is often conducted with a manualized form of the therapy in order to establish a consistent treatment approach across therapists. Analytic therapy is a complex, nuanced undertaking that requires years of training and experience to develop the requisite skills, experience, judgment, intuition, and emotional responsiveness to practice it effectively. Therefore, it is difficult to create research designs that establish sufficient parameters for the type of therapy being evaluated and to recruit analysts or analytic therapists who are sufficiently experienced to adequately represent analytic therapy. These research issues are particularly pronounced with a specific technique, such as interpretation, which can vary widely in how it is implemented by different analytic therapists with different patient populations. However, despite these obstacles, some relevant research has been conducted on the subject of interpretation.

The research on analytic interpretation typically involves a sampling of sessions across the course of the therapy or analysis. The selected sessions are recorded for later viewing or verbatim transcriptions are created from recordings. Typically, the session content is evaluated by independent raters who assess the patient–therapist interaction for a variety of factors, including the therapist's adherence to a particular analytic approach, type of intervention, the patient's reaction to interpretations, and level of therapeutic alliance or collaboration. Ratings of interactional variables are correlated with other measures of change in therapy such as overall life satisfaction, reduction in reported symptomatology, or improvement in relational functioning. Baseline measures of functioning are taken both before treatment begins and at the conclusion of treatment, but may also be assessed at several additional points during longer therapies.

Allen et al. (1996) investigate the relationship between the type of therapist intervention (such as interpretation, clarification, confrontation, encouragement to elaborate, empathy, advice, or praise) and the level of patient collaboration. The transcripts of single psychotherapy sessions for thirty-nine patients were rated for the type of intervention used by the therapist and degree of patient collaboration in the therapeutic process. Higher levels of interpretation and clarification interventions by the therapist were associated with better patient collaboration, whereas a higher proportion of advice and praise was associated with poorer patient collaboration. In short, higher levels of therapist interpretation resulted in higher patient participation in the therapeutic process. The findings underscore the therapeutic value of the patient and therapist jointly making psychological meaning through the process of interpretation.

Ackerman and Hilsenroth (2003) review research on therapist characteristics and techniques that positively impact the therapeutic alliance. The studies reviewed provide evidence that accurate interpretation by the therapist improves the therapeutic alliance. A number of additional studies indicate that the quality, or accuracy, of therapist interventions successfully predicts treatment outcome (Crits-Christoph, Cooper, & Luborsky, 1988; Crits-Christoph, Gibbons, Temes, Elkin, & Gallop, 2010; Piper, Joyce, McCallum, & Azim, 1993; Norville, Sampson, & Weiss, 1996) and the development of a productive therapeutic alliance (Crits-Christoph, Barber, & Kurcias, 1993) in psychodynamic psychotherapy. These researchers determine that when therapists provide well-crafted, accurate interpretations (i.e., articulating a good understanding of the patient's psychological situation at the moment of the interpretation), the therapeutic alliance is enhanced, and such interpretations are predictive of positive therapeutic outcomes.

Research also demonstrates that high emphasis on interpretation of the transference in brief psychoanalytic psychotherapy is correlated with less favorable outcomes (Piper et al., 1991; Høglend, 1993) or deterioration of therapeutic alliance (Henry et al., 1993). Based on these findings, it has been recommended that overactive use of transference interpretations should be avoided in short-term analytic therapy. Høglend et al. (2008) identify transference interpretations as an essential core competency for analytic therapists and investigate its impact on the outcome of psychoanalytic therapies. They demonstrate that treatment that includes ongoing interpretation of the transference yields more favorable results than treatment using no transference interpretations, especially with patients with less developed object relationship structures. Transference interpretation seems to be especially important for patients with more severe, long-standing interpersonal problems. The positive impact attributable to transference interpretation remained in effect during one-year and three-year follow-up evaluations conducted after the conclusion of treatment (Høglend et al., 2008). Taken together, this group of studies suggests that the utilization of transference interpretation is a complex activity in which multiple factors must be considered: the length of the treatment in which transference interpretations are used, the frequency of transference interpretations, and the overall level of psychological functioning of the patient.

Peräkylä (2004) utilizes a qualitative research design,[1] rather than a quantitative design, to evaluate interpretive interaction sequences between analyst and patient. Through a micro-analytic examination of verbal exchanges between the analytic dyad, Peräkylä demonstrates how analyst–patient interpretive exchanges result from a back and forth collaboration, with the analyst offering an interpretation and then modifying or deepening the interpretive focus based upon the patient's responses to the interpretation. Peräkylä also demonstrates how interpretations are often made after a relatively long stretch of interaction that leads up to an interpretation. According to Peräkylä's research, the focus of an analytic interpretation is not created from a position of independent authority, but rather co-constructed through interaction with the patient. He indicates, in about 50 percent of the interpretational sequences examined, that the primary function of the interpretation involves the analyst's effort to create connections between domains of experience for the patient. These domains would include past, present, and future, as well as past relationships, current relationships, and the analytic relationship. He also indicates that many interpretations focus on making connections between an unconscious feeling, a defense against that feeling, and the anxiety associated with the possibility of the unconscious feeling becoming known. Overall, Peräkylä's qualitative analysis of analytic interactions presents a picture of the complex interpersonal and intrapsychic engagement underlying the interpretive process. Peräkylä's analysis supports contemporary views of analytic interpretation which embrace the co-created, mutually influencing model of analytic interaction that Jung (1946) depicts in *The Psychology of the Transference*.

One of the largest and most stimulating empirical research programs into the function of psychoanalytic therapy was conducted by the Mt. Zion Psychotherapy Research Group[2] led by psychoanalysts Joseph Weiss and Harold Sampson (Weiss & Sampson, 1986; Weiss, 1993). Research emerging from this program by Curtis and Silberschatz (1986) and Silberschatz and Curtis (1986, 1993) indicate that the therapist's interpretations that are most closely matched to the patient's unconscious plan[3] for improvement in therapy are closely correlated with the most positive therapeutic outcomes. Broadly stated, positive transformations occur when the therapist's interventions are consistent with the patient's unconscious goals for therapy and simultaneously disconfirm the patient's unconscious situational expectations originating from past interactions that have inhibited the patient's progress toward achieving these goals (Silberschatz, Fretter, & Curtis, 1986).

In summary, it is clear that the quantitative and qualitative research on analytic interpretation supports the use of interpretation in analytic therapy, especially in terms of increasing therapeutic efficacy, deepening the therapeutic alliance, and increasing patient collaboration. The finding that an over-reliance on providing praise and advice to the patient actually undermines the progress of analytic therapy is quite revealing and provides support for the emphasis on interpretation as a core characteristic of analytic therapy. The research on interpretation also underscores the importance of sensitivity, accuracy, and timing during interpretive intervention, as well as the need for awareness of the patient's level of psychological development and unconscious motivations for therapy.

Notes

1 Peräkylä utilizes a qualitative methodology referred to as "conversation analysis" which evaluates "how" interaction is organized to produce coordinated engagements between individuals. Conversation analysis has been applied to a wide variety of research settings and populations.
2 Later renamed the San Francisco Psychotherapy Research Group.
3 Based on the research program conducted at the Mt. Zion Psychotherapy Research Group, Weiss and Sampson propose that patients have an unconscious plan for their psychotherapy, that is, an unconsciously organized way that they intend to go about working on their problems. At times, this plan may be partially conscious, but the plan often differs significantly from their stated goals for therapy and may even be the diametric opposite of their conscious position. Often, their perceptions of interpersonal danger and the risk of being re-traumatized will determine when and which aspects of the unconscious plan will be tackled. The therapist, based on their understanding or lack of understanding of the patient's unconscious plan, will either act in ways that support this plan or unknowingly oppose it. Interpretations that support the patient's unconscious plan for change are referred to as pro-plan interventions, while interpretations that are opposed to the patient's unconscious plan for change are referred to as anti-plan interpretations. See Weiss and Sampson (1986) and Weiss (1993) for fuller discussions of the patient's unconscious plan.

Bibliography

Ackerman, S., & Hilsenroth, M. (2003). A review of therapist characteristics and techniques positively impacting the therapeutic alliance. *Clinical Psychology Review*, 23: 1–33.

Adler, G. (1967). *Studies in Analytical Psychology*. New York: Putnam.

Adler, G., & Myerson, P. (Eds.) (1991). *Confrontation in Psychotherapy*. New York: Aronson.

Alexander, F., & French, T. (Eds.) (1946). *Psychoanalytic Therapy: Principles and Application*. New York: Ronald Press.

Allen, J., Coyne, L., Colson, D., Horwitz, L., Gabbard, G., Frieswyk, S., & Newson, G. (1996). Pattern of therapist interventions associated with patient collaboration. *Psychotherapy: Theory, Research, Practice, Training*, 33: 254–261.

Allphin, C. (2005). An ethical attitude in the analytic relationship. *Journal of Analytical Psychology*, 50: 451–468.

Arlow, J. A. (1979). Metaphor and the psychoanalytic situation. *Psychoanalytic Quarterly*, 48: 363–385.

Astor, J. (1995). *Michael Fordham: Innovations in Analytical Psychology*. London: Routledge.

Astor, J. (1998). Some Jungian and Freudian perspectives on the Oedipus myth and beyond. *International Journal of Psycho-Analysis*, 79: 697–712.

Astor, J. (2011). Saying what you mean, meaning what you say: Language, interaction and interpretation. *Journal of Analytical Psychology*, 5: 203–216.

Atwood, G., & Stolorow, R. (1993). *Faces in a Cloud: Intersubjectivity in Personality Theory*. Northvale, NJ: Aronson.

Auld, F., & Hyman, M. (1991). *Resolution of Inner Conflict: An Introduction to Psychoanalytic Psychotherapy*. Washington, DC: American Psychological Association.

Baranger, M. (1993). The mind of the analyst: From listening to interpretation. *International Journal of Psycho-Analysis*, 74: 15–24.

Barrett, F. J. (2000). Cultivating an aesthetics of unfolding: Jazz improvisation as self-organizing system. In S. Linstead & H. J. Hopfl (Eds.), *The Aesthetics of Organizations*. London: Sage Press.

Bauer, G. (1993). *The Analysis of the Transference in the Here and Now*. New York and London: Aronson.

Beebe, B., & Lachmann, F. (2002). *Infant Research and Adult Treatment*. Mahwah, NJ: Lawrence Erlbaum.

Benjamin, J. (2004). Beyond doer and done to: An intersubjective view of thirdness. *Psychoanalytic Quarterly*, 73: 5–46.

Bernstein, J. (2014). Healing our split: Participation mystique and C. G. Jung. In Mark Winborn (Ed.), *Shared Realities: Participation Mystique and Beyond* (pp. 167–185). Skiatook, OK: Fisher King Press.

Bion, W. R. (1959). Attacks on linking. *International Journal of Psycho-Analysis*, 40: 308–315.

Bion, W. R. (1962). *Learning from Experience*. New York and London: Aronson, 1983.

Bion, W. R. (1965). *Transformations*. Northvale, NJ: Aronson.

Bion, W. R. (1967a), Notes on memory and desire. *Psychoanalytic Forum*, 3: 272–280.

Bion, W. R. (1967b). *Second Thoughts*. London: Karnac, 1993.

Bion, W. R. (1970). *Attention and Interpretation*. Northvale, NJ: Aronson, 1983.

Bion, W. R. (1990). *Brazilian Seminars*. London: Karnac.

Bion, W. R. (1992). *Cogitations*. London: Karnac.

Bion, W. R. (1994). *Clinical Seminars and Other Works*. London: Karnac.

Bisagni, F. (2013). On the impact of words: Interpretation, empathy and affect regulation. *Journal of Analytical Psychology*, 58: 615–635.

Blue, D., & Harrang, C. (2016). *From Reverie to Interpretation: Transforming Thought into the Action of Psychoanalysis*. London: Karnac.

Bly, R. (1975). *Leaping Poetry*. Boston: Beacon Press.

Bollas, C. (1987). *The Shadow of the Object*. New York: Columbia University Press.

Bollas, C. (1992). *Being a Character*. New York: Hill and Wang.

Bollas, C. (1996). Figures and their functions: On the oedipal structure of a psychoanalysis. *Psychoanalytic Quarterly*, 65: 1–20.

Bollas, C. (2009). *The Infinite Question*. London: Routledge.

Bolognini, S. (2002). The analyst at work: Two sessions with Alba. *International Journal of Psycho-Analysis*, 83: 753–759.

Bolognini, S. (2009). The complex nature of psychoanalytic empathy. *Fort Da*, 15: 35–56.

Borbely, A. F. (1998). A psychoanalytic concept of metaphor. *International Journal of Psycho-Analysis*, 79: 923–936.

Borbely, A. F. (2009). The centrality of metaphor and metonymy in psychoanalytic theory and practice. *Psychoanalytic Inquiry*, 29: 58–68.

Boston Change Process Study Group (2010). *Change in Psychotherapy: A Unifying Paradigm*. New York: W. W. Norton.

Botella, C., & Botella, S. (2005). *The Work of Psychic Figurability: Mental States without Representation*. London: Routledge.

Bovensiepen, G. (2002). Symbolic attitude and reverie. *Journal of Analytical Psychology*, 47: 241–257.

Bovensiepen, G. (2006). Attachment-dissociation network: Some thoughts about a modern complex theory. *Journal of Analytical Psychology*, 51: 451–466.

Bowlby, J. (1969). *Attachment and Loss*: Vol. 1, *Attachment*. New York: Basic Books.

Bunster, J. (1993). The patient difficult to reach. *Journal of Analytical Psychology*, 31: 153–171.

Busch, F. (2011). The workable here and now and the why of there and then. *International Journal of Psycho-Analysis*, 92: 1159–1181.

Cambray, J. (2009). *Synchronicity: Nature and Psyche in an Interconnected Universe*. College Station, TX: Texas A&M University Press.

Carsky, M., & Chardavoyne, J. (2017). Transference-focused psychotherapy and the language of action. *Psychoanalytic Psychology*, 34: 397–403.

Casement, A. (2007). Psychodynamic therapy: The Jungian approach. In Windy Dryden (Ed.), *Dryden's Handbook of Individual Therapy*. New York: Sage Publications.

Charlton, R. S. (1986). Free association and Jungian analytic technique. *Journal of Analytical Psychology*, 31: 153–171.

Civitarese, G. (2015). *The Necessary Dream: New Theories and Techniques of Interpretation in Psychoanalysis*. London: Karnac.

Colman, W. (2005). Sexual metaphor and the language of unconscious phantasy. *Journal of Analytical Psychology*, 50: 641–660.

Colman, W. (2009). Theory as metaphor: Clinical knowledge as communication. *Journal of Analytical Psychology*, 54: 199–215.

Colman, W. (2010). The analyst in action: An individual account of what Jungians do and why they do it. *International Journal of Psycho-Analysis*, 91: 287–303.

Colman, W. (2016). *Act and Image: The Emergence of Symbolic Imagination*. New Orleans, LA: Spring.

Connolly, A. (2008). Some brief considerations on the relationship between theory and practice. *Journal of Analytical Psychology*, 53: 481–499.

Connolly, A. (2013). Out of the body: Embodiment and its vicissitudes. *Journal of Analytical Psychology*, 58: 636–656.

Connolly, A. (2014). Review of *Transformations: Jung's Legacy and Clinical Work Today* by Cavelli, Hawkins, & Stevens. *Journal of Analytical Psychology*, 59: 448–451.

Connolly, A. (2015). Bridging the reductive and the synthetic. *Journal of Analytical Psychology*, 60: 159–178.

Cooper, J. (1949). Foreword to M. Rukeyser, *The Life of Poetry*. Retrieved from https://www.poets.org/poetsorg/text/life-poetry-chapter-1.

Cooper, S. (2008). Privacy, reverie, and the analyst's ethical imagination. *Psychoanalytic Quarterly*, 77: 1045–1073.

Covington, C. (1995). No story, no analysis? The role of narrative in interpretation. *Journal of Analytical Psychology*, 40: 405–417.

Crits-Christoph, P., Cooper, A., & Luborsky, L. (1988). The accuracy of therapists' interpretations and the outcome of dynamic psychotherapy. *Journal of Consulting and Clinical Psychology*, 56: 490–495.

Crits-Christoph, P., Barber, J., & Kurcias, J. (1993). The accuracy of therapists' interpretations and the development of the therapeutic alliance. *Psychotherapy Research*, 3: 25–35.

Crits-Christoph, P., Gibbons, M., Temes, C., Elkin, I., & Gallop, R. (2010). Interpersonal accuracy of interventions and the outcome of cognitive and interpersonal therapies for depression. *Journal of Consulting and Clinical Psychology*, 78: 420–428.

Curtis, J., & Silberschatz, G. (1986). Clinical implications of research on brief dynamic psychotherapy: I. Formulating the patient's problems and goals. *Psychoanalytic Psychology*, 3: 13–25.

Cwik, A. (2011). Associative dreaming: Reverie and imagination. *Journal of Analytical Psychology*, 56: 14–36.

Damasio, A. (1994). *Descartes' Error: Emotion, Reason, and the Human Brain*. New York: Avon Books.

Davey, C. G., Pujol, J., & Harrison, B. J. (2016). Mapping the self in the brain's default mode network. *Neuroimage*, 132: 390–397. https://www.ncbi.nlm.nih.gov/pubmed/26892855.

Davidson, D. (1966). Transference as a form of active imagination. *Journal of Analytical Psychology*, 11: 135–146.

Davies, J. M. (1994). Love in the afternoon: A relational reconsideration of desire and dread in the countertransference. *Psychoanalytic Dialogues*, 4: 153–170.

Davis, P. (2007). *Shakespeare Thinking*. London: Continuum.

Dehing, J. (1992). The therapist's interventions in Jungian analysis. *Journal of Analytical Psychology*, 37: 29–47.

Dieckmann, H. (1991). *Methods in Analytical Psychology: An Introduction*. Wilmette, IL: Chiron.

Dieckmann, H. (1999). *Complexes: Diagnosis and Therapy in Analytical Psychology*. Wilmette, IL: Chiron.

Doctors, S. R. (2009). Interpretation as a relational process. *International Journal of Psycho-Analytic Self Psychology*, 4: 449–465.

Doty, M. (2008). Tide of voices: Why poetry matters now. *Presentation at Key West Literary Seminar*. Retrieved from https://www.poets.org/poetsorg/text/tide-voices-why-poetry-matters-now.

Edinger, E. (1984). *The Creation of Consciousness*. Toronto: Inner-City Books.

Edinger, E. (1991). *Anatomy of the Psyche: Alchemical Symbolism in Psychotherapy*. Chicago: Open Court.

Eigen, M. (1981). The area of faith in Winnicott, Lacan and Bion. *International Journal of Psycho-Analysis*, 62: 413–433.

Ellman, S. (1991). *Freud's Technique Papers*. New York: Other Press.

Ellman, S. (2010). *When Theories Touch: A Historical and Theoretical Integration of Psychoanalytic Thought*. London: Karnac.

Enthoven, R. (2011). On reverie. Excerpted from *New York Times* online, April 6, 2011. https://opinionator.blogs.nytimes.com/2011/08/06/on-reverie/.

Epstein, L. (1977). The function of hate in the countertransference. *Contemporary Psychoanalysis*, 13: 442–460.

Etchegoyen, R. H. (2005). *Fundamentals of Psychoanalytic Technique*. London: Karnac.

Fast, I. (1992). The embodied mind: Toward a relational perspective. *Psychoanalytic Dialogues*, 2: 389–409.

Fenichel, O. (1941). *Problems of Psychoanalytic Technique*. New York: The Psychoanalytic Quarterly.

Ferro, A. (1999). *The Bi-Personal Field*. London: Routledge.

Ferro, A. (2006). Trauma, reverie, and the field. *Psychoanalytic Quarterly*, 75: 1045–1056.

Ferro, A. (2013). *Supervision in Psychoanalysis*. London: Routledge.

Ferro, A., & Civitarese, G. (2015). *The Analytic Field and Its Transformations*. London: Karnac.

Firestein, S. K. (2001). Teaching with tape-recorded psychoanalysis. *Psychoanalytic Quarterly*, 70: 655–663.

Fonagy, P. (1991). Thinking about thinking. *International Journal of Psycho-Analysis*, 72: 639–656.

Fonagy, P. (2000). Attachment and borderline personality disorder. *Journal of the American Psychoanalytic Association*, 48: 1129–1146.

Fonagy, P. (2013). There is room for even more doublethink: The perilous status of psychoanalytic research. *Psychoanalytic Dialogues*, 23: 116–122.

Fonagy, P., Gergely, G., Jurist, E., & Target, M. (Eds.) (2002). *Affect Regulation, Mentalization, and the Development of Self*. New York: Other Press.

Fordham, M. (1958). Individuation and ego development. *Journal of Analytical Psychology*, 3: 115–130.

Fordham, M. (Ed.) (1974a). *Technique in Jungian Analysis*. London: Karnac.

Fordham, M. (1974b). Defences of the self. *Journal of Analytical Psychology*, 19: 192–199.

Fordham, M. (1976). *The Self and Autism*. London: Heinemann.

Fordham, M. (1978). *Jungian Psychotherapy*. London: Karnac.

Fordham, M. (1979). Analytical psychology and countertransference. *Contemporary Psychoanalysis*, 15: 630–646.

Fordham, M. (1991a). The supposed limits of interpretation. *Journal of Analytical Psychology*, 36: 165–175.

Fordham, M. (1991b). Rejoinder to Nathan Schwartz-Salant. *Journal of Analytical Psychology*, 36: 367–369.

Fordham, M. (1998). *Freud, Jung, Klein: The Fenceless Field*. London: Routledge.

Fosshage, J. L. (1994). Toward reconceptualising transference: Theoretical and clinical considerations. *International Journal of Psycho-Analysis*, 75: 265–280.

Frayn, D. (1987). An analyst's regressive reverie: A response to the analysand's illness. *International Journal of Psycho-Analysis*, 68: 271–277.

Frederickson, J. (1990). Hate in the countertransference as an empathic position. *Contemporary Psychoanalysis*, 26: 479–495.

Freud, A. (1967). *The Ego and the Mechanisms of Defence*. Madison, CT: International Universities Press.

Freud, S. (1895). *Studies on Hysteria*. In the *Standard Edition of the Complete Psychological Works of Sigmund Freud, Volume II* (pp. 1–323). London: Hogarth.

Freud, S. (1900). *The Interpretation of Dreams*. New York: Basic Books, 2010.

Freud, S. (1910). "Wild" psycho-analysis. In the *Standard Edition of the Complete Psychological Works of Sigmund Freud, Volume XI* (pp. 219–228). London: Hogarth.

Freud, S. (1912). Recommendations to physicians practising psychoanalysis. In the *Standard Edition of the Complete Psychological Works of Sigmund Freud, Volume XII* (pp. 109–120). London: Hogarth.

Freud, S. (1914). Remembering, repeating and working-through. In the *Standard Edition of the Complete Psychological Works of Sigmund Freud, Volume XII* (pp. 145–156). London: Hogarth.

Freud, S. (1915). The unconscious. In the *Standard Edition of the Complete Psychological Works of Sigmund Freud, Volume XIV* (pp. 159–215). London: Hogarth.

Freud, S. (1917). *Introductory Lectures on Psycho-Analysis*. In the *Standard Edition of the Complete Psychological Works of Sigmund Freud, Volume XVI* (pp. 241–463). London: Hogarth.

Freud, S. (1918). From the history of an infantile neurosis. In the *Standard Edition of the Complete Psychological Works of Sigmund Freud, Volume XVII* (pp. 1–122). London: Hogarth.

Freud, S. (1959). *Collected Papers, Volume II: Clinical Paper and Papers on Technique*. New York: Basic Books.

Friedman, L. (1996). Overview: Knowledge and authority in the psychoanalytic relationship. *Psychoanalytic Quarterly*, 65: 254–265.

Frost, R. (1923). Nothing gold can stay. Public domain, retrieved from http://www.public-domain-poetry.com/robert-lee-frost/nothing-gold-can-stay-1213.

Frost, R. (1972). *The Robert Frost Reader: Poetry and Prose*, ed. E. G. Lathem & L. Thompson. New York: Henry Holt.

Frudakis, Z. (n.d.) *Freedom* sculpture. http://www.zenosfrudakis.com/freedom-sculpture.

Gabbard, G., & Ogden, T. (2009). On becoming a psychoanalyst. *International Journal of Psycho-Analysis*, 90: 311–327.

Geary, J. (2011). *I is an Other: The Secret Life of Metaphor and How It Shapes the Way We See the World*. New York: Harper.

Ghent, E. (1989). Credo: The dialectics of one-person and two-person psychologies. *Contemporary Psychoanalysis*, 25: 169–211.

Ghent, E. (2001). Need, paradox, and surrender. *Psychoanalytic Dialogues*, 11: 23–41.

Gill, M. (1954). Psychoanalysis and exploratory psychotherapy. *Journal of the American Psychoanalytic Association*, 2: 771–797.

Gill, M., & Hoffman, I. (1982). *Analysis of Transference*: Vol. 2, *Studies of Nine Audio-Recorded Psychoanalytic Sessions*. Madison, CT: International Universities Press.

Gill, M., Simon, J., Endicott, N., & Paul, I. (1968). Studies in audio-recorded psychoanalysis, 1: General considerations. *Journal of the American Psychoanalytic Association*, 16: 230–244.

Giordanelli, L. (1990). On technique: Interpretation as a structuring function in relational space. *Rivista Psicoanalisis*, 36: 4–24.

Giustino, G. (2009). Memory in dreams. *International Journal of Psycho-Analysis*, 90: 1057–1073.

Glover, E. (1930). The "vehicle" of interpretations. *International Journal of Psycho-Analysis*, 11: 340–344.

Goodheart, W. (1980). Theory of analytic interaction. *The San Francisco Jung Institute Library Journal*, 1(4): 2–39.

Gordon, R. (1985). Losing and finding. *Journal of Analytical Psychology*, 30: 117–133.

Greenson, R. (1967). *The Technique and Practice of Psychoanalysis*. Madison, CT: International Universities Press.

Groesbeck, C. J. (1975). The archetypal image of the wounded healer. *Journal of Analytical Psychology*, 20: 122–145.

Grotstein, J. (2009). *But at the Same Time and on Another Level*, Vols. 1 and 2. London: Karnac.

Guggenbuel-Craig, A. (1971). *Power in the Helping Professions*. Dallas, TX: Spring.

Haggard, E., Hiken, J., & Isaacs, K. (1965). Some effects of recording and filming on the psychotherapeutic process. *Psychiatry*, 28: 169–191.

Hart, A. (1999). Reclaiming the analyst's disruptive role. *Contemporary Psychoanalysis*, 35: 185–211.

Heisenberg, W. (1927). "Ueber den anschaulichen inhalt der quantentheoretischen kinematik and mechanik", *Zeitschrift für Physik*, 43: 172–198.

Henry, W., Strupp H., Butler, S., Schacht, T., & Binder, J. (1993). Effects of training in time-limited dynamic psychotherapy: Changes in therapist behavior. *Journal of Consulting and Clinical Psychology*, 61: 434–440.

Hillman, J. (1975). *Re-Visioning Psychology*. New York: Harper & Row.

Hillman, J. (1983). *Interviews*. Dallas, TX: Spring.

Hogenson, G. B. (2009). Archetypes as action patterns. *Journal of Analytical Psychology*, 54: 325–337.

Høglend P. (1993). Transference interpretations and long-term change after dynamic psychotherapy of brief to moderate length. *American Journal of Psychotherapy*, 47: 494–507.

Høglend, P., Bøgwald, K., Amlo, S., Marble, A., Ulberg, R., Sjaastad, M., Sørbye, O., Heyerdahl, O., & Johansson, P. (2008). Transference interpretations in dynamic psychotherapy: Do they really yield sustained effects? *American Journal of Psychiatry*, 165: 763–771.

Holy Bible (1960). *New American Standard Version*. Nashville: Holman.

Honan, D. (2011). This is your brain on Shakespeare. Retrieved from http://bigthink.com/how-to-think-like-shakespeare/this-is-your-brain-on-shakespeare.

Hooberman, R. (2007). *Competing Theories of Interpretation: An Integrative Approach*. Northvale, NJ: Aronson.

Horne, M., Sowa, A., & Isenman, D. (2000). Philosophical assumptions in Freud, Jung and Bion: Questions of causality. *Journal of Analytical Psychology*, 45: 109–121.

Huxley, A. (1933). *Texts and Pretexts*. New York and London: Harper & Brothers.

Imber, R. R. (2000). The dilemma of relational authority. *Contemporary Psychoanalysis*, 36: 619–638.

Jacoby, M. (1996). Reductive analysis in the light of modern infant research. *Journal of Analytical Psychology*, 41: 387–398.

Johnson, M. (1987). *The Body in the Mind*. Chicago: University of Chicago Press.

Johnson, M. (2007). *The Meaning of the Body: Aesthetics of Human Understanding*. Chicago: University of Chicago Press.

Johnson, M. (2017). *Embodied Mind, Meaning, and Reason: How Our Bodies Give Rise to Understanding*. Chicago: University of Chicago Press.

Jones, Raya (Ed.) (2011). *Body, Mind and Healing after Jung*. London: Routledge.

Josephs, L. (1995). *Balancing Empathy and Interpretation*. Northvale, NJ: Aronson.

Jung, C. G. (1916). The transcendent function. *Collected Works*, Vol. 8 (CW8) (pp. 67–91). Princeton, NJ: Princeton University Press.

Jung, C. G. (1917). *Collected Papers on Analytical Psychology*. London: Bailliere, Tindall and Cox.

Jung, C. G. (1946). The psychology of the transference. CW16 (pp. 163–323). Princeton, NJ: Princeton University Press.

Jung, C. G. (1950). *The Symbolic Life*. CW18. Princeton, NJ: Princeton University Press, 1976.

Jung, C. G. (1953a). *Two Essays on Analytical Psychology*. CW7. Princeton, NJ: Princeton University Press, 1966.

Jung, C. G. (1953b). *Psychology and Alchemy*. CW12. Princeton, NJ: Princeton University Press, 1968.

Jung, C. G. (1954a). *The Development of Personality*. CW17. Princeton, NJ: Princeton University Press.

Jung, C. G. (1954b). *The Practice of Psychotherapy*. CW16. Princeton, NJ: Princeton University Press, 1966.

Jung, C. G. (1956). *Symbols of Transformation*. CW5. Princeton, NJ: Princeton University Press.

Jung, C. G. (1958a). A review of the complex theory. CW8 (pp. 92–104). Princeton, NJ: Princeton University Press.

Jung, C. G. (1958b). *Psychology and Religion*. CW11. Princeton, NJ: Princeton University Press, 1969.

Jung, C. G. (1959a). *Aion*. CW9ii. Princeton, NJ: Princeton University Press.

Jung, C. G. (1959b). *The Archetypes and the Collective Unconscious*. CW9i. Princeton, NJ: Princeton University Press, 1969.

Jung, C. G. (1960a). *The Psychogenesis of Mental Disease*. CW3. Princeton, NJ: Princeton University Press.

Jung, C. G. (1960b). *The Structure and Dynamics of the Psyche*. CW8. Princeton, NJ: Princeton University Press, 1969.

Jung, C. G. (1961). *Freud and Psychoanalysis*. CW4. Princeton, NJ: Princeton University Press.

Jung, C. G. (1963). *Mysterium coniunctionis*. CW14. Princeton, NJ: Princeton University Press, 1970.

Jung, C. G. (1964). *Civilization in Transition*. CW10. Princeton, NJ: Princeton University Press, 1970.

Jung, C. G. (1965). *Memories, Dreams, Reflections*. New York: Vintage.

Jung, C. G. (1966). *The Spirit in Man, Art, and Literature*. CW15. Princeton, NJ: Princeton University Press.

Jung, C. G. (1967). *Alchemical Studies*. CW13. Princeton, NJ: Princeton University Press.

Jung, C. G. (1971). *Psychological Types*. CW6. Princeton, NJ: Princeton University Press.

Jung, C. G. (1973). *Experimental Researches*. CW2. Princeton, NJ: Princeton University Press.

Jung, C. G. (1983). *The Zofingia Lectures*. CW, Supplementary Vol. A. Princeton, NJ: Princeton University Press.

Jung, C. G. (1988). *Nietzsche's Zarathustra*, Vol. 1. Princeton, NJ: Princeton University Press.

Jung, C. G., & Kerenyi, K. (1949). *Essays on a Science of Mythology*. Princeton, NJ: Princeton University Press.

Kadinsky, D. (1970). The meaning of technique. *Journal of Analytical Psychology*, 15: 165–176.

Kalsched, D. (1996). *The Inner World of Trauma*. London: Routledge.

Kalsched, D. (2010). Defenses in dreams: Clinical reflections on the multiplicity necessary for survival in pieces. Paper presented at the XVIIIth Congress of the International Association for Analytical Psychology, August 22–27, Montreal, Canada.

Kalsched, D. (2013). *Trauma and the Soul*. London: Routledge.

Karp, J. G., Hyler, I., Wald, M., Whitman, L., Herschkowitz, S., and Goldberger, M. (1993). The use of an audiotaped analysis in a continuous case seminar. *Psychoanalytic Quarterly*, 62: 263–269.

Keats, J. (1820). Ode on a Grecian urn. Public domain, retrieved from http://www.public domainpoems.com/odegrecianurn.html.

Kerényi, K. (1986). *Hermes: Guide of Souls*. Dallas, TX: Spring.

Kernberg, O. (1996). The analyst's authority in the psychoanalytic situation. *Psychoanalytic Quarterly*, 65: 137–157.

Khan, M. R. (1983). *Hidden Selves*. London: Hogarth Press.

Kirsch, T. (2000). *The Jungians: A Comparative and Historical Perspective*. London: Routledge.

Klein, M. (1946). Notes on some schizoid mechanisms. *International Journal of Psycho-Analysis*, 27: 99–110.

Klein, M. (1950). On the criteria for the termination of a psycho-analysis. *International Journal of Psycho-Analysis*, 31: 78–80.

Klerman, G., Weissman, M., Rounsaville, B., & Chevron, E. (1984). *Interpersonal Psychotherapy of Depression*. New York: Basic Books.

Knight, Z. (2007). The analyst's emotional surrender. *Psychoanalytic Review*, 94: 277–289.

Knoblauch, S. (2000). *The Musical Edge of Therapeutic Dialogue*. Hillsdale, NJ: The Analytic Press.

Knox, J. (2003). *Archetype, Attachment, Analysis: Jungian Psychology and the Emergent Mind*. London: Brunner-Routledge.

Knox, J. (2007). Who owns the unconscious? Or why psychoanalysts need to "own" Jung. In A. Casement (Ed.), *Who Owns Jung?* (pp. 315–337). London: Karnac.

Kohut, H. (1959). Introspection, empathy, and psychoanalysis: An examination of the relationship between mode of observation and theory. *Journal of the American Psychoanalytic Association*, 7: 459–483.

Kohut, H. (1971). *The Analysis of the Self*. New York: International Universities Press.

Kohut, H. (1984). *How Does Analysis Cure?* Chicago: University of Chicago Press.

Kradin, R. (2005). The roots of empathy and aggression in analysis. *Journal of Analytical Psychology*, 50: 431–449.

Kugler, P. (1982). *The Alchemy of Discourse*. Lewisberg, PA: Bucknell University Press.

Labije, J., & Neborsky, R. (2012). *Mastering Intensive Short-Term Dynamic Psychotherapy*. London: Karnac.

Lacey, S., Stilla, R., & Sathian, K. (2012). Metaphorically feeling: Comprehending textural metaphors activates somatosensory cortex. *Brain and Language*, 120: 416–421.

Lakoff, G., & Turner, M. (1989). *More than Cool Reason: A Field Guide to Poetic Metaphor*. Chicago: University of Chicago Press.

Lakoff, G., & Johnson, M. (1980). *Metaphors We Live By*. Chicago: University of Chicago Press.

Lakoff, G., & Johnson, M. (1999). *Philosophy in the Flesh: The Embodied Mind and Its Challenge to Western Thought*. New York: Basic Books.

Lambert, K. (1981). *Analysis, Repair and Individuation*. London: Academic Press.

Langs, R. (1992). *A Clinical Workbook for Psychotherapists*. London: Karnac.

Langs, R., & Searles, H. (1980). *Intrapsychic and Interpersonal Dimensions of Treatment*. Northvale, NJ: Aronson.

Lear, J. (2009). Technique and final cause in psychoanalysis. *International Journal of Psycho-Analysis*, 90: 1299–1317.

Ledermann, R. (1995). Thoughts on interpreting. *Journal of Analytical Psychology*, 40: 523–529.

Lee, R., & Martin, J. (1991). *Psychotherapy after Kohut*. Hillsdale, NJ: The Analytic Press.

Levine, S. (2009). *Loving Psychoanalysis: Technique and Theory in the Therapeutic Relationship*. Northvale, NJ: Aronson.

Levy, S. (1990). *Principles of Interpretation: Mastering Clear and Concise Interventions in Psychotherapy*. Northvale, NJ: Aronson.

Lichtenberg, J. D. (2009). The clinical power of metaphoric experience. *Psychoanalytic Inquiry*, 29: 48–57.

Loewald, H. W. (1980). *Papers on Psychoanalysis*. New Haven, CT: Yale University Press.

Malan, D. H. (1995). *Individual Psychotherapy and the Science of Psychodynamics*. London: Butterworth-Heinemann.

Mann, D. W. (2010). Practical poetry. *Psychoanalytic Review*, 97: 717–732.

Maroda, K. (2010). *Psychodynamic Techniques: Working with Emotions in the Therapeutic Relationship*. New York: Guilford.

Mars, R. B., Neubert, F.-X., Noonan, M. P., Sallet, J., Toni, I., & Rushworth, M. F. S. (2012). On the relationship between the "default mode network" and the "social brain." *Frontiers in Human Neuroscience*, 6, 189. http://doi.org/10.3389/fnhum.2012.00189

Martin-Vallas, F. (2013). Are archetypes transmitted or emergent? A response to Christian Roesler. *Journal of Analytical Psychology*, 58: 278–285.

Mathew, M. (2005). Reverie: Between thought and prayer. *Journal of Analytical Psychology*, 50: 383–393.

McWilliams, N. (2004). *Psychoanalytic Psychotherapy*. New York: Guilford.

Mead, G. R. S. (1919). *The Doctrine of the Subtle Body in Western Tradition*. London: Jack Watkins.

Meissner, W. W. (1998). The self and the body: The embodied self. *Psychoanalysis and Contemporary Thought*, 21: 85–111.

Merchant, J. (2009). A reappraisal of classical archetype theory and its implications for theory and practice. *Journal of Analytical Psychology*, 54: 339–358.

Merriam-Webster (n.d.). *Merriam-Webster online dictionary*. Retrieved from https://www.merriam-webster.com/dictionary/hermeneutics.

Micati, L. (1990). Hate and destructiveness in analysis: On the function and use of the analyst's hatred. *Rivista Di Psicoanalisi*, 6: 58–94.

Miller, H. (1969). *The Books in My Life*. New York: New Directions.

Mitchell, S. (1998). *Relational Concepts in Psychoanalysis: An Integration*. Cambridge, MA: Harvard University Press.

Mitrani, J. L. (2001). Taking the transference. *International Journal of Psycho-Analysis*, 82: 1085–1104.

Modell, A. (1997). The synergy of memory, affects and metaphor. *Journal of Analytical Psychology*, 42: 105–117.

Modell, A. (2003). *Imagination and the Meaningful Brain*. Cambridge, MA: MIT Press.

Modell, A. (2009). Metaphor – the bridge between feelings and knowledge. *Psychoanalytic Inquiry*, 29: 6–11.

Moore, B., & Fine, B. (1990). *Psychoanalytic Terms and Concepts*. New Haven, CT: Yale University Press.

Muller, J., & Tillman, J. (2007). *The Embodied Subject: Minding the Body in Psychoanalysis*. Northvale, NJ: Aronson.

Nin, A. (1976). *In Favor of the Sensitive Man, and Other Essays*. New York: Harcourt Brace.

Norville, R., Sampson, H., & Weiss J. (1996). Accurate interpretations and brief psycho-therapy outcome. *Psychotherapy Research*, 6: 16–29.

Ogden, T. (1994). *Subjects of Analysis*. Northvale, NJ: Aronson.

Ogden, T. (1996). Reconsidering three aspects of psychoanalytic technique. *International Journal of Psycho-Analysis*, 77: 883–899.

Ogden, T. (1997). *Reverie and Interpretation*. Northvale, NJ: Aronson.

Ogden, T. (2001). *Conversations at the Frontier of Dreaming*. Northvale, NJ: Aronson.

Ogden, T. (2003). On not being able to dream. *International Journal of Psycho-Analysis*, 84: 17–30.

Ogden, T. (2004). The analytic third: Implications for psychoanalytic theory and tech-nique. *Psychoanalytic Quarterly*, 73(1): 167–195.

Ogden, T. (2005). *This Art of Psychoanalysis: Dreaming Undreamt Dreams and Interrupted Cries*. London: Routledge.

Ogden, T. (2009). *Rediscovering Psychoanalysis: Thinking and Dreaming, Learning and Forgetting*. London: Routledge.

Ogden, T. (2017). Dreaming the analytic session: A clinical essay. *Psychoanalytic Quarterly*, 86: 1–20.

Oremland, J. (1991). *Interpretation and Interaction: Psychoanalysis or Psychotherapy?* Hillsdale, NJ: Analytic Press.

Ornstein, A. (2009). Do words still matter? Further comments on the interpretive process and the theory of change. *International Journal of Psychoanalytic Self Psychology*, 4: 466–484.

Osofsky, J. (1988). Attachment theory and research and the psychoanalytic process. *Psychoanalytic Psychology*, 5: 159–177.

Otto, R. (1923). *The Idea of the Holy*. New York: Oxford University Press, 1965.

Parsons, M. (2000). *The Dove that Returns, the Dove that Vanishes*. London: Routledge.

Pecher, D., & Zwaan, R. (Eds.) (2005). *Grounding Cognition: The Role of Perception and Action in Memory, Language, and Thinking*. Cambridge: Cambridge University Press.

Pelled, E. (2007). Learning from experience: Bion's concept of reverie and Buddhist meditation, *International Journal of Psycho-Analysis*, 88: 1507–1526.

Peräkylä, A. (2004). Making links in psychoanalytic interpretations. *Psychotherapy Research*, 14: 289–307.

Piattelli-Palmarini, M. (Ed.) (1980). *Language and Learning: The Debate between Jean Piaget and Noam Chomsky*. Cambridge, MA: Harvard University Press.

Pine, F. (1990). *Drive, Ego, Object, and Self*. New York: Basic Books.

Piper, W., Azim, H., Joyce, A., & McCallum, M. (1991). Transference interpretations, therapeutic alliance, and outcome in short-term individual psychotherapy. *Archives of General Psychiatry*, 48: 946–953.

Piper, W., Joyce, A., McCallum, M., & Azim, H. (1993). Concentration and correspondence of transference interpretations in short-term psychotherapy. *Journal of Consulting and Clinical Psychology*, 61: 586–595.

Plaut, A. (1966). Reflections about not being able to imagine. *Journal of Analytical Psychology*, 11: 113–134.

Plaut, A. (1974). Part-object relations and Jung's luminosities. *Journal of Analytical Psychology*, 19: 165–181.

Poland, W. S. (2002). The interpretive attitude. *Journal of the American Psychoanalytic Association*, 50: 807–826.

Poland, W. S. (2008). The best thing in me: The analyst's courage in clinical practice. *Psychoanalytic Psychology*, 25: 556–559.

Ponsi, M. (1997). Interaction and transference. *International Journal of Psycho-Analysis*, 78: 243–263.

Quinodoz, D. (2003). *Words that Touch: A Psychoanalyst Learns to Speak*. Trans. P. Slotkin. London: Karnac.

Racker, H. (1968). *Transference and Countertransference*. Madison, CT: International Universities Press.

Rangell, L. (2006). *The Road to Unity in Psychoanalytic Theory*. New York: Aronson.

Redfearn, J. W. (1982). When are persons things and things persons? *Journal of Analytical Psychology*, 27: 215–237.

Redfearn, J. W. (1985). *My Self, My Many Selves*. London: Academic Press.

Redfearn, J. W. (1994). Introducing subpersonality theory. *Journal of Analytical Psychology*, 39: 283–309.

Reik, T. (1948). *Listening with the Third Ear*. New York: Harcourt.

Riesenberg-Malcolm, R. (1995). The three W's: What, where and when – The rationale of interpretation. *International Journal of Psycho-Analysis*, 76: 447–456.

Roazen, P. (1976). *Freud and His Followers*. London: Penguin.

Roesler, C. (2012). Are archetypes transmitted more by culture than biology? *Journal of Analytical Psychology*, 57: 223–246.

Roesler, C. (2013). Evidence for the effectiveness of Jungian psychotherapy: A review of empirical studies. *Behavioural Science*, 3: 562–575.

Rose, G. (2004). *Between Couch and Piano: Psychoanalysis, Music, Art and Neuroscience*. New York, Sussex: Brunner- Routledge.

Rothstein, A. (1995). *Psychoanalytic Technique and the Creation of Analytic Patients*. Madison, CT: International Universities Press.

Rubovits-Seitz, P. (1998). *Depth-Psychological Understanding: The Methodologic Grounding of Clinical Interpretations*. Hillsdale, NJ: Analytic Press.

Rubovits-Seitz, P. (2001a). *The Interpretative Process in Clinical Practice: Progressive Communication of Latent Meanings*. Northvale, NJ: Aronson.

Rubovits-Seitz, P. (2001b). *A Primer of Clinical Interpretation*. Northvale, NJ: Aronson.

Rubovits-Seitz, P. (2002). The fate of interpretation in postclassical schools of psychoanalysis. *Psychoanalysis and Contemporary Thought*, 25: 363–432.

Samuels, A. (1986). *Jung and the Post-Jungians*. London: Routledge.

Samuels, A. (1996). Jung's return from banishment. *Psychoanalytic Review*, 83: 469–489.

Sandler, J., & Dreher, A. (1996). *What Do Psychoanalysts Want? The Problem of Aims in Psychoanalytic Therapy*. London: Routledge.

Saxbe, D., Yang, X., Borofsky, L., & Immordino-Yang, M. (2013). The embodiment of emotion: Language use during the feeling of social emotions predicts cortical somatosensory activity. *Social, Cognitive and Affective Neuroscience*, 8: 806–812.

Schafer, R. (1976). *A New Language for Psychoanalysis*. New Haven, CT: Yale University Press.

Schafer, R. (1983). *The Analytic Attitude*. New York: Basic Books.

Schafer, R. (1993). *Retelling a Life: Narration and Dialogue in Psychoanalysis*. New York: Basic Books.

Scharff, D., & Scharff, J. (1992). *Scharff Notes: A Primer of Object Relations Therapy*. Northvale, NJ: Aronson.

Schaverien, J. (2007). Countertransference as active imagination: Imaginative experiences of the analyst. *Journal of Analytical Psychology*, 52: 413–431.

Schenk, R. (1992). *The Soul of Beauty: A Psychological Investigation of Appearance*. Lewisburg, PA: Bucknell University Press.

Schenk, R. (2016). Falling into language life. *Journal of Analytical Psychology*, 61: 676–692.

Schermer, V. L. (2011). Interpreting psychoanalytic interpretation. *Psychoanalytic Review*, 98: 817–842.

Schwartz-Salant, N. (1989). *The Borderline Personality: Vision and Healing*. Wilmette, IL: Chiron.

Schwartz-Salant, N. (1991a). Vision, interpretation, and the interactive field. *Journal of Analytical Psychology*, 36: 343–365.

Schwartz-Salant, N. (1991b). *Mythology and clinical practice*. Lecture given at the C. G. Jung Institute of Chicago, Illinois, USA.

Schwartz-Salant, N. (1998). *The Mystery of Human Relationship: Alchemy and the Transformation of the Self*. London: Routledge.

Sedgwick, D. (1994). *The Wounded Healer: Countertransference from a Jungian Perspective*. London: Routledge.

Sedgwick, D. (2001). *Introduction to Jungian Psychotherapy: The Therapeutic Relationship*. London: Routledge.

Seinfeld, J. (1993). *Interpreting and Holding*. Northvale, NJ: Aronson.

Shalit, E. (2002). *The Complex: Path of Transformation from Archetype to Ego*. Toronto: Inner-City Books.

Shamdasani, S. (2003). *Jung and the Making of Modern Psychology: The Dream of a Science*. Cambridge: Cambridge University Press.

Sharp, D. (1991). *C. G. Jung Lexicon*. Toronto: Inner-City Books.

Sharpe, E. F. (1940). Psycho-physical problems revealed in language: An examination of metaphor. *International Journal of Psycho-Analysis*, 21: 201–213.

Shedler, J. (2010). The efficacy of psychodynamic psychotherapy. *American Psychologist*, 65: 98–109.

Shengold, L. (1981). Insight as metaphor. *Psychoanalytic Study of the Child*, 36: 289–305.

Siegelman, E. (1990). *Metaphor and Meaning in Psychotherapy*. New York: Guilford.

Siegelman, E. (1994). Reframing "reductive" analysis. *Journal of Analytical Psychology*, 39: 479–496.

Silberschatz, G., & Curtis, J. T. (1986). Clinical implications of research on brief dynamic psychotherapy: II. How the therapist helps or hinders therapeutic progress. *Psychoanalytic Psychology*, 3: 27–37.

Silberschatz, G., & Curtis, J. T. (1993). Measuring the therapist's impact on the patient's therapeutic progress. *Journal of Consulting and Clinical Psychology*, 61: 403–411.

Silberschatz, G., Fretter, P. B., & Curtis, J. T. (1986). How do interpretations influence the process of psychotherapy? *Journal of Consulting and Clinical Psychology*, 54: 646–652.

Simon, J., Fink, G., Endicott, N., Paul, I., & Gill, M. (1970). Studies in audio-recorded psychoanalysis, 2: The effect on the analyst. *Journal of the American Psychoanalytic Association*, 18: 86–101.

Skar, P. (2004). Chaos and self-organization: Emergent patterns at critical life transitions. *Journal of Analytical Psychology*, 49: 245–264.

Smith, H. (2016). Confrontation and the fool's method. *Psychoanalytic Inquiry*, 36: 323–345.

Solomon, H. M. (1991). Archetypal psychology and object relations theory. *Journal of Analytical Psychology*, 36: 307–329.

Spence, D. (1982). *Narrative Truth and Historical Truth: Meaning and Interpretation in Psychoanalysis*. New York: W. W. Norton.

Speziale-Bagliacca, R. (2008). Reverie and metaphor: A particular way to investigate the unconscious. *American Journal of Psychoanalysis*, 68: 350–359.

Stark, M. (1999). *Modes of Therapeutic Action*. Northvale, NJ: Aronson.

Sterba, R. (1934). The fate of the ego in analytic therapy. *International Journal of Psycho-Analysis*, 15: 117–126.

Stern, D. N. (1985). *The Interpersonal World of the Infant*. New York: Basic Books.

Stern, D. N., Sander, L. W., Nahum, J. P., Harrison, A. M., Lyons-Ruth, K., Morgan, A. C., Bruschweilerstern, N., & Tronick, E. Z. (1998). Non-interpretive mechanisms in psychoanalytic therapy: The "something more" than interpretation. *International Journal of Psycho-Analysis*, 79: 903–921.

Stolorow, R. (1992). Closing the gap between theory and practice with better psychoanalytic theory. *Psychotherapy*, 29: 159–166.

Stone, L. (1961). *The Psychoanalytic Situation*. Madison, CT: International Universities Press.

Strachey, J. (1934). The nature of the therapeutic action of psychoanalysis. *International Journal of Psycho-Analysis*, 15: 117–126.

Sullivan, B. S. (2009). *The Mystery of Analytical Work: Weavings from Jung and Bion*. London: Routledge.

Taylor, T. (Trans.) (1792). *The Hymns of Orpheus*. London: B. White & Son.

Tettamanti, M., Buccino, G., Saccuman, M. C., Gallese, V., Danna, M., Scifo, P., et al. (2005). Listening to action-related sentences activates fronto-parietal motor circuits. *Journal of Cognitive Neuroscience*, 17: 273–281.

Thierry, G., Martin, C. D., Gonzalez-Diaz, V., Rezaie, R., Roberts, N., & Davis P. (2008). Event-related potential characterisation of the Shakespearean functional shift in narrative sentence structure. *Neuroimage*, 40: 923–931.

Thoma, H., & Kächele, H. (1998). *Psychoanalytic Practice*: Vol. 2, *Clinical Studies*. Northvale, NJ: Aronson.

Tronick, E. (1998). Dyadically expanded states of consciousness and the process of therapeutic change. *Infant Mental Health Journal*, 19: 290–299.

Tubert-Oklander, J. (2006). I, thou, and us: Relationality and the interpretive process in clinical practice. *Psychoanalytic Dialogues*, 16: 199–216.

Tuch, R. (2001). Questioning the psychoanalyst's authority. *Journal of the American Psychoanalytic Association*, 49: 491–513.

Ulanov, A. (1999). Countertransference and the self. *Journal of Jungian Theory and Practice*, 1: 5–26.

Van Eenwyk, J. R. (1991). The analysis of defences. *Journal of Analytical Psychology*, 36: 141–163.

Varla, F., Thompson, E., & Rosch, E. (1991). *The Embodied Mind: Cognitive Science and Human Experience*. Cambridge, MA: MIT Press.

Villeneuve, D. (Director) (2016). *Arrival* [Motion Picture]. Paramount Pictures.

Vivona, J. M. (2003). Embracing figures of speech: The transformative potential of spoken language. *Psychoanalytic Psychology*, 20: 52–66.

Vivona, J. M. (2006). From developmental metaphor to developmental model: The shrinking role of language in the talking cure. *Journal of the American Psychoanalytic Association*, 54: 877–902.

Vivona, J. M. (2009). Embodied language in neuroscience and psychoanalysis. *Journal of the American Psychoanalytic Association*, 57: 1327–1360.

Vivona, J. M. (2013). Psychoanalysis as poetry. *Journal of the American Psychoanalytic Association*, 61: 1109–1137.

von der Tann, M. (1999). The myth of the "correct" interpretation. *Journal of Analytical Psychology*, 44: 57–67.

von Franz, M. L. (1970). *Interpretation of Fairytales*. Dallas, TX: Spring.

Waska, R. (2006). *The Danger of Change*. London: Routledge.

Waska, R. (2007). *The Concept of Analytic Contact*. London: Routledge.

Weir, H. (1996). Analytic reverie and poetic reverie. *Free Associations*, 6: 315–333.

Weiss, J. (1993). *How Psychotherapy Works: Process and Technique*. New York: Guilford.

Weiss, J., & Samson, H. (1986). *The Psychoanalytic Process: Theory, Clinical Observation, and Empirical Research*. New York: Guilford.

Werman, D. S. (1984). *The Practice of Supportive Psychotherapy*. New York: Psychology Press.

Whitmont, E. (1987). Archetypal and personal interaction in the clinical process. In N. Schwartz-Salant & M. Stein (Eds.), *Archetypal Processes in Psychotherapy* (pp. 1–25). Wilmette, IL: Chiron.

Wilde, O. (1881). *A Vision*. Public domain, retrieved from http://www.publicdomainpoems.com/vision.html.

Wilkinson, M. (2004). The mind–brain relationship: The emergent self. *Journal of Analytical Psychology*, 49: 83–101.

Wilkinson, M. (2005). Undoing dissociation: Affective neuroscience. *Journal of Analytical Psychology*, 50: 483–501.

Willeford, W. (1975). Towards a dynamic concept of feeling. *Journal of Analytical Psychology*, 20: 18–40.

Williams, M. (1963). The indivisibility of the personal and collective unconscious. *Journal of Analytical Psychology*, 8: 45–50.

Winborn, M. (Ed.) (2014). *Shared Realities: Participation Mystique and Beyond*. Skiatook, OK: Fisher King Press.

Winborn, M. (2015a). Aesthetic experience and analytic process. *International Journal of Jungian Studies*, 7: 94–107.

Winborn, M. (2015b). Revisiting the left brain–right brain metaphor. *Bulletin of the C. G. Jung Society of Atlanta*, Winter, http://www.jungatlanta.com/articles/winter15-left-brain.pdf.

Winborn, M. (2016). Analytical psychology and science: Adversaries or allies? *Psychological Perspectives*, 59: 490–508.

Winborn, M. (2017a). The colorless canvas: Non-representational states and implications for analytical psychology. In *Kyoto 2016: Anima mundi in Transition – Cultural and Professional Challenges, Proceedings of the 20th IAAP Congress* (pp. 430–439). Einsiedeln, Switzerland: Daimon-Verlag.

Winborn, M. (2017b). The aesthetics of being. In S. Lord (Ed.), *Moments of Meeting in Psychoanalysis: Interaction and Change in the Therapeutic Encounter* (pp. 84–99). London: Routledge.

Winborn, M. (2018). Jung and Bion: Intersecting vertices. In R. S. Brown (Ed.), *Re-Encountering Jung: Analytical Psychology and Contemporary Psychoanalysis* (pp. 85–112). London: Routledge.

Winnicott, D. W. (1949). Hate in the countertransference. *International Journal of Psycho-Analysis*, 30: 69–74.

Winnicott, D. W. (1994). *Holding and Interpretation: Fragment of an Analysis*. New York: Grove Press.

Wolf, E. (1988). *Treating the Self*. New York: Guilford.

Wolkenfeld, F. (1990). The parallel process phenomenon revisited. In R. C. Lane (Ed.), *Psychoanalytic Approaches to Supervision* (pp. 95–109). New York: Brunner/Mazel.

Zinkin, L. (1969). Flexibility in analytic technique. *Journal of Analytical Psychology*, 14: 119–132.

Zinkin, L. (1979). The collective and the personal. *Journal of Analytical Psychology*, 24: 227–250.

Index